THE PUZZLE MOUNTAIN

GYLES BRANDRETH

ALLEN LANE

ALLEN LANE
Penguin Books Ltd
536 King's Road
London SW10 0UH

First published 1981
Published simultaneously by Penguin Books

Conceived, designed and produced by
Shuckburgh Reynolds Ltd.
8 Northumberland Place, London W2 5BS, England
Designed by Roger Pring

Printed in Hong Kong by
Dai Nippon Printing Co Ltd

ISBN 0 7139 1431 9

The author is grateful to the following authors, publishers and copyright owners for permission to reproduce their material in the sections indicated: 14, 76 Language on Vacation, *D. A. Borgmann, Scribner, © 1965. 22 the first puzzle, © Simon & Schuster. 33, 43, 51, 67 © British Mensa Ltd. 45 Metric Puzzles, S. Morgenstern, © Sterling Publishing 1978. 55* Figure It Out, *D. St. P. Barnard, Pan Books, © 1973. 61 Mind Teasers, G. J. Summers, Sterling Publishing, © 1977. 70, 93 The Moscow Puzzles, B. Kordemsky, Scribner, © 1972. 76 Creative Puzzles of the World, P. van Delft and J. Botermans, Cassell, © 1978. 78, 89, 96, 98 Your Move, D. Silverman, Kaye & Ward, © 1973. 87 © Victor Serebriakoff, 91 150 Puzzles in Cryptarithmetic, M. Brooke, Dover, © 1969. 94 Polyominoes, S. Golomb, Allen & Unwin, © 1966. 95 Word Recreations, A. Ross Eckler, Dover, © 1979. 97 E. Kingsley, © The Saturday Review; Torquemada and Ximenes, © The Observer; Afrit, © The Listener. For other puzzles, crosswords and mazes thanks are also due to Eric Chalkley, Dave Crossland, Michael Curl, David Farris, Darryl Francis, Paul James and Peter Newby.*

Contents

		page
	INTRODUCTION	6
1	Seeing is Believing	8
2	Out For The Count	10
3	Words, Words, Words	11
4	Unmatchable	12
5	Amazing	14
6	The Silver Screen	16
7	World Word Ways	18
8	Victoriana	20
9	Money Matters	22
10	Our Island Story	24
11	Dudeney's Gems	26
12	Paper Posers	28
13	Age Old Problems	30
14	The Brilliance of Borgmann	32
15	There was a Young Lady from Crewe	34
16	Artistic Endeavour	35
17	Draw, O Coward!	36
18	Domino Delights	38
19	Clocking In	40
20	Word Search	42
21	Patience is a Virtue	44
22	Word Cross/Cross Word	46
23	Reading Between the Lines	48
24	Words at Play	50
25	Time for Tangrams	52
26	The Food of Love	55
27	Fair and Square	56
28	Verse and Worse	58
29	In for a Spell	59
30	Mixed Bag	60
31	King Lear	62
32	Out of Shape	64
33	Mensa Gymnastics	66
34	Fly the Flag	68
35	Number Classics	70
36	True or False?	72
37	Watch the Birdie	76
38	Hide and Seek	78
39	Heads or Tails?	80
40	Missing Numbers	82
41	That is the Question	84
42	A Riot of Rebuses	86
43	Suitably Puzzling	88
44	A Man's Rag	90
45	Metric Mixture	91
46	Letter by Letter	92
47	Moviola	94
48	The Puzzles of Sam Loyd	96
49	Definitively	98
50	Literary Lapses	100
51	Perfectly Perplexing	102
52	Mixed Blessings	104
53	Play at Words	106
54	Puzzles Through The Looking Glass	108
55	Mathematical Marvels	110
56	Antiquarian Excursions	111
57	Amazing Follicles	112
58	Full Marx	113
59	Mountain Retreat	114
60	Anatomical Atrocities	116
61	That's Logical	118
62	It Must be a Sign	119
63	Around The World in 80 Seconds	120
64	Of a Literary Bent	122
65	Crosswords with a Difference	124
66	Push Button Brainteasers	126
67	Problematic	128
68	Visual Variations	130
69	Hidden Words	132
70	Boris Kordemsky's Puzzles	134
71	Eye Catching	136
72	Indomitable	138
73	What's Yours?	140
74	Ins and Outs	142
75	Solitaire Sensations	144
76	Parlez-Vous?	146
77	Logical Logograms	148
78	Silverman's Gold	150
79	Sam Loyd Classics	152
80	Questions of Science	154
81	Round in Circles	156
82	Weigh Out	158
83	Crossland's Crosswords	160
84	More of Crossland	162
85	Mental Gymnastics	164
86	An Olio of Orthographical Oddities	166
87	Cerebrial Serebriakoff	168
88	Countdown/Countup	170
89	Criss-Cross	172
90	For the Numerate	174
91	Alphametics and Cryptarithms	176
92	Poet's Corner	178
93	Never Say Die!	180
94	Polyominoes	182
95	A. Ross Eckler's Cryptology	186
96	Noughts and Crosses?	188
97	Classic Crosswords	190
98	The Philadelphia Maze	194
99	No Solution	196
100	The Summit	198
	Answers	204
	Acknowledgements	256

Introduction

This book is not the first of its kind. Just over 80 years ago, my great-great-grandfather published *Brandreth's Puzzle Book*, a slim volume featuring brainteasers, mindbenders and mental entertainments of all sorts – a few of which you can sample here.

Brandreth's Puzzle Book was intended to promote the sales of Brandreth's Pills – *'a medicine that acts directly on the stomach, bowels and liver, and through them purifies the blood: they cure rheumatism, headache, biliousness, constipation, dyspepsia and liver complaint'* – but having tasted the medicine and visited the old Pill Factory in Sing Sing, New York, I am inclined to think that my forefathers were better puzzlers than they were pharmacists.

What my great-great-grandfather did at the turn of the century I have tried to do today: that is produce a comprehensive collection of quizzes, crosswords, conundra, mazes and cerebral challenges of every description that will both please and puzzle you. I am afraid you won't find many cures for rheumatism, biliousness, constipation, dyspepsia and liver complaint in the pages that follow (and one or two of the sections may even *give*

Your Grandfather Used Them.

Brandreth's Pills had a reputation before you were born. They have been for sale in the markets of the world since 1770—130 years. Those who regard them with the greatest favor are those who have used them the longest. They are the safest pills for old or young because they are *pure, harmless, effective.* The same dose always produces the same effect.

How would you divide this design into 6 parts with 2 cuts of the scissors, so that one round dot appears on each part?

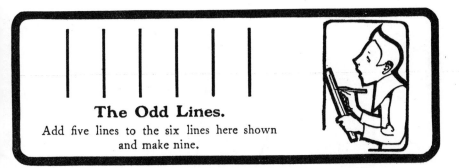

The Odd Lines.

Add five lines to the six lines here shown
and make nine.

you a headache), but if you do happen to be suffering from any real ailments I hope the book may help you take your mind off them for a while.

I have done my best to make the collection as varied as possible, featuring the classics of old masters like H. E. Dudeney and Sam Loyd as well as copious contributions from contemporary puzzlers. There are puzzles here from all over the world and you will find both British and American spellings according to the nationality of the person setting the puzzle in question. I have tried to include material to suit most tastes and talents and, if you don't have a head for heights, you will be relieved to know that you can ascend *The Puzzle Mountain* quite gradually because, generally speaking, the puzzles become more difficult as you make your way through the book.

This is a book full of challenges and I hope you will find them appropriately rewarding. As the poet says: *'Great things are done when men and mountains meet.'*

PS: *Which poet?*

THE GREAT CHECKER BOARD PUZZLE.

Start on the square occupied by the figure 1 and moving over every square on the board end by arriving on the square occupied by the figure 2.

Seeing is Believing

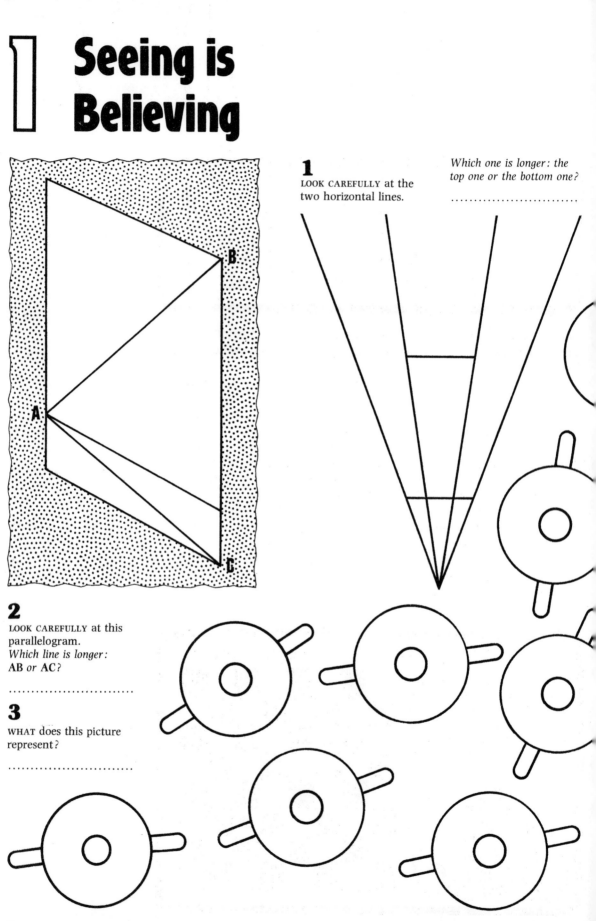

2

LOOK CAREFULLY at this parallelogram.
Which line is longer:
AB *or* **AC**?

....

3

WHAT does this picture represent?

....

1

LOOK CAREFULLY at the two horizontal lines.

Which one is longer: the top one or the bottom one?

....

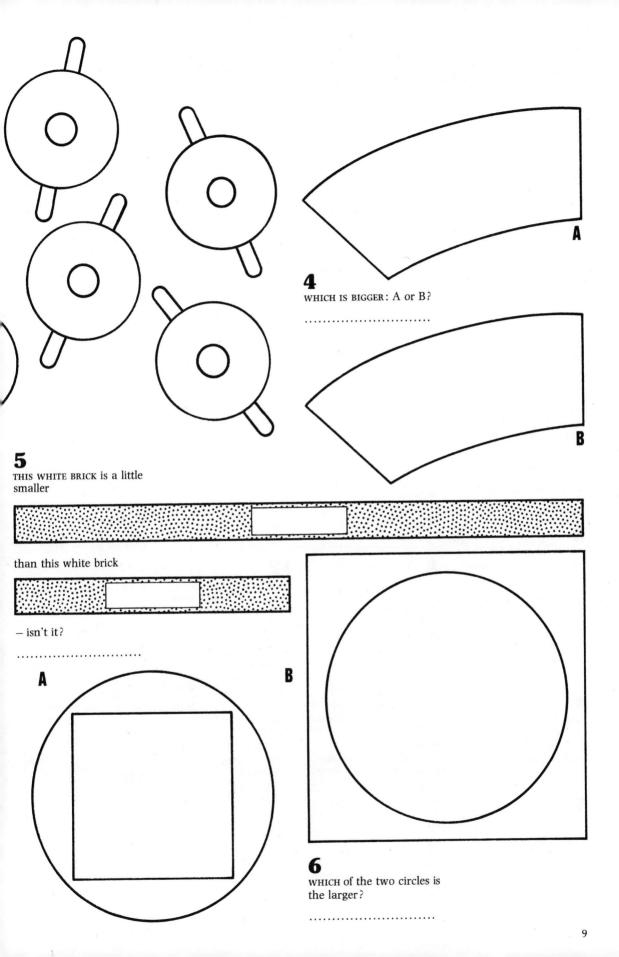

4

WHICH IS BIGGER: A or B?

A

B

....

5

THIS WHITE BRICK is a little smaller

than this white brick

– isn't it?

....

A

B

6

WHICH of the two circles is the larger?

....

2 Out For The Count

1

A HUSBAND AND WIFE have the combined ages of 91. The husband is now twice as old as his wife was when he was as old as she is now.
How old are the husband and wife?

Husband is...............

Wife is....................

2

THERE IS A NUMBER made up of four digits. The last digit is twice the first digit. The second digit is three less than the third. If you add the first digit to the last digit the answer you get will be twice the third digit.
What is the number?

....

3

THE RIVER KWAI is 760 feet wide and is spanned by a famous bridge. One-fifth of the bridge stands on one side of the river and one-sixth over the River Kwai.
How long is the bridge over the River Kwai?

....

4

HOW MUCH EARTH is there in a freshly-dug hole that is 22 cm deep, 18 cm wide and 41 cm long?

....

5

IF A MOTOR CYCLIST travels a certain distance at 40 mph and back again at 20 mph,
what is his average speed for the round trip?

....

6

IF A QUARTER OF 20 isn't 5 but 4, *what's a third of 10?*

....

7

THERE IS A NUMBER under 3000 that when divided by 2 leaves a remainder of 1, when divided by 3 leaves a remainder of 2, when divided by 4 leaves a remainder of 3, when divided by 5 leaves a remainder of 4, when divided by 6 leaves a remainder of 5, when divided by 7 leaves a remainder of 6, when divided by 8 leaves a remainder of 7, when divided by 9 leaves a remainder of 8, and when divided by 10 leaves a remainder of 9.
What's the number?

....

8

WHEN THEY WERE very young lovers, the combined ages of Helen of Troy and her friend Paris totalled 44 years. Paris was twice as old as Helen was when Paris was half as old as Helen was to be when Helen was three times as old as Paris was when Paris was three times as old as Helen.
When their combined ages totalled 44, how old were they?

Paris was..................

Helen was..................

9

WHAT TWO FIGURES multiplied together will equal 7?

....

10

RONALD SET OUT to walk from Camp David to Baltimore at precisely 12 noon and Nancy set out to walk from Baltimore to Camp David at exactly 2.00 pm and they passed each other on the high-way at 4.05 in the afternoon.
At what time would they each have reached their destination, given that they both arrived at the very same moment?

....

11

IN SQUARE FEET, what is the area of a triangle in which one side measures 2.5 metres, the second side measures 3.14 metres and the third side measures 4.98 metres?

....

12

IF A COLLECTION OF ANIMALS, including both birds and beasts, has 43 heads and 120 feet,
how many birds and how many beasts are there in the collection?

......................birds

......................beasts

13

WHAT IS THE NEXT NUMBER in this series?
589638
597532
605426
613320
621214
629108
637002
644896
652790
660684

....

14

WHAT ARE THE EIGHT consecutive numbers that multiplied together will give you a sum of 34,459,425?

....

15

IF A CHICKEN and a half lays an egg and a half in a day and a half, *how many eggs can 6 chickens lay in 6 days?*

....

16

A MAN HAS FOUR YOUNG SONS. The eldest is 4 years older than the second son, who is 4 years older than the third, who is 4 years older than the youngest, who is half the age of the oldest.

How old are the sons?

Eldest son is ....

second son is...............

third son is..................

youngest son is.............

17

IF A BABY MONKEY weighs three-quarters of a baby monkey plus three-quarters of a pound, *how much does a baby monkey weigh?*

....

18

TAKE THESE DIGITS:

1, 2, 3, 4, 5, 6, 7,

and arrange them in a simple sum that will add up to 100.

....

3 Words, Words, Words

1
WHAT ONE NINE-LETTER WORD could I use to explain that between nine and eleven you had a snack?

....

2
LOOK CLOSELY AT THIS VERSE and see if you can make thirteen different fruits ap*pear*.

Ah! If I get my good ship home
I'll find a tempting rural spot,
Where mayhap pleasant flowers will bloom,
And there I'll shape a charming cot.

Where bees sip nectar in each flower,
And Philomel on hawthorn rests,
I'll shape a rustic, sun-kissed bower —
A bower meet for angel guests.

Then she who lives and loves with me,
Full snug our days of calm repose,
Sole monarch of the flowers will be —
For Myra is indeed a rose.

....
FIG, DATE, APPLE, PEACH,
NECTARINE, MELON, PEAR,
ORANGE, OLIVE, GOURD
LEMON, RAISIN, MR
....
....

3
THERE ARE TEN WORDS missing here. They are all spelled exactly alike, except that the initial letter is different in every case, as in taste, waste, haste, paste, etc.

The EIGHT men sail around the SIGHT

Eagerly waiting for the LIGHT

To put an end to that dread NIGHT

In which the mate, that fearsome.......... ?

Had tried to prove that MIGHT was RIGHT

The rum he'd doped and made their SIGHT

A useless thing; they were too TIGHT

To FIGHT

4
CAN YOU CREATE five familiar English words by rearranging the letters in each of the following sentences?

'Tis ye govern
On real catgut
Made in pint pots
Into my arm
There we sat

....
....
....

5
THE WORD 'FACETIOUSLY' contains the six vowels a, e, i, o, u, in their alphabetical order. Can you think of another English word that does the same? To find the correct word calls for self-discipline.

....

6
CAN YOU COMPLETE the following words? The three missing letters in each case will spell the name of a different animal.

EDU***ION   BR***RY

PRE***SOR   PY***ID

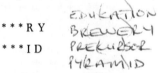
EDUKATION
BREWERY
PREKURSOR
PYRAMID

7
IF YOU TAKE AWAY the first letter, I murder. If you take away two, I may die, unless my whole should save me.

.... SKILL ....

8
A FAMILIAR QUOTATION from Shakespeare is buried in the following paragraph and each word is buried in its proper order. Can you unearth the quotation?

'Strange weather! What could equal it? Yesterday sunshine and soft breezes; to-day a summer cyclone raging noisily; then other changes, as floods of the fiercest rain eddy beneath the blast.'

....

9
CAN YOU THINK of a word which contains the letters TCHPHR grouped together in the middle?

....

4 Unmatchable

1

TAKE TWELVE MATCHSTICKS and arrange them like this:

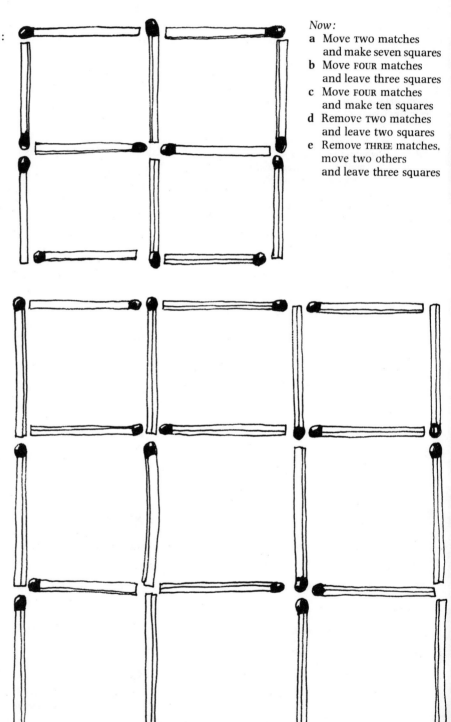

Now:

a Move TWO matches
and make seven squares

b Move FOUR matches
and leave three squares

c Move FOUR matches
and make ten squares

d Remove TWO matches
and leave two squares

e Remove THREE matches,
move two others
and leave three squares

2

TAKE TWO DOZEN matchsticks and arrange them like this:

Now:

a Remove FOUR matches
and leave five squares

b Remove SIX matches
and leave three squares

c Remove SIX matches
and leave five squares

d Remove EIGHT matches
and leave two squares

e Remove EIGHT matches
and leave three squares

f Remove EIGHT matches
and leave four squares

3

Move just ONE match and make this Roman sum work:

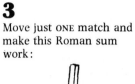

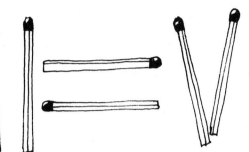

4

FOR EACH of the next seven puzzles you will need two dozen matchsticks:

Now:

a With the 24 matchsticks construct FOUR Squares

b With the 24 matchsticks construct FIVE squares

c With the 24 matchsticks construct SIX squares

d With the 24 matchsticks construct SEVEN squares

e With the 24 matchsticks construct EIGHT squares

f With the 24 matchsticks construct NINE squares

g With the 24 matchsticks construct TWENTY squares

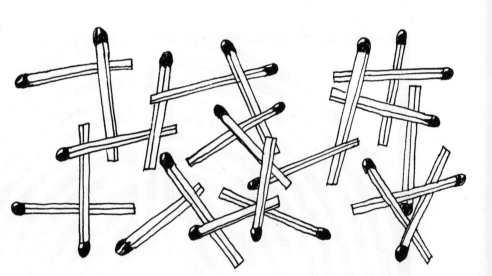

5

TAKE SIX MATCHES and arrange them on the table so that each match is touching the other five.

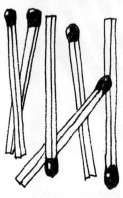

5 Amazing

The Cretan Labyrinth

PERHAPS THE FIRST and certainly the most famous of all the ancient mazes was the Cretan Labyrinth designed by Daedalus, the wizard of Knossos, as a devilish den for the monstrous Minotaur. If you want to know the story in full, you will have to dig out a volume of Bacchylides. If you are content with the essence, this is it.

A long, long time ago, when Minos was king of Knossos, he extracted a cruel tribute from the people of Athens by having seven Athenian youths and seven Athenian maidens shipped across to Knossos every nine years. These hapless lads and lasses would be dropped into the centre of the Labyrinth and before they could begin to make their escape the mighty Minotaur, half-man, half-bull, would devour and destroy them. This nasty business went on for

twenty-seven years and would doubtless be going on to this day but for the courage of young Theseus, the son of the king of Athens. Theseus persuaded his father to let him become one of the fourteen unfortunates and set boldly off for Knossos. There he found time to fall in love with Ariadne, the daughter of Minos, before being cast into the Labyrinth, where he quickly slew the miserable Minotaur (with a sword kindly supplied by the fair princess) and made a miraculous escape (thanks to some helpful thread, also provided by the amorous Ariadne). As you can tell, he was a great Greek.

To emulate him — and to do so without benefit of sword or thread — simply start at the centre of the Labyrinth and work your way out.

The Somerton Maze

The Ancients built mythical
labyrinths out of stone.
The English grow real ones
in their gardens. At
Somerton, near Banbury
in Oxfordshire, there is a
turf path one foot wide
and twelve hundred feet long
that's quite easy to walk
down, but somewhat mind-
boggling to look at in replica.

In the case of this maze,
the white paths will get you
nowhere. It's the black
line you have to follow.

6 The Silver Screen

1

WHO HAVE WE HERE?

1 CLARK GABLE
2 VIVIEN LEIGH
3 JAYNE RUSSELL
4 JOHN TRAVOLTA
5 SNOOPY
6 RUDOLPH VALENTINO
7 LIZA MINNELLI
8 LASSIE

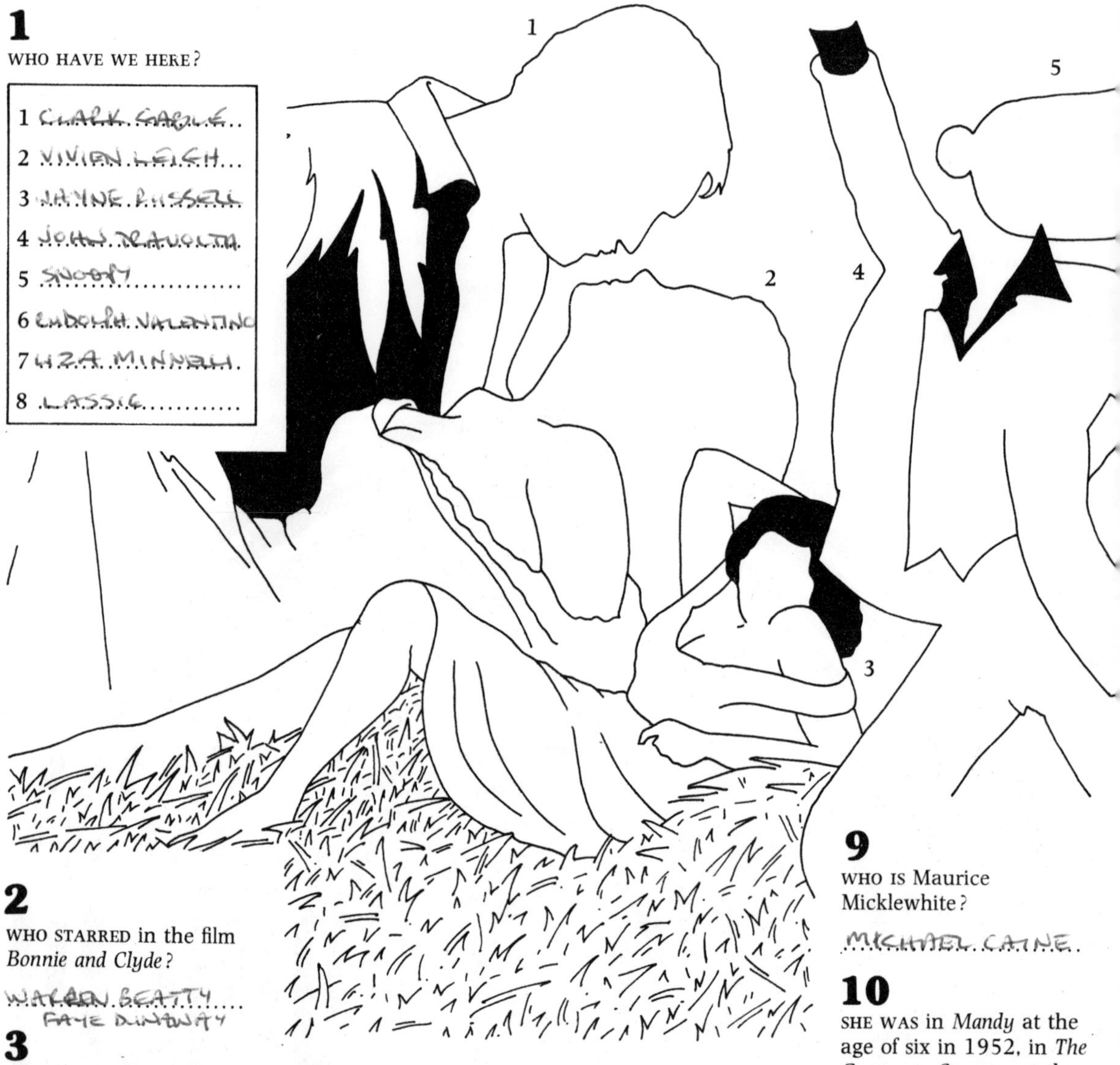

2

WHO STARRED in the film *Bonnie and Clyde*?

WARREN BEATTY
FAYE DUNAWAY

3

WHO PLAYED OPPOSITE Marlon Brando in *Last Tango in Paris*?

MARIE SCHNEIDER

4

NEIL DIAMOND starred in a re-make of *The Jazz Singer*. Who was in the first version and what year was it made?

AL JOLSON
....

5

WHAT WAS Barbra Streisand's first film called?

FUNNY GIRL

6

WHILE HE WAS writing the screenplay for *Brief Encounter*, another Noel Coward film was made. Which one?

....

7

HER MOTHER was an Oscar winner. Her father is a film director. Her first film was *Charlie Bubbles*. What is her name?

LIZA MINNELLI

8

WHEN WAS Mickey Mouse first seen on the silver screen?

....

9

WHO IS Maurice Micklewhite?

MICHAEL CAINE

10

SHE WAS in *Mandy* at the age of six in 1952, in *The Greengage Summer* at the age of fourteen in 1960, in *The Masque of the Red Death* at the age of eighteen in 1964 and in *Alfie* at the age of twenty in 1966. What is her name?

JANE ASHER

11

WHO STARRED in *The Ghost goes West*?

12

WHO STARRED in *Tommy* with Oliver Reed?

…THE WHO……… *(handwritten)*

13

WHO WAS the second actor to play the role of James Bond on screen?

GEORGE LAZENBY *(handwritten)*

14

HOW IS Richard Starkey better known? And what was his first film?

RINGO STARR
HARD DAYS NIGHT *(handwritten)*

15

WHAT IS the name of the actress-singer who starred in *Darling Lili* and *She Loves Me*, although she is much better known for a film she made in the late 1960s in which she co-starred with Christopher Plummer?

JULIE ANDREWS *(handwritten)*

16

TWIGGY STARRED in the film version of Sandy Wilson's *The Boyfriend*, but what was the name of the Oscar-winning actress who made an unannounced guest appearance in this film?

……………………

17

WHAT DID Carole Lombard and Sylvia Ashley have in common?

CLARK GABLE *(handwritten)*

18

THEODOSHIA GOODWIN of Chillicothe, Ohio, was one of the great stars of the silent era. She is much better known by her screen name, which formed an appropriate anagram.
What was it?

……………………

19

THEIR COMEDY partnership began in 1930. Their many movies included *Rio Rita*. They were friends for years, but not at the end. By the time one of them died of a heart attack in 1959 he was suing his partner for $222,000 in unpaid royalties.
Who were they?

……………………

20

CARY GRANT was the original casting for the part of the debonair Wall Street broker in *Sabrina*. But when the film came to be made who in fact did star with Audrey Hepburn?

……………………

7 World Word Ways

1

WHAT DO these Australian turns of phrase mean?

a Don't come the raw prawn
b Rattle your dags
c She's apples
d Am I ever!
e A one-pot screamer
f Beyond the rabbit-proof fence
g Rafferty's Rules

a ....

b ....

c ....

d ....

e ....

f ....

g ....

2

YOU WILL FIND these words and phrases in an English dictionary, but what are their languages of origin?

a Pince-nez
b Cul-de-sac
c Ad nauseam
d Pro tempore
e Mañana
f Fait accompli
g Allegro

a ..FRENCH..........

b ..FRENCH..........

c ..LATIN............

d ....LATIN..........

e ..SPANISH........

f ..FRENCH..........

g ..ITALIAN........

3

CAN YOU THINK OF:

a A seven-lettered English word which does not use any of the five vowels?
b A perambulatory English word that has the letters 'shch' grouped together in the middle?
c A word with more than 15 letters in which the only vowel is E?
d The longest word in the Oxford English Dictionary?

a ....

b ..PUSHCHAIR........

c ....

d ....

4

HERE ARE 20 American words. *Can you give the British equivalents?*

1 Apartment
2 Back-up lights
3 Band-aid
4 Bathrobe
5 Bill
6 Checkers
7 Closet
8 Cream of wheat
9 Elevator
10 Faucet
11 Flashlight
12 Hamburger meat
13 Lima bean
14 Molasses
15 Nightstick
16 Odometer
17 Panty hose
18 Private school
19 Raisin
20 Sidewalk

1 ....FLAT..........

2 REVERSING LIGHT

3 ELASTO PLAST PLASTER

4 ....

5 ..BANK NOTE....

6 ..DRAUGHTS......

7 ..CUPBOARD......

8 ....

9 ..LIFT..........

10 ..TAP..........

11 ..TORCH..........

12 ..MINCE..........

13 ....

14 ..TREACLE........

15 ....

16 ....

17 ..TIGHTS........

18 ....

19 ....

20 ..PAVEMENT....

18

5

IN ANY COUNTRY in the
world you might discover
a menu written in
French, but could you
understand it? *Can you
name the dishes here?*

1 Caneton	16 Bouillabaisse
2 Artichauts	17 Tournedos
3 Consommé	18 Foies de volaille
4 Patisserie	19 Laitue
5 Epinards	20 Gratinée
6 Petits pois	21 Chouxfleur
7 Escargots	22 Pommes de terre
8 Vichysoisse	23 Rognons
9 Macédoine	24 Côtes de veau
10 Fruits de mer	25 Framboises
11 Coquilles	26 Poivre
12 Ris de veau	27 En gelée
13 Pêche	28 Agneau
14 Blanquette	29 Fraises
15 Choucroute	30 Bifteck

1 DUCKLING
2 ARTICHOKES
3 CLEAR SOUP
4 PASTRY
5 SPINACH
6 PEAS
7 SNAILS
8 COLD SOUP (CHICKEN) (POTATO)
9 MIX VEG OR FRUIT
10 SEA FOOD
11 SCALLERS
12 ....
13 PEACH
14 STEW WITH CREAM
15 ....
16 SEA FOOD SOUP
17 SMALL THICK STEAK
18 ....
19 ....
20 CHEESE TOPPING
21 CAULIFLOWER
22 POTATOES
23 KIDNEYS
24 ....
25 RASPBERRIE
26 PEPPER
27 IN ASPIC JELLY
28 ....
29 STRAWBERRIES
30 BEEFSTEAK

6

IF YOU GO DOWN UNDER
and hope to sound like a
native, you'll need to be
able to speak Australian.
*Can you turn these British
words and phrases into
colloquial Australian ones?*

a Australian soldier
b Belongings
c Certainty
d Countryside
e Die
f Englishman
g Girl
h Honest
i Off licence
j Petrol pump
k Pond
l Well done
m Yellow Pages

a ....
b SWAG
c ....
d BUSH
e ....
f PAMMY
g SHEILA
h FAIR DINKUM
i BOTTLE SHOP
j ....
k ....
l GOOD ON YA
m ....

8 Victoriana

Contrary to popular belief, Queen Victoria was frequently amused, particularly by puzzles like these created by 'Tom Hood and his Sister' in 1879.

1

A Proverb in Rhyme

A chronicler from times of old,
The rolling years above me pass:
Throned on a stone, my dial cold
Gathers the lichens, weeds, or grass;
No sign shows on my placid face
Where moss obscures long centuries' trace!

Can you unearth the proverb?

...... A ROLLING STONE GATHERS NO MOSS ......

2

A Pictorial Acrostic Charade

LOOK AT THE PICTURES. The first four will give you all the letters you need. The next two are the acrostic charades. The flower makes the whole.

3

A handful of October flowers

Here is my example:

| Two thirds of | an aspirate | and half of |
| 24 hours; **Da**(y) | **h** | 'subject to'; **lia**(ble) |

= DAHLIA

And here are four flowers for you to find:

1 Porcelain: two-thirds of a donkey; and a classical word meaning 'thrice'.

...... CHINA ASTER ......

2 A precious metal; a headless fowl; and an implement of punishment.

...... GOLDEN ROD ......

3 A note in music; to sell; and two-fifths of a mistake.

...... LAVENDER ......

4 Three-fourths of an orifice; two-thirds of an insect; and a German wine.

...... HOLLY HOCK ......

4

A Valentine Puzzle

IN OLD TIMES the rule of St Valentine's Day was that you became the Valentine for the day of the first person of the opposite sex whom you saw on the morning of the fourteenth of February; and the gentleman was expected to give the lady some little present – a brooch or a ribbon – in honour of the occasion. I am going to give you a diamond. But I will tell you first it is a Puzzledom diamond, which you will have to cut, polish and set for yourselves. As you have never had any before, I will cut, polish, and set one for you.

1 A consonant
2 A lad
3 A flavour
4 A quill
5 A consonant

When you have found these out and placed them under one another they will make a diamond, for the consonant is of course only one letter, the second step contains three; the third, five; the fourth, three; and the fifth, one. Reading from the top point of the diamond to the bottom you will get one word – certain sweet flowers. Reading from the left to the right you will get another word – an appreciation of the beautiful.

Well, the first consonant is 'R', the lad is 'BOY', the flavour is 'TASTE', the quill is 'PEN' and the last consonant is 'S'. Place these in the proper order and you find the diamond:

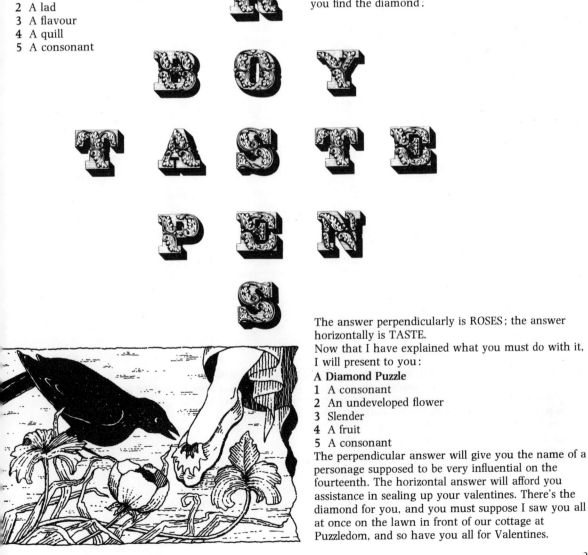

The answer perpendicularly is ROSES; the answer horizontally is TASTE.

Now that I have explained what you must do with it, I will present to you:

A Diamond Puzzle

1 A consonant
2 An undeveloped flower
3 Slender
4 A fruit
5 A consonant

The perpendicular answer will give you the name of a personage supposed to be very influential on the fourteenth. The horizontal answer will afford you assistance in sealing up your valentines. There's the diamond for you, and you must suppose I saw you all at once on the lawn in front of our cottage at Puzzledom, and so have you all for Valentines.

Money Matters

Money can't buy happiness, but these financial teasers, ancient and modern, should prove an enriching challenge.

1

AN ENGLISHMAN sold a dog for £35 and half as much as he gave for it, and gained thereby £10.50.
What did he pay for the dog?

....

2

THE MAN BOUGHT another dog and sold him again at 5% on his purchase; if he had given 5% less for the dog, and sold him for 5p less, he would have gained 10%.
What was the original cost?

....

3

THREE AMERICAN MEN, A, B and C, went into a bar together. After sundry glasses of whisky they got into a dispute as to who had the most cash, and since not one of them was willing to show his hand, the landlord was called upon to adjudicate. He found that A's money and half of B's money added to one third of C's just came to $32. Again that one-third of A's with one-fourth of B's and one-fifth of C's made up $15. Again he found that one-fourth of A's together with one-fifth of B's and one-sixth of C's totalled $12.
How much money had they each got?

A had............ B had............ C had............

4

A MAN HAS four cows, for which he gave $800; the first cow cost as much as the second and half of the third, the second cost as much as the fourth minus the cost of the third, the third cost one-third of the first, and the fourth cost as much as the second and third together.
What was the price of each cow?

1st......... 2nd......... 3rd......... 4th.........

5

TWO ENGLISH GENTLEMEN, A and B, with £100 and £48 respectively, having to perform a journey through a lonely part of the country decided to travel together for purposes of company. As they were walking through a wood a gang of youths jumped out and threatened them. The gang leader was satisfied with taking twice as much from A as from B, and left to A three times as much as to B.
How much was taken from each?

From A.................... from B....................

6

A GENTLEMAN, dying, left his property in this way: To his wife, three fifths of his son's and younger daughter's shares; to his son, four-fifths of his wife's and elder daughter's shares; to his elder daughter, two-sevenths of his wife's and son's shares; to his younger daughter, one-sixth of his son's and elder daughter's shares. The wife's share was £4,650.
What did the gentleman leave and how much did each receive?

The gentleman left ....

The son received ....

The elder daughter received...............................

The younger daughter received ....

7

THREE AMERICANS were in a restaurant and decided to split the bill equally between them. By doing so Joe had to pay an extra 15 cents, Jack saved 21 cents. They turned to Tom and said: 'What you had would have cost you a dollar sixty-five, so you don't lose much.'
Can you work out the total bill?

....

8

AN ENGLISH WOMAN bought a piece of meat for £2.16. If the meat had been a penny a pound more expensive, she would have received three pounds less for the same money.
How many pounds did she buy?

....

9

HOW MUCH MONEY would I have originally had in my wallet, if in spending one-fifth and then one-fifth of what remained, I altogether spent $36.00 somewhere?

....

12

AT THE BEGINNING of January little Willie told his parents that he had decided to save all his pocket money. He knew he had been spending far too much and he realised that the time had come to put by some of the money his parents gave him for a rainy day. His plan was this:

> On the first day of the month he wanted to save 1 penny.
> On the second day of the month he wanted to save twice as much, 2 pennies.
> On the third day of the month he wanted to save twice as much again, 4 pennies.
> On the fourth day of the month he wanted to save twice as much again, 8 pennies.
> On the fifth day of the month he wanted to save twice as much again, 16 pennies.

And so he went on right through the month, each day saving twice as much as he'd saved on the day before. Little Willie's parents, being sensible people, decided to encourage his thrift and gave him all the money he needed.
Do you know how much little Willie had managed to save by the end of January?

....

10

IF YOU TAKE $20 from the first and put it into the second of three purses, the second would then contain 4 times as much as remains in the first. If $60 of what is now in the second is put into the third, the third will contain twice what is in the first and second together. Now, if $40 be removed from the third and put into the first, there will be half as much as in the third.
What did each purse originally hold?

First purse........ second purse........ third purse........

11

NINE MEN earned in a certain time $333.60. One received $5.00, others $3.75 and the rest $1.35 for a day's work.
How long did they work?

....

13

IF A FARMER buys chicken feed for £5 per ton, pigs' swill for £3 per ton and cattle fodder for 50p per ton and gets a total of 100 tons for a £100, *how much chicken feed, pigs' swill and cattle fodder did he get?*

Chicken feed........ pigs' swill........ cattle fodder........

14

AN AUNT decided to leave her five nieces $1,000, but her last will and testament specified that the girls had to divide the money according to their ages, so that each niece received $20 more than the niece next younger to her.
How much did the youngest of the five nieces get?

....

10 Our Island Story

Here are the outlines of eighteen islands and island groupings. Can you identify them?

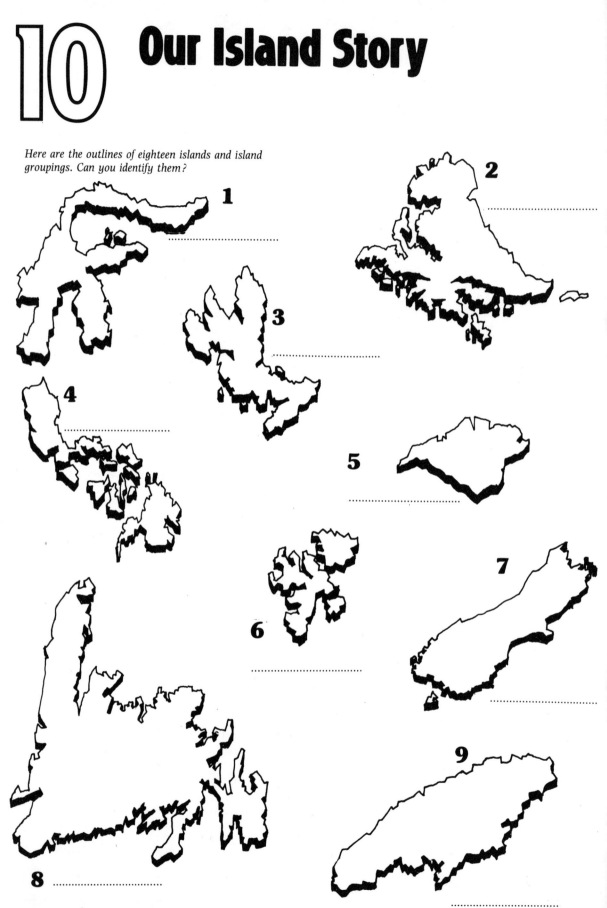

1 ....

2 ....

3 ....

4 ....

5 ....

6 ....

7 ....

8 ....

9 ....

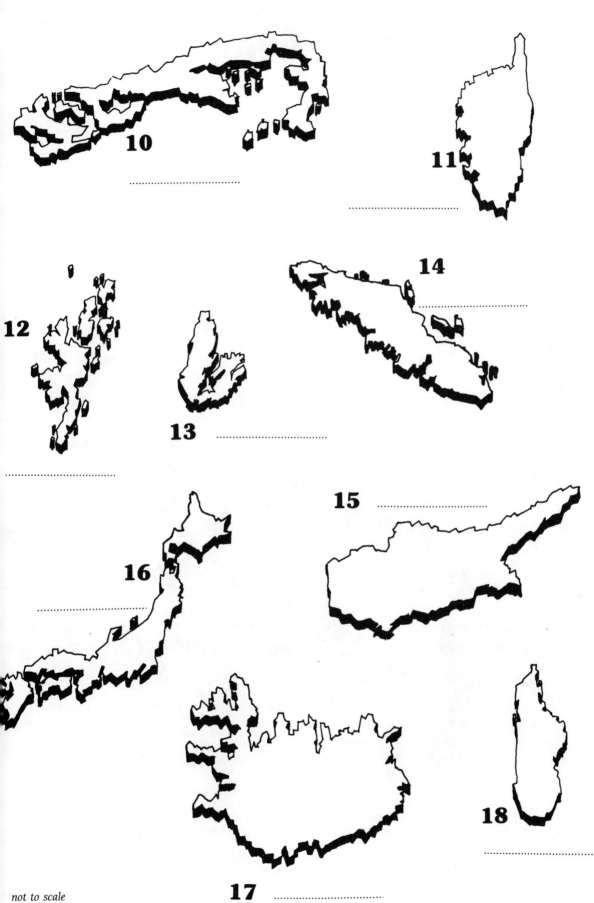

10

....

11

....

12

....

13 ....

14 ....

15 ....

16 ....

not to scale

17 ....

18

....

25

11 Dudeney's Gems

Henry Ernest Dudeney (1857–1930) was a self-taught mathematician and puzzler extraordinary. Here are seven of his gems.

1

WHAT NUMBER is it that, when multiplied by 18, 27, 36, 45, 54, 63, 72, 81, or 99, gives a product in which the first and last figures are the same as those in the multiplier, but which multiplied by 90 gives a product in which the last two figures are the same as those in the multiplier?

....

2

Twice four and twenty blackbirds
  Were sitting in the rain;
I shot and killed a seventh part,
  How many did remain?

....

3

A TRAVELLING MENAGERIE contained two freaks of nature – a four-footed bird and a six-legged calf. An attendant was asked how many birds and beasts there were in the show and he said: *'Well, there are 36 heads and 100 feet altogether. You can work it out for yourself.'* How many were there?

.....................*birds* ....*beasts*

4

A MAN'S PROPERTY has a 99-year lease. Two-thirds of the time past is equal to four-fifths of the time to come. *How much of the lease has already expired?*

....

5

A MAN MARRIED a widow, and they each already had children. Ten years later there was a pitched battle engaging the present family of twelve children. The mother ran to the father and cried, *'Come at once! Your children and my children are fighting our children!'* As the parents now had each nine children of their own, *how many were born during the ten years?*

....

6

WE'VE ALL DONE crossword puzzles, but here is one of Dudeney's fiendish cross-**number** puzzles. What you have to do is place numbers in the spaces across and down, so as to satisfy the following conditions:

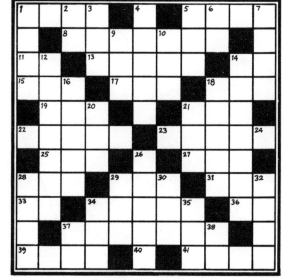

7

CAN YOU re-arrange the playing cards, moving as few as possible, so that the two columns should add up alike?

ANSWER

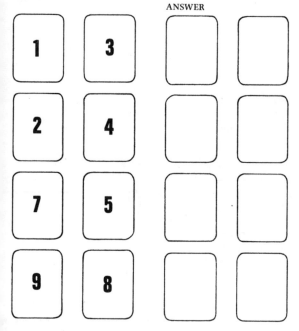

Across

1. a square number
4. a square number
5. a square number
8. the digits sum to 35
11. square root of 30 across
13. a square number
14. a square number
15. square of 36 across
17. square of half 11 across
18. three similar figures
19. product of 4 across and 33 across
21. a square number
22. five times 5 across
23. all digits alike except the central one
25. square of 2 down
27. see 20 down
28. a fourth power
29. sum of 18 across and 31 across
31. a triangular number
33. one more than 4 times 36 across
34. digits sum to 18 and the three middle numbers are 3
36. an odd number
37. all digits even, except one, and their sum is 29
39. a fourth power
40. a cube number
41. twice a square

Down

1. reads both ways alike
2. square root of 28 across
3. sum of 17 across and 21 across
4. digits sum to 19
5. digits sum to 26
6. sum of 14 across and 33 across
7. a cube number
9. a cube number
10. a square number
12. digits sum to 30
14. all similar figures
16. sum of digits is 2 down
18. all similar digits except the first, which is 1
20. sum of 17 across and 27 across
21. multiple of 19
22. a square number
24. a square number
26. square of 18 across
28. a fourth power of 4 across
29. twice 15 across
30. a triangular number
32. digits sum to 20 and end with 8
34. six times 21 across
35. a cube number
37. a square number
38. a cube number

12 Paper Posers

1
Folding an Octagon
Can you cut a regular octagon from a square piece of paper without using compasses or ruler or anything but scissors? You can fold the paper so as to make creases.

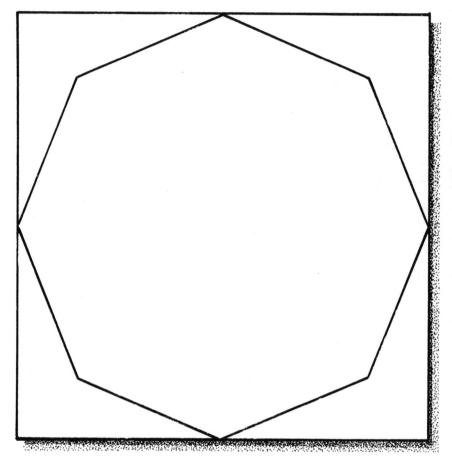

2
Square and Triangle
Take a perfectly square piece of paper and fold it so as to form the largest possible equilateral triangle. The triangle in which the sides are the same length as those of the square, as shown in the diagram, will *not* be the largest possible. No markings or measurements may be made except by the creases themselves.

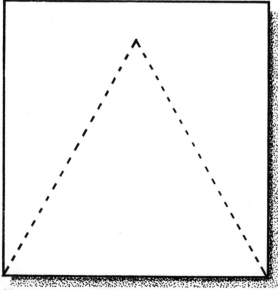

3
Strip to Pentagon
Given a ribbon of paper, as in the illustration, of any length — say more than four times as long as broad — it can be folded into a perfect pentagon, with every part lying within the boundaries of the figure. The only condition is that the angle *ABC* must be the correct angle of two contiguous sides of a regular pentagon. *How are you to fold it?*

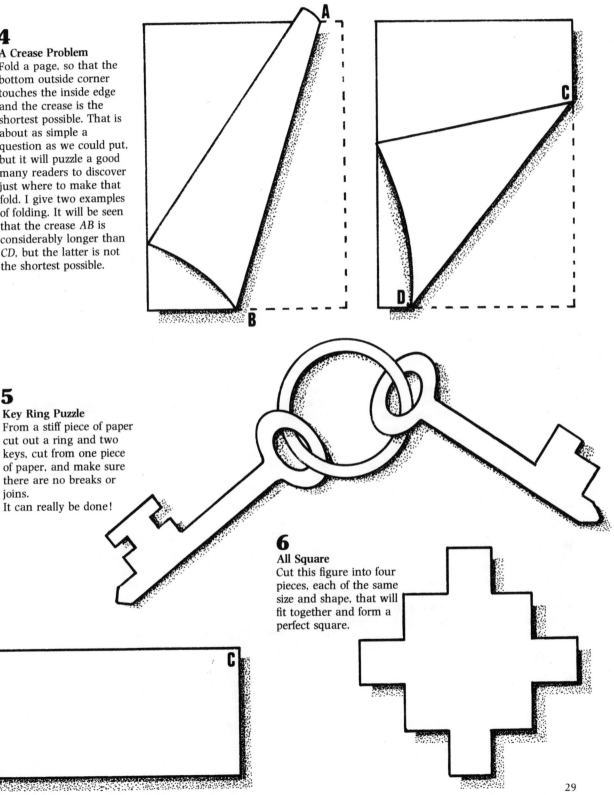

4
A Crease Problem
Fold a page, so that the bottom outside corner touches the inside edge and the crease is the shortest possible. That is about as simple a question as we could put, but it will puzzle a good many readers to discover just where to make that fold. I give two examples of folding. It will be seen that the crease AB is considerably longer than CD, but the latter is not the shortest possible.

5
Key Ring Puzzle
From a stiff piece of paper cut out a ring and two keys, cut from one piece of paper, and make sure there are no breaks or joins.
It can really be done!

6
All Square
Cut this figure into four pieces, each of the same size and shape, that will fit together and form a perfect square.

13 Age Old Problems

1

NEXT WEEK on her wedding anniversary, which is her birthday and her husband John's birthday too, Jane will have been married half her life. John will be married half his life in five years, on his silver wedding anniversary.
How old is Jane?

....

2

A MAN WAS BORN in the year 50 BC.
How old was he on his birthday in 50 AD?

....

3

IF YOU ADD THE SQUARE of Tom's age to the age of Mary, the sum is 62, but if you add the square of Mary's age to the age of Tom, the result is 176.
Can you say what are the ages of Tom and Mary?

Tom is..................... Mary is.....................

4

MRS. DICKENS had three children: Edgar, James and John. Their combined ages were half of hers. Five years later, during which time Ethel was born, Mrs. Dickens' age equalled the total of all her children's ages. Then years more have passed, Daisy appearing during that interval. At the latter event Edgar was as old as John and Ethel together. The combined ages of all the children are now double Mrs. Dickens' age, which is, in fact, only equal to that of Edgar and James together. Edgar's age also equals that of the two daughters.
Can you work out all their ages?

Mrs. Dickens is........ Edgar is........ James is........

John is............ Ethel is............ Daisy is..........

5

TWO SIMPLETONS were asked their ages, and to test their arithmetical powers were asked to add them together. The first one by mistake subtracted one age from the other and gave the answer 44, while the other multiplied the two together and gave the answer 1,280.
What were their real ages?

First was................... second was...................

6

I HAVE LIVED a quarter of my life as a boy, one-fifth as a youth, one-third as a man, and I've been going steadily down-hill for the thirteen years since then.
How old am I?

....

7

A MAN on being asked the ages of his two sons stated that eighteen more than the sum of their ages is double the age of the elder, and six less than the difference of their ages is the age of the younger.
What are their ages?

Elder son is.................. younger son is..............

8

A BOY on being asked his age and that of his sister replied: 'Three years ago I was seven times as old as my sister; two years ago I was four times as old; last year I was three times as old; and this year I am two and one-half times as old.'
What are their ages?

Boy is....................... sister is...................

9

A MAN HAD NINE CHILDREN all born at regular intervals, and the sum of the squares of their ages was equal to the square of his own.
What was the age of each child? Every age was an exact number of years.

Child no. 1........ 2........ 3........ 4........ 5........

6........ 7........ 8........ 9........ Father.............

10

BOADICEA DIED one hundred and twenty-nine years after Cleopatra was born. Their combined ages were one hundred years. Cleopatra died in 30 BC.
When was Boadicea born?

....

11

'How old are you, Robinson?' asked Colonel Crackham one morning. 'Well, I forget exactly,' was the reply; 'but my brother is two years older than I; my sister is four years older than he; my mother was twenty when I was born; and I was told yesterday that the average age of the four of us is 39 years.'
What is Robinson's age?

....

12

A MAN AND HIS WIFE had three children, John, Ben, and Mary, and the difference between their parents' ages was the same as between John and Ben, and between Ben and Mary. The ages of John and Ben multiplied together equalled the age of the father, and the ages of Ben and Mary multiplied together equalled the age of the mother. The combined ages of the family amounted to 90 years.
What was the age of each person?

Father was........ Mother was........ John was........

Ben was.......... Mary was..........

13

I AM FOUR TIMES AS OLD as my son. In twenty years time I will be twice as old as my son.
How old am I and how old is he?

I am........................... he is......................

14

MY AGE and that of my daughter are the same with the digits reversed. A year ago I was twice as old as my daughter.
How old am I and how old is she today?
I am.......................... she is.....................

15

IF YOU ADD THE AGE of Punch to the age of Judy you get a combined age of 91 years. Punch is now twice as old as Judy was when he was as old as she is now.
How old are Punch and Judy?

Punch is...................... Judy is......................

14 The Brilliance of Borgmann

Dimitri Borgmann is one of the modern masters of wordplay. Here he is at his brilliant best.

1

Homonymic Humdingers

Some words, differing in spelling, are pronounced alike. Words of this type are called homonyms. Thus, WRITE, RITE, RIGHT and WRIGHT are homonyms, as are ROAD, RODE, ROWED, ROED and RHODE (in Rhode Island). English, remarkable language that it is, affords examples of as many as ten different words and/or names pronounced alike.

To heighten your homonymic sensitivity, we have worked up a group of ten mutually homonymous English words, but are not revealing them to you directly. We are going to give you their dictionary definitions, expecting you to deduce the words from the definitions. Because the words sound alike, finding one or two of them will enable you to guess many of the rest, or at least to look for them intelligently. Consequently, it has been incumbent upon us to select definitions difficult to recognise, and we have not shirked our duty. If this sounds apologetic, it was meant to be precisely that.

The definitions:

1 rather than.

....

2 utterance abroad.

....

3 the Saxon and Bavarian name for the Teutonic god Tiwaz.

....

4 in any conceivable way.

....

5 a court of circuit judges.

....

6 a.

....

7 a town in Massachusetts, USA.

....

8 a town in Scotland.

....

9 a point on the Isle of Man.

....

10 that which is produced: a term used by Shakespeare.

....

The typography for these definitions has skilfully been modified to conceal the differentness of one of the ten terms, in two respects.

Can you identify the term and point out the two typographical features involved in this deception?

2

A Jug of Wine, a Loaf of Bread – and Thou
Lovers of poetry with definitely mystical overtones
will immediately recognise this stanza:

*'Wake! For the Sun behind yon Eastern height
Has chased the Session of the Stars from Night;
And, to the field of Heav'n ascending, strikes
The Sultan's Turret with a Shaft of Light.'*

It is the opening quatrain of the *Rubaiyat of Omar
Khayyam*, quoted from the second edition of the
famous translation by Edward Fitzgerald.
*What is the essence, substance, or distinctive quality of
this passage?*

....

A pregnant question, indeed!

3

Sight and Sound
This lesson in the logic of language concerns its two
parallel aspects: how it is written, and how it is
pronounced. We are challenging you to prove your
mastery of English – a prerequisite to any exploration
of what lies beyond – by composing two perfectly
grammatical and perfectly sensible sentences. In one,
all words are to begin with the same sound, although
no two begin with the same letter. In the other, all
words are to begin with the same letter, although no
two begin with the same sound. Suggested length:
about six words each.

1 ....

   ....

2 ....

   ....

4

Un-French French
We use all sorts of words
and phrases in English
that have been borrowed
from French, and we
delude ourselves into
thinking that this
upgrades our speech. The
funny thing about this is
that, often, the 'French'
words we use are *not*
used by Frenchmen, or at
least not with the
meanings we assign to
them. For example, we
shout *vive!*, meaning
'long live!' To the
Frenchman, a *vive* is an
edible fish, the weever.
What is the French
equivalent for our 'long
live!'? Either *hourras!* or
bravo! or *vivat!* – but
never *vive!*

Here are another seven
terms, supposedly French
but not used in French as
we use them in English.
*Can you translate them
into French correctly?*

1 brassiere

   ....

2 double entendre

   ....

3 encore!

   ....

4 lingerie

   ....

5 menu

   ....

6 morale

   ....

7 nom de plume

   ....

5

An Odd Problem
For many years,
mathematicians have
suspected that any odd
number whatever,
multiplied by a factor of
two, will yield an even
number as a product.
Since there is an infinite
sequence of odd numbers,
it is impossible to prove
this theorem empirically,
even with the aid of the
most advanced electronic
computers.

We have discovered an
elegant verbal proof for
the proposition.
Can you duplicate it?

....

....

....

....

....

....

*If you want a hint, read on.
America is a nation of 50
states. How would you go
about proving this state-
ment? By replacing each
letter in the name* AMERICA
*with its numerical position
in our alphabet:*

A   M   E   R   I   C   A

1   13   5   18   9   3   1

*Add the seven numerical
values. Their sum is 50.*

15 There was a Young Lady from Crewe

These limericks might drive you demented:
They're the oddest I ever invented.
    You'll see they're not long,
    For something is wrong:
The last line of each has absented.

Can you supply the missing last lines?

1

There was once a woman from Churston
Who thought her third husband the worst 'un
    For he justly was reckoned
    Far worse than the second,

....

2

There was a young girl from Devizes
Whose ears were quite different sizes.
    The one that was small
    Was of no use at all,

....

3

Said an envious erudite ermine:
'There's one thing I cannot determine:
    When a dame wears my coat
    She's a person of note,

....

4

A skeleton once in Khartoum
Invited a ghost to his room.
    They spent the whole night
    In the eeriest fight

....

5

There was an old man known as Keith
Who sat on his set of false teeth.
    Said he with a start,
    'Oh Lor' bless my heart!

....

6

There was a young lady named Maud
Who was a society fraud:
    In the drawing-room she
    Was as staid as could be,

....

7

There was a lady named Muir
Whose mind was so frightfully pure
    That she fainted away
    At a friend's house one day

....

8

There was an old fellow of Rosham
Who took out his false teeth to wash 'em.
    But his wife said: 'Dear Jack,
    If you don't put them back,

....

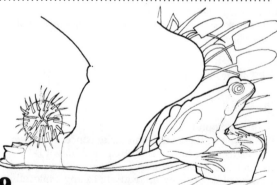

9

There was a young girl known as Sue
Who carried a frog in each shoe.
    When asked to stop
    She replied with a hop,

....

10

There once was a fellow called Sydney
Who ate lots of pie - steak and kidney.
    He ate so much crust
    That he thought he would bust

....

16 Artistic Endeavour

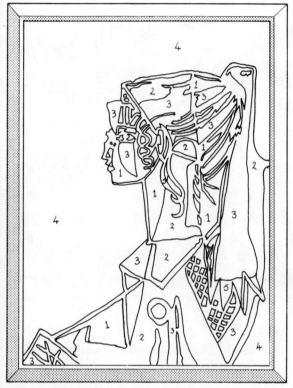

2

WHAT NATIONALITY are these artists?

a Whistler

b Bruegel

c Cézanne

d Corot

e Delacroix

f Van Gogh

g Goya

h Holbein

i Manet

j Millais

k Picasso

l Raphael

m Rembrandt

n Rubens

o Titian

p Van Dyck

q Velasquez

r Watteau

1

WHO PAINTED the following?

a *The Laughing Cavalier*

b *Mrs Siddons*

c *Madonna of the Rocks*

d *Massacre of the Innocents*

e *The Starry Night*

f *Christ in the Carpenter's Shop*

g *The Rake's Progress*

h *Dignity and Impudence*

i *The Night Watch*

j *The Blue Boy*

k *Assassination of Marat*

l *Miracle of St Mark*

m *The Gleaners*

n *Primavera*

o *Marriage at Cana*

p *Lesson in Anatomy*

q *Henry VIII*

3

IN THE LAST seventy days of his life he painted seventy pictures. He shot himself at the age of 37 in 1890.
Who was he?

4

WHO WERE the two most famous painters knighted by Charles I?

5

WHICH OF THE FOLLOWING artists were also architects?
Underline the architects
Raphael, Bernini, Michelangelo, Titian, Goya, Reynolds, Turner

17 Draw, O Coward!

A PALINDROME is a word or phrase that reads the same backwards as it does forwards – for example '*Madam I'm Adam*', or '*Able was I ere I saw Elba.*'

1

THESE CLUES should lead you to some simple one-word palindromes.

a A feat or exploit

...DEED...

b Mid-day

...NOON...

c Holy woman

NUN

d Males and females

...SEXES...

e Musical compositions for a single instrument

...SOLOS...

f Not sloping

LEVEL

g Heroic tales

SAGAS

h Take a look

PEEP

i Former rulers of Iran

SHAHS

j To cover a wall again

REPAPER

k Addressing the Queen

MA'AM

l Blushing even more

REDDER

m It goes round and round

n It brings you round

o It gives strength to your arms

2

COMPLETE the following palindromic sentences:

a Live not..

b Sums are not set as a ....

c Not New York ....

d Niagara, o roar......................................

e Yawn a more...

f No, misses ordered..................................

g Was it a car or......................................

h Evil bats in a cave, sides reversed...................

....

i Dennis, Nell, Edna, Leon............................

j Some men interpret ....

k Stiff, o dairy-man, in...............................

l No, it is opposed; art ....

m Now stop, major-general ....

....

n No, it's a bar of gold...............................

o Desserts I desire not, so long ....

....

p No sot nor Ottawa law ....

3

IN THE FOLLOWING PASSAGE the dots indicate a palindrome. The dots are, however, no indication as to the number of letters. Your task is to fill in the gaps:

It was a lovely day, between .... and ...., when ...., his sister ...., and their father decided to have a .... at their pet ....

'Look, ...,' said the children, *'there is a blue* .... *in the tree.* ....! *If it* .... *us it will fly away, for it will soon have its* .... *on us.'*

They called at a cottage to get a young .... that they had bought, and had a .... at the baby while they put on it a new ...., and made it some .... The children so worshipped the little .... that they nearly .... it. The boy was eating an orange and allowed a .... to fly in the eye of a demure .... who appeared at the door. Her face grew ...., and she said, '.......!

But I am sure you did it by accident.' 'I am *very sorry,* ....,' he replied. *'Of course it was not an intentional* ....', The lady did not further .... to the matter. Then they walked along the .... seashore, to .... out their time, and saw a ship in the distance with the captain on the .... and the boatswain in the ...., and they shouted '.................!' The children were a little tired so they had a bathe, and found it an excellent .... The boy boasted of his swimming, and his father advised him to keep .... on the subject, or he would have to .... him, as he is apt to ....on his own trumpet. They met a gentleman who was an alderman, or holder of some such .... post, with whom the father discussed the question of the equality of the ...., and many a doctrine and .... was uttered that seemed strange to their juvenile ears.

⅛ Domino Delights

1

First Square

Here's a puzzle you shouldn't have to puzzle over for too long. Take the 6 lowest dominoes in the set – the 0/0, the 0/1, the 0/2, the 1/1, the 1/2 and the 2/2 – and arrange them in a square so that all the joins match in number. The shape of the square should be just like this one:

2

Second Square

Take the same 6 dominoes as you used for the First Square – the 0/0, the 0/1, the 0/2, the 1/1, the 1/2, and the 2/2 – and arrange them in exactly the same shaped square, but this time *do it so that each of the four sides of the square contains the same number of pips.*

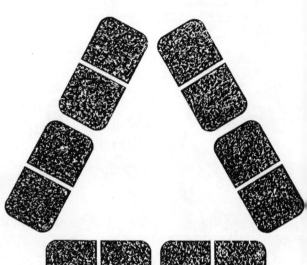

3

Triangular Trouble

For this puzzle you will need the same 6 dominoes as you used for the first two – that's to say the 0/0, the 0/1, the 0/2, the 1/1, the 1/2 and the 2/2. Arrange the 6 dominoes to form an equilateral triangle.

The puzzling part is that you have to make sure that each of the three sides of the triangle contains exactly the same number of pips, but at the same time you must make sure that none of the joins match.

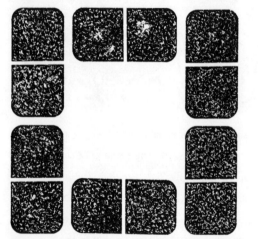

4

First Rectangle

Since we've had a couple of square problems and a triangular one, it's probably about time we had a rectangular puzzle. For this one you'll need the same 6 dominoes – the 0/0, the 0/1, the 0/2, the 1/1, the 1/2, the 2/2, – and the same quick-wittedness you've used before. *You have got to use the dominoes to create a rectangle that looks exactly like this:*

The puzzling part of the problem comes in making sure that each of the four sides of the rectangle contains precisely the same number of pips.

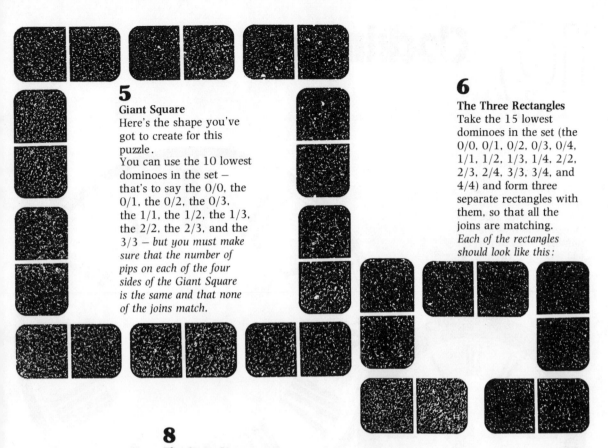

5

Giant Square

Here's the shape you've got to create for this puzzle.
You can use the 10 lowest dominoes in the set — that's to say the 0/0, the 0/1, the 0/2, the 0/3, the 1/1, the 1/2, the 1/3, the 2/2, the 2/3, and the 3/3 — *but you must make sure that the number of pips on each of the four sides of the Giant Square is the same and that none of the joins match.*

6

The Three Rectangles

Take the 15 lowest dominoes in the set (the 0/0, 0/1, 0/2, 0/3, 0/4, 1/1, 1/2, 1/3, 1/4, 2/2, 2/3, 2/4, 3/3, 3/4, and 4/4) and form three separate rectangles with them, so that all the joins are matching.
Each of the rectangles should look like this:

7

Three More Rectangles

Using the same 21 dominoes, form three rectangles. Each rectangle should contain 7 dominoes and should look like this. The problem is to make sure that all twelve sides — that is to say each of the four sides on each of the three triangles — *contain exactly the same number of pips.*

8

The Seven Lines

Take a complete set of dominoes and discard all the pieces in the 6 suit. You are now left with 21 dominoes. Arrange the 21 dominoes in seven lines with 3 dominoes in each line, *so that each line contains exactly the same number of pips and all the joins match.*

9

The Five Lines

With the same 15 dominoes you used to make the Three Rectangles, form 5 lines, with 3 dominoes in each line, like this:

In each of the 5 lines *the joins must match and there must be exactly the same number of pips in each line.*

10

The Seven Squares

Take all 28 dominoes and make them into seven squares with each square formed like this:
All the joins in each of the seven squares must match, but your solution to the puzzle must *not* include the example given here.

Clocking In

ON A CLOCK with Roman numerals – where the fourth hour is marked IIII and not IV – see if you can draw in cracks which break the face into four parts so that the numbers on each part will add up to twenty.

Here is an example which fails:

1

A sets out from his home on foot and travels at 5 miles an hour.
B sets out $4\frac{1}{2}$ hours after A and travels in the same direction 3 miles in the first hour, $3\frac{1}{2}$ miles in the second hour, 4 miles in the third hour and so on.
In how many hours will B overtake A?

....

2

IF AN ORDINARY striking clock was turned into a 24-hour clock, so that at midnight it struck 24 times, how many times would the clock strike in a full 24-hour day?

....

3

IN A STRANGE far-off land there is a curious clock, similar to our own, except that the minute hand moves in the opposite direction to the hour hand. The hands started together at noon, so what was the real time when they were exactly together between the hours of four and five o'clock?

....

4

AT A LATE-NIGHT PARTY it seemed to the guests that the clock had stopped half-way through the party because the hands appeared in exactly the same position as when the party started. In fact they had only changed places. The party began between 10 and 11 o'clock.
What were the two times?

....

5

AT WHAT TIME between three and four o'clock will the minute hand be as far from twelve on the left side of the clock face as the hour hand is from twelve on the right side of the clock face?

....

6

BETWEEN TWO and three o'clock in the afternoon a man looked at his watch and mistook the minute hand for the hour hand, and he thought the time was fifty-five minutes earlier than it actually was.
What was the correct time?

....

7

WHAT should be the next number in this sequence:

712595812595913....?

8

ON A CLOCK where the hour hand and minute hand are the same length and identical, if it were set at noon what would be the first time that it would be possible to be sure of the correct time?

....

9

BETWEEN EIGHT and nine o'clock in the morning a man crossing over Westminster Bridge noted the time on Big Ben. On his return between four and five o'clock he noticed the hands were exactly reversed.
What were the exact times he made the two crossings?

....

10

IF IT TAKES 3 minutes to boil one egg how long will it take to boil 2?

....

11

IF A MAN CAN LOAD a cart in five minutes, and a friend can load it in two-and-a-half minutes, how long will it take them both to load it, working together?

....

12

IF A CHURCH BELL takes two seconds to strike the hour at 2 o'clock, how many seconds will it take to strike 3 o'clock?

....

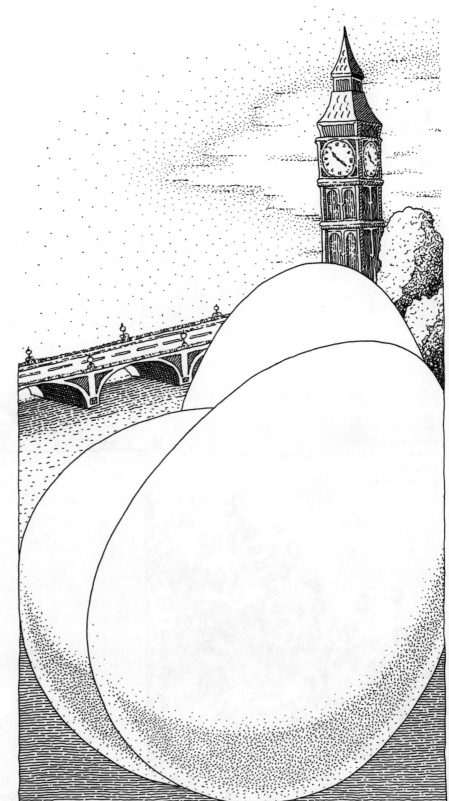

20 Word Search

THE CHALLENGE here is to find the words that have been specially hidden in the diagrams. The words themselves may be written forwards or backwards. upwards or downwards. or even diagonally.

1

Needle in a Haystack
There is only one NEEDLE in this diagram. *Can you find it?*

2

Nation in a Muddle
THIRTY-FIVE AMERICAN TOWNS are hidden in this diagram.
Can you locate them all?

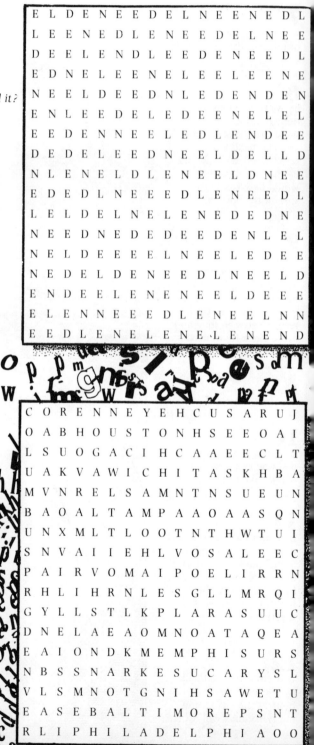

```
E L D E N E E D E L N E E N E D L
L E E N E D L E N E E D E L N E E
D E E L E N D L E E D E N E E D L
E D N E L E E N E L E E L E E N E
N E E L D E E D N L E D E N D E N
E N L E E D E L E D E E N E L E L
E E D E N N E E L E D L E N D E E
D E D E L E E D N E E L D E L L D
N L E N E L D L E N E E L D N E E
E D E D L N E E D L E N E E D L
L E L D E L N E L E N E D E D N E
N E E D N E D E D E E D E N L E L
N E L D E E E E L N E E L E D E E
N E D E L D E N E E D L N E E L D
E N D E E L E N E N E E L D E E E
E L E N N E E E D L E N E E L N N
E E D L E N E L E N E L E N E N D
```

```
C O R E N N E Y E H C U S A R U J
O A B H O U S T O N H S E E O A I
L S U O G A C I H C A A E E C L T
U A K V A W I C H I T A S K H B A
M V N R E L S A M N T N S U E U N
B A O A L T A M P A A O A A S Q N
U N X M L T L O O T N T H W T U I
S N V A I I E H L V O S A L E E C
P A I R V O M A I P O E L I R R N
R H L I H R N L E S G L L M R Q I
G Y L L S T L K P L A R A S U U C
D N E L A E A O M N O A T A Q E A
E A I O N D K M E M P H I S U R S
N B S S N A R K E S U C A R Y S L
V L S M N O T G N I H S A W E T U
E A S E B A L T I M O R E P S N T
R L I P H I L A D E L P H I A O O
```

3

Author!

FIRST identify the authors of these forty-two books. Then, *find their surnames in the diagram.*

Great Expectations

....

War and Peace

....

Treasure Island

....

Ivanhoe

....

Robinson Crusoe

....

Animal Farm

....

Wuthering Heights

....

Alice in Wonderland

....

Tom Jones

....

A Farewell To Arms

....

Moby Dick

....

Sons and Lovers

....

Room at the Top

....

The Hobbit

....

Madame Bovary

....

From Russia With Love

....

Watership Down

....

The Good Companions

....

Ulysses

....

```
L Y B O D A R N O C H E K R A Y A L L
R W O L L N E T S H O C N Y S I M A L
M E X T U T O L K I E N A R D O W M Y
A D A M S O B S I B L M P C E R C K B
H W M U L L I G N O L D I S E V A R G
G L A F C Y O I T E I D N N O C S H N
U N W R I S E T H A V L C I G C O B I
A O I G F T H W A L L E W R O W P A L
M T O M S E Z I C H E Z T T Y J A M P
F H N W E B I G K R M A T S O G S Y I
B G U Y E L T S E I R P A Y F I T S K
B I G H R I F O R R K Y C I L D E N I
J E R O M E V L A P A E E L A G R E T
F D N G T H T S Y D D L U L U B N K E
W M A N N O N S E N D T D O B E A C N
B E O B E O A F R I Y R B R E B K I I
C R L I M T O V N O K A T R R Y A D A
B U R L B E T G H O F H G A T W Y O R
F O R T S N O B B I G L Y C T H L I B
```

Huckleberry Finn

....

Far From The Madding Crowd

....

Vanity Fair

....

Doctor Zhivago

....

The War of the Worlds

....

Pride and Prejudice

....

The Go-Between

....

Of Human Bondage

....

The Cruel Sea

....

The Spy Who Came In From The Cold

....

Tender Is The Night

....

The Grapes of Wrath

....

A Passage To India

....

Clayhanger

....

Kim

....

Cold Comfort Farm

....

Death in Venice

....

Around The World in Eighty Days

....

Three Men in a Boat

....

Lucky Jim

....

Brighton Rock

....

Nostromo

....

I. Claudius

....

21 Patience is a Virtue

1

FROM A PACK OF CARDS take the four Aces, Kings, Queens, Jacks, making a total of 16 cards. The problem is to arrange them in four rows so that in each horizontal, vertical and diagonal row you have one of each suit and also one of each denomination. Thus you will have eight rows and two diagonals, each of four cards, without duplicating a suit or a value in any single series of four.

2

ARRANGE EIGHT RED AND EIGHT BLACK playing cards like this:

The object is to convert this pattern into a chessboard arrangement of alternating red and black cards, the top left card being black. A move consists of abstracting any card, placing it outside the grid at either end of the line it came from, and then closing the line up again. If only columns are considered, i.e. all such moves are made vertically, a solution in eight moves is easily found. But with the stipulation that moves are to be alternately vertical and horizontal, *what is the smallest number of extra moves required?*

3

A TOTAL OF 21 CARDS consisting of

4 Kings
4 Queens
4 Jacks
4 Tens
4 Nines and
1 Joker

were dealt to Alec, Bill and Carl. Then all Jacks, Tens, and Nines were discarded.

At that point:

The combined hands consisted of 4 Kings, 4 Queens, and 1 Joker.

Alec had 2 cards, Bill had 3 cards, and Carl had 4 cards.

The man with the most singletons did not have the Joker.

No man had more than 2 Kings.

Who had the Joker?

(A hand contains a singleton when it contains only one King or only one Queen, or the Joker.)

Take the cards from the pack and lay them out in three groups so that each condition is observed and you should find the solution.

4

HERE ARE THREE playing cards —
can you spot the deliberate mistakes?

5

TAKE THE ACES, Kings, Queens and Jacks from a pack. Place them in four rows, each row with four cards, in such a way that the sequence King, Queen, Jack, Ace or Ace, Jack, Queen, King shall make up each side of your quadrilateral (horizontally and perpendicularly), and one of each denomination be found in the two middle rows.

6

AFTER REMOVING the Aces, Kings, Queens, and Jacks from an ordinary pack of cards, arrange the remaining thirty-six cards in a quadrilateral, so that:

The pips of each row, both horizontal and perpendicular, amount to thirty-six.

No two cards of the same value occur in any row or diagonal.

Each row contains three red and three black cards.

Crosswords Ancient

1

The world's first crossword puzzle appeared in the *New York World* newspaper on Sunday, December 21, 1913. It was devised by Arthur Wynne who called it a *Word-cross Puzzle*.

2–3   What bargain hunters enjoy
4–5   A written acknowledgement
6–7   Such and nothing more
10–11 A bird
14–15 Opposed to less
18–19 What this puzzle is

22–23 An animal of prey
26–27 The close of a day
28–29 To elude
30–31 The plural of is
8–9   To cultivate
12–13 A bar of wood or iron

N–8   A fist
24–31 To agree with
3–12 Part of a ship
20–29 One
5–27 Exchanging
9–25 To sink in mud
13–21 A boy

16–17 What artists learn to do
20–21 Fastened
24–25 Found on the seashore
10–18 The fibre of the gomuti palm
6–22 What we all should be
4–26 A day dream
2–11 A talon
19–28 A pigeon
F–7   Part of your head
23–30 A river in Russia
1–32 To govern
33–34 An aromatic plant

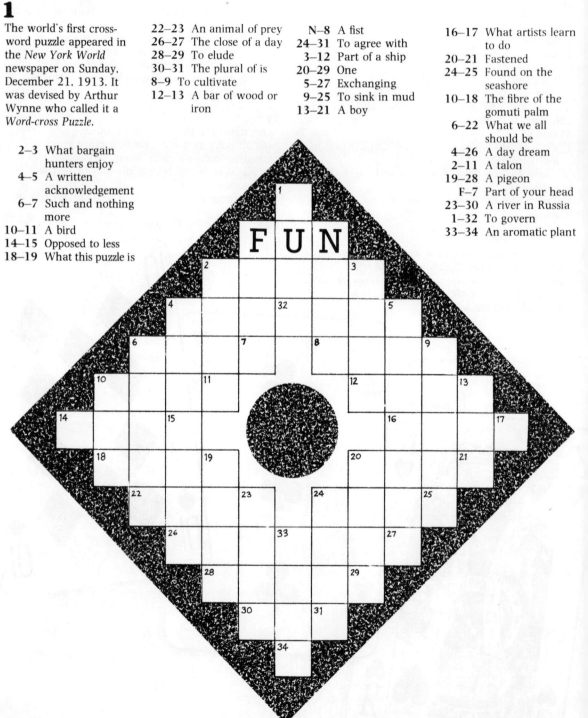

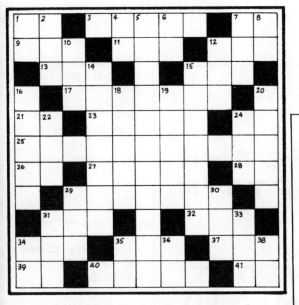

The first ever book of crossword puzzles was published by Dick Simon and Lincoln Schuster in New York in 1924. And the first puzzle in the first book was this one:

HORIZONTAL
1 Pronoun
3 Albumin from castor-oil bean
7 Exist
9 Aged
11 Negative
12 Incite, hasten
13 Remote
15 Obstruction
17 Bivalves
21 Father
23 Tree
24 River in Italy
25 Owners
26 Printer's measure
27 Tree
28 Personal pronoun
29 Legislative bodies
31 Compact mass
32 Moved rapidly
34 Walk about
35 Toss
37 Small child
39 On
40 Small openings
41 Act

VERTICAL
1 Exclamation
2 Fairy
4 Preposition
5 Plotter
6 Pronoun
7 Express generally
8 Pronoun
10 Obstruct
12 Owns
14 Disarranged
15 Voluble talkativeness
16 Above
18 The bow of Vishnu
19 Choose
20 Assumed an attitude
22 Limb
24 Peer
29 Sorrowful
30 Rested
31 Pale
33 Incline the head
34 Move
35 Behold
36 Exist
38 Preposition

Crosswords Modern

These puzzles are neither as old nor as easy as the two 'firsts' on the left. In fact they are brand-new and, while they feature far fewer words than the other puzzles, solving them will probably take you twice as long.

MINIATURE CROSSWORD 1

ACROSS
1 Sirius follows sailor
5 It's taught in schools in Berkshire
6 Plead for demonology?
7 Eli dyes loose covers for viewers

DOWN
1 Creatures found in frozen bedroom?
2 King George has fruit to lay hold of
3 Stumble on crude oil in Libya
4 River birds showing sorrow

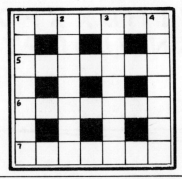

MINIATURE CROSSWORD 2

DOWN
1 Some slimmers eat duck
2 A cutter is a ship
3 Hurried up, gaining speed, to tell a story
4 In the centre a tramp is seen to beg

ACROSS
1 Anger? Holy smoke!
5 Detective's ragtime composition
6 Put back two kinds of material
7 Sincere listener finds shelter

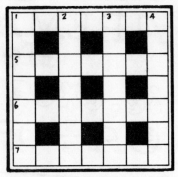

23 Reading Between the Lines

You will find deciphering these messages ylevitaler elpmis!

1
Vowel Play
When you have found what's missing, you should be able to make sense of these sentences:

a P R S V R Y P E F C T M N
   V R K P T H S P R C P T S T N

   ....

   ....

b R T H D X X F D D N S D N T
   K N W L D P R T F R M L G W D

   ....

   ....

3
Numbers Up

a 16 -21-26-26-12-5
   13-15-21-14-20-1-9-14
   9-19 20-8-5
   2-5-19-20
   16-21-26-26-12-5
   2-15-15-11 5-22-5-18

   ....

   ....

   ....

b 3-15-4-5-19 1-18-5
   5-1-19-25
   23-8-5-14 25-15-21
   11-14-15-23
   8-15-23

   ....

   ....

   ....

2
Fine Phrases
Yes, *but what are they?*

a *murohado*

b 2amin3pm

c *Enutrof*

d A REMAINDER
   He is

e *ie,* cXCEPT

f ⑤GA－$\frac{s}{G}$ OFₚPₚPₚPₚP

g (musical notation)

48

4

Pig Latin

What's it all about?

a hetayaveragewayengthlayofway
ordsaywinwayhetayenglishway
anguagelayiswayaboutway
ourfayandwayawayalfhay
etterslay

....

....

b inwayallwayhetaycommoncay
anguageslayofwayesternway
europewayandwayamericaway
ewayiswayhetayetterlayhattay
iswayusedwayhetayostmay
oftenway

....

....

....

5

Morse the Merrier

Translate these messages:

a

....

....

b

....

....

c

....

....

....

6

Natural Break

Can you make sense of this?

al Lou rliv
eswea recru
she dbythewei
ghtofw ords

....

....

....

7

False Start

Can you work out what is phoney about this message?

GALLB GTHEY RFIRSTQ
HANDX TALLY STHEJ
KLASTH YLETTERS
WARET PFALSEM

....

....

24 Words at Play

1

Dual Duel

Homophones are words (like DUAL and DUEL) which have different meanings and which are spelled differently but which sound identical.

Can you find twenty pairs of homophones to fit these definitions?

1 entirely/sacred

...W.HOLLY... / ...HOLY...

2 correct/ceremonial procedure

...RIGHT... / ...RITE...

3 pick/masticates

...CHOOSE... / ...CHEWS...

4 forsake/sweet course

...DESERT... / ...DESSERT...

5 connections/wildcat

...LINKS... / ...LYNX...

6 sluggish/blackthorn

...SLOW... / ...SLOE...

7 napped leather/moved to and fro

...SUEDE... / ...SWAYED...

8 gorse/trees

.... / ....

9 sphere/cry lustily

...BALL... / ...BAWL...

10 narrow/direct

...STRAIT... / ...STRAIGHT...

11 agreement/crammed

...PACT... / ...PACKED...

12 agreement/climb

...ASSENT... / ...ASCENT...

13 virgin/created

...MAID... / ...MADE...

14 vile/bird

...FOUL... / ...FOWL...

15 a cereal/labyrinth

...MAIZE... / ...MAZE...

16 forbidden/ring

...BANNED... / ...BAND...

17 careless/deficiencies

...LAX... / ...LACKS...

18 route/indelicate

...COURSE... / ...COARSE...

19 chop/colour

...HEW... / ...HUE...

20 praise/peer

...LAUD... / ...LORD...

2

'Ologies'

The left-hand column contains twenty branches of study ending with the suffix -OLOGY. The right-hand column shows, in random sequence, the subjects studied.

Can you match each 'OLOGY' with its corresponding subject? Fill in the correct letter.

1 Pharmacology ...DRUGS...   **a** Insects

2 Cardiology ...HEARTS...   **b** Fungi

3 Conchology ...SHELLS...   **c** Caves

4 Campanology ...BELLS...   **d** Ferns

5 Horology ...CLOCKS...   **e** Hair

6 Dermatology ...SKIN...   **f** ~~Whales~~

7 Phonology ...SOUNDS...   **g** ~~Clocks~~ ✓

8 Seismology ...EARTHQUAKES...   **h** Trees

9 Entomology ...INSECTS...   **i** ~~Drugs~~ ✓

10 Oology ....   **j** ~~Hearts~~ ✓

11 Dendrology.................   **k** Dreams

12 Trichology ...HAIR...   **l** ~~Rocks~~

13 Mycology.................   **m** ~~Sounds~~ ✓

14 Spelaeology ....   **n** ~~Bells~~ ✓

15 Bryology ....   **o** ~~Teeth~~ ✓

16 Odontology...TEETH...   **p** Shells

17 Petrology...ROCKS...   **q** Eggs

18 Cetology ...WHALES...   **r** Mosses

19 Pteridology.................   **s** ~~Earthquakes~~

20 Oneirology ...DREAMS...   **t** ~~Skin~~ ✓

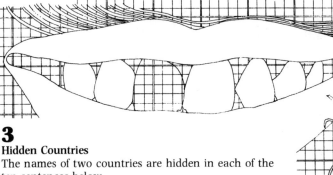

3

Hidden Countries

The names of two countries are hidden in each of the ten sentences below.

Can you discover them?

For instance, in the sentence 'Interpol and the FBI discover hidden marksmen', POLAND is concealed in the first two words and DENMARK is concealed in the last two words.

Underline the countries.

1 Vladimir and Olga are Soviet names.
2 Have you ever heard an animal talk in dialect?
3 In letters to the press we denounce the wholesale ban on luxury imports.
4 Evening classes may help an amateur to improve his painting.
5 Children put on galoshes to go out in the rain.
6 Rash decisions may cause trouble so thorough analysis is a necessity.
7 The viscount has not found a home yet and he regrets leaving his fine palace.
8 If your exhaust pipe rusts you just have to shrug and accept it.
9 Such a display could be either grand or rather vulgar.
10 Give the dog a bone and give him a little water.

4

Alphabetic Extractions

The 26 words below have each had a different letter removed wherever it occurs in the word. One word has had two or more As extracted, one word has had two or more Bs extracted, and so on through the alphabet. Thus FLUFFY, for example, might appear as LUY.

Can you discover the 26 original words?

1 VRGRN
....
2 RYTM
....
3 INIU
....
4 UINUIREME
....
5 NGRM
....
6 IETEE
....
7 ARLIN
....
8 IGAM
....
9 YLI
....
10 UIES
....
11 INY
....

12 GPS
....
13 UCCE
....
14 ERES
....
15 HIRY
....
16 ANARE
....
17 EASIE
....
18 SUUR
....
19 HOO
....
20 IABE
....
21 JAY
....
22 AMNE
....
23 LLATE
....
24 EUNE
....
25 VD
....
26 RONC
....

25 Time for Tangrams

TO ATTEMPT THIS ANCIENT CHINESE PUZZLE you will need a set of tangrams – seven pieces of card that can be cut from a single square.

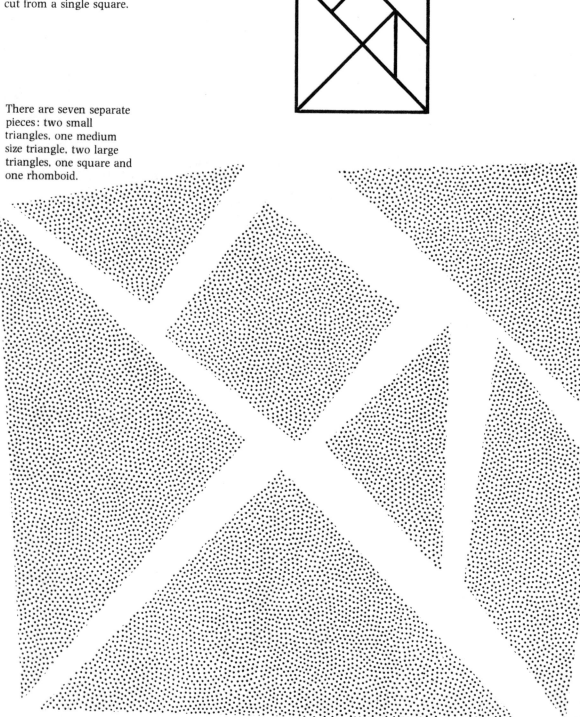

There are seven separate pieces: two small triangles, one medium size triangle, two large triangles, one square and one rhomboid.

The medium sized triangle, the square and the rhomboid are all twice the area of one of the small triangles. Each of the large triangles is four times the area of one of the small triangles. All the angles in the pieces are either right angles or angles of 45° or 135°. You may feel that making a set of tangrams is challenge enough, but it is only when you have your set that the puzzling part begins.

With your tangrams try to construct, one at a time, the numbers one, two, three, four, five, six, seven and eight as shown. *You must use all seven pieces and none of them must overlap.*

HAVING LEARNED TO COUNT from one to eight the tangram way, now attempt to construct these eight shapes.

In each case you must use all seven pieces and make sure that none of them overlaps.

1

2

3

4

6

5

7

8

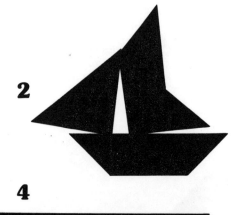

The Food of Love

1

WHAT WAS THE NATIONALITY of each of the following great composers?

a J. S. Bach

....

b Charles Ives

....

c H. Berlioz

....

d Johannes Brahms

....

e Frédéric Chopin

....

f C. W. Gluck

....

g G. F. Handel

....

h Gustav Holst

....

i A. Khachaturyan

....

j F. Liszt

....

k F. Mendelssohn

....

l W. A. Mozart

....

m Henry Purcell

....

n Maurice Ravel

....

o F. Schubert

....

p J. P. Sousa

....

q P. I. Tchaikovsky

....

r Richard Wagner

....

2

WHO COMPOSED the following?

a *The Barber of Seville*

....

b *The Dream Gerontius*

....

c *I Pagliacci*

....

d *Oberon*

....

e *The Ring of the Nibelung*

....

f *The Golden Cockerel*

....

g *The Fairy Queen*

....

h *Fidelio*

....

i *La Bohème*

....

j *The Tales of Hoffman*

....

k *Russlan and Ludmilla*

....

l *Belshazzar's Feast*

....

3

IDENTIFY THE COMPOSER:

a Born in Hamburg on February 3, 1809. Wrote music that has great emotion, one particular piece that many lovers hear. He died in Berlin on November 4, 1847 — never really recovering from the shock of his sister's death six months earlier.

....

b Born on June 8, 1810, the youngest of a family of four boys and a girl. Embarked on his musical career in Leipzig in 1828, and was profoundly distressed by the death of Schubert in the same year. He lived in constant fear of death or insanity. He set Byron's *Manfred* to music. In 1854 he tried to commit suicide and spent the remainder of his life in a mental asylum. He died in July 1856.

....

c Born on March 1, 1810, in the village of Zelazowa Wola, 28 miles from Warsaw. His music is regarded as some of the most romantic ever written. He died on October 17, 1849, and his friends filled the death chamber with flowers.

....

d Born in Bergen, Norway on June 15, 1843. His music reflects the love he had for his country — the mountains, fjords, and valleys. He died on September 3, 1907. His burial place is as romantic as his music, cut fifty-feet high into a cliff, projecting over a fjord near his home, in a natural grotto that can only be reached by boat.

....

e Born in Vienna, January 31, 1797. In a short life he composed over 600 songs, eight symphonies, several operas, chamber works and masses. Beethoven said of him 'He has the divine fire'. He suffered a break-down in October, 1828, and died on November 19, 1828. He is buried close to Beethoven, his tomb bearing the inscription: 'Music has here emtombed a rich treasure, but much fairer hopes.'

....

27 Fair and Square

1

HERE IS THE SKELETON of a
word square.
Can you complete it?
The words you are
looking for are quite
straightforward and
remember that there are
only five of them because
the words in the rows
must be the same as the
words in the columns.

```
S _ _ _ S
_ D _ _ _
_ _ U _ _
_ _ _ E _
S _ _ _ Y
```

2

USING THESE VERSIFIED
CLUES, create a five-letter
word square.

My *first* are very lovely to the eye,
Though superstitious men refuse to buy.
My *second* too is beautious to behold,
When closed or when it happens to unfold.
Those, who perchance, have fallen into sin,
Should try to do my *third*, their peace to win.
My *fourth*'s a weapon soldiers bear today,
Though used by ancient warriors in the fray.
To be exposed before my *last*, you'll say,
Is not delightful, any time of day.

```
_ _ _ _ _
_ _ _ _ _
_ _ _ _ _
_ _ _ _ _
_ _ _ _ _
```

3

ALL THE LINES of four
figures in this square
ought to add up to 34,
whether read across,
down or diagonally. By
mistake, two have been
placed wrongly.
*Can you discover which
two?*

16	3	2	13
5	10	11	8
9	6	12	7
4	15	14	1

4

FILL THE SQUARES with the
numbers 1 to 9. Obviously
no number can be used
twice. When you have
finished the numbers
must add up to 15 in **all**
directions.

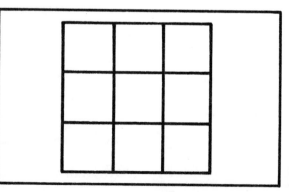

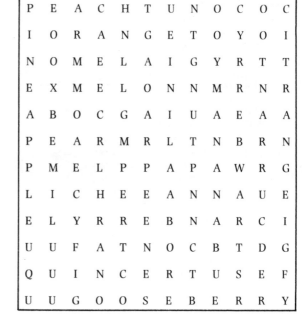

6

THIS SQUARE is full of fruit.
How many?
What are they?
Where are they?

5

WITH TANGRAMS fresh in your memory, look what the great Chinese puzzler, T'ung Hsiehkeng, managed to do with a square piece of card. He cut it into fifteen pieces like this:

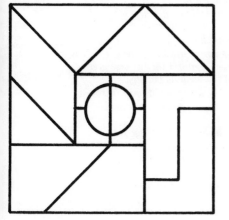

and used those fifteen pieces to create the figure above.
How did he position his fifteen pieces?

P	E	A	C	H	T	U	N	O	C	O	C
I	O	R	A	N	G	E	T	O	Y	O	I
N	O	M	E	L	A	I	G	Y	R	T	T
E	X	M	E	L	O	N	N	M	R	N	R
A	B	O	C	G	A	I	U	A	E	A	A
P	E	A	R	M	R	L	T	N	B	R	N
P	M	E	L	P	P	A	P	A	W	R	G
L	I	C	H	E	E	A	N	N	A	U	E
E	L	Y	R	R	E	B	N	A	R	C	I
U	U	F	A	T	N	O	C	B	T	D	G
Q	U	I	N	C	E	R	T	U	S	E	F
U	U	G	O	O	S	E	B	E	R	R	Y

28 Verse and Worse

1

A PARADOX to explain . . .

> Four jolly men sat down to play,
> And played all night till break of day.
> They played for gold and not for fun,
> With separate scores for everyone.
> Yet when they came to square accounts,
> They all had made quite fair amounts.
> Can you the paradox explain,
> If no one lost, how could all gain?

....

2

A MUTILATED POEM to make sense of . . .

> Hewn I saw young dan ni my ripem,
> I doluc tea a finfum nay item.
> Tub won I'm dol dan noggi regy,
> It skate me learny fahl a ady.

....

....

....

....

3

A CHARADE to perform . . .

> My First _ _ _ _ for that consult the cook,
> She'll know the reason why;
> She, without this, by hook or crook
> Could never make a pie.
>
> My Second _ _ _ is not very hard,
> You'll be upon the track,
> If only you've the proper card
> Selected from the pack.
>
> My Third _ _ _ you'll find that each true Scot
> With that contrives to see,
> And in the alphabet I wot
> It's pretty sure to be.
>
> My Last _ _ _ in some things 'tis a first,
> I give a clear suggestion,
> And oftentimes, when you've conversed,
> You've met it as a question.
>
> My Whole _ _ _ are dwellers in the sea,
> And frequently you meet 'em,
> And now if you'll come home with me,
> I'll show you how to eat 'em.

....

4

AN ACROSTIC CREATURE and four words to find . . .

> Twinkle, twinkle little star,
> I can guess, though, what you are,
> As you shine not up on high,
> But among the hedgerows nigh.
> > i
> It's a shame and disgrace
> > Beyond a doubt
> > To laugh right out
> > In anyone's face;
> And in manners you make a shocking flaw
> With a 'ho! ho! ho!' and a 'haw! haw! haw!'
> > ii
> The Indian who courses
> And catches wild horses,
> Is apt at the use
> Of the flying noose,
> Which is one of his chief resources.
> > iii
> Down as Heaven's first law, lay
> > 'Always obey
> > What your masters say!'
> > iv
> The chief of the tribe of Snakes
> He always with him takes
> The squaw he chose to marry
> In order that she might carry
> His dwelling of skins and stakes.

....

5

A WORD TO FIND . . .

> In early spring, one silent night,
> The bold Sir Wilfred strayed,
> Beneath his lady's lattice bright,
> To sing a serenade.
> He sat him down upon my First,
> And there his loving lay rehearsed.
>
> A silvery mist hung o'er the scene
> Where thus he breathed his vows;
> And dewdrops gemmed the herbage green,
> And decked the budding boughs.
> But ah! Sir Wilfred should have reckoned
> The grass was sure to be my Second.
>
> Next morn he did his foot-page call,
> And bade at once repair
> To gay Lord Guthlac's festive hall,
> And him this message bear —
> Al Cal't to-dight atteld by Whole!

....

29 In for a Spell

1

HERE ARE 50 WORDS. Some are spelt correctly, but some are not.
Mark the incorrect ones with an x.

diptheria
hitchhiker
irresistable
violoncello
definately
wierd
batallion
dissapointment
beseige
managable
guage
embarrassed
apochryphal
threshold
dissipate
pursue
rarify
harrassment
category
gaiety
desiccated
accomodate
ecstacy
chagrined
drunkenness
putrefied
parallellogram
supercede
idiosyncrasy
fricassee
ocurrence
obbligato
bizarre
straitjacket
appropriate
hara-kiri
picnicking
recommendation
irridescent
stacatto
woolly
coolly
benifited
perserverance
intercede
catarrh
niece
sacreligious
rythm
numskull

2

BELOW ARE THE *pronounciations* of a dozen familiar words. *Can you give the correct spelling?*

a an es the zi a

....

b Ka kof o ni

....

c Kro nol ogi

....

d Do be ous

....

e e lips

....

f for fit

....

g freekwen see

....

h fu ror i

....

i idi o sink racy

....

j nu row hip nol o ji

....

k a j ern ment

....

l vish us

....

3

HERE ARE 30 WORDS, correctly spelt.
Can you write down the plurals of each word?

1 Daughter-in-law

....

2 Attorney general

....

3 Brigadier general

....

4 Judge advocate

....

5 Chargé d'affaires

....

6 Potato

....

7 Notary public

....

8 Law merchant

....

9 Opus

....

10 Pelvis

....

11 Sergeant major

....

12 Teaspoonful

....

13 Piccolo

....

14 Table d'hôte

....

15 Court-martial

....

16 Paymaster general

....

17 Mister

....

18 Madam

....

19 Crisis

....

20 Man-of-war

....

21 Lieutenant colonel

....

22 Bandit

....

23 Cannon

....

24 Phenomenon

....

25 Aviatrix

....

26 Manservant

....

27 Oboe

....

28 Ox

....

29 Valet de chambre

....

30 Datum

....

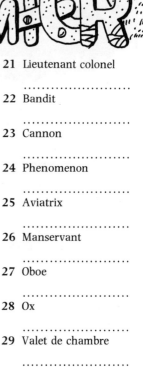

30 Mixed Bag

1

USING THE FIGURE 4 four times, and simple mathematical symbols, the number 12 can be represented as follows:

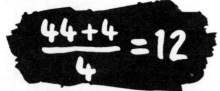

$$\frac{44+4}{4}=12$$

And 15, 16, and 17 can be represented by the following expressions:

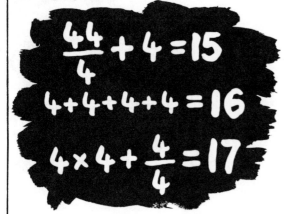

$$\frac{44}{4}+4=15$$

$$4+4+4+4=16$$

$$4\times4+\frac{4}{4}=17$$

Using the same approach, can you devise representations for the numbers from 0 to 10?

You ought to be able to stick with addition signs, subtraction signs, multiplication signs, and division signs.

2

I AM A WORD of ten letters.

My **1, 2, 8** is rainy
My **1, 5, 6, 7** is part of a bird's body
My **8, 9, 10** is a weight
My **1, 2, 3, 4** is a spring
My **7, 5, 4, 8** is a golden surface
My **10, 9, 8, 2** is a short letter
My **whole** is a celebrated warrior

Who or what am I?

....

3

I HAVE TWO COINS whose sum is 55 pence. One of them is not a 50 pence piece.
What two coins do I have?

....

4

a Which is heavier: 1000 kilograms *or* 1 ton?

....

b Which is longer: 250 centimetres *or* 8 feet?

....

c Which is larger: 3 raised to the 5th power *or* 5 raised to the 3rd power?

....

d Which is hotter: zero degrees Centigrade *or* zero degrees Fahrenheit?

....

e Which are there more of: ounces in a ton *or* inches in a kilometre?

....

f Which is colder: $-40°$ Centigrade *or* $-40°$ Fahrenheit?

....

5

```
F I V
I F E
V E F
F I V F I V
I E V I F E
E E V V I F
      I F I V F I
      V F I F E V
      E F V I E E
            E E V I F I
            V F I I F V
            E V F I F F
                  V E F I V V
                  V E F V I F
                  E I V E F I
```

The word FIVE appears just five times in this arrangement of letters. Find the five FIVES.

6

Take the word ORIENTALS. Delete one letter and rearrange the remaining letters to make another word. Now delete one letter from this new word and rearrange the remaining letters to make another word. Keep doing this until there is only one letter left.

```
O R I E N T A L S
..................................................
..............................................
.........................................
...................................
.............................
.......................
.................
...........
......
```

7

THIS QUOTATION is a muddled version of a quotation by George Bernard Shaw. *What was the original quotation?*

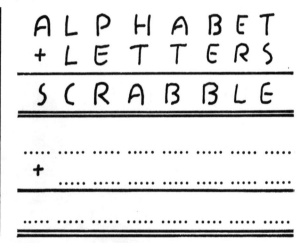

"they clever are
time making
expedient foolish
doing wasting very
something for idle
is a they chess
people when their
are only believe."

....
....
....

8

EACH OF THE LETTERS below corresponds uniquely to a numerical digit. Find the correspondence to make this addition correct.

$$\begin{array}{r} A L P H A B E T \\ + L E T T E R S \\ \hline S C R A B B L E \end{array}$$

```
..... ..... ..... ..... ..... ..... ..... .....
+
     ..... ..... ..... ..... ..... ..... .....
_____
..... ..... ..... ..... ..... ..... ..... .....
```

9

THIS ARRANGEMENT of letters contains only the letters of the word C-R-E-A-T-I-O-N-S. How many words of five letters or more can you spell out from the diagram? There are at least twenty.

N	E	R	I	S	C	A	N	T	A
S	S	E	C	R	E	T	I	O	N
S	I	N	C	E	T	I	C	E	R
R	A	N	O	I	T	C	E	R	E
T	R	E	S	I	N	A	R	O	C
T	R	S	I	N	T	E	R	O	E
C	R	A	T	E	R	C	N	A	I
E	E	E	C	E	R	T	A	I	N
R	E	I	R	E	C	A	T	E	R
E	C	I	R	T	N	A	C	E	R

31 King Lear

AMAZING is as good a word as any to use to describe the talents of Edward Lear (1812–88), an ordinary artist and an extraordinary nonsense writer, who taught drawing to Queen Victoria and pioneered the limerick. These mazes by David Farris were inspired by him.

To work your way through them go in at one arrow and come out at the other.

There was an old man in a barge,
Whose nose was exceedingly large;
    But in fishing by night,
    It supported a light,
Which helped that old man in a barge.

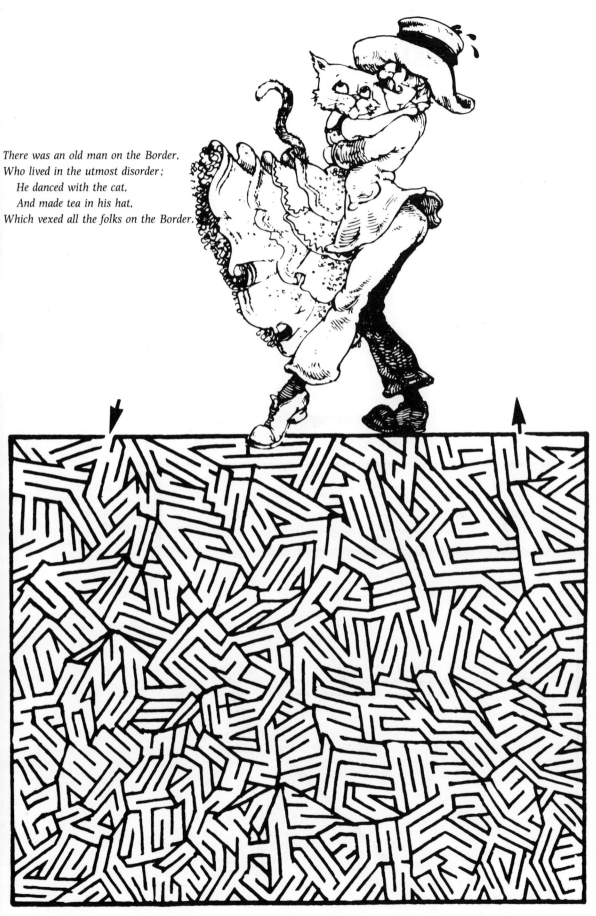

There was an old man on the Border,
Who lived in the utmost disorder;
   He danced with the cat,
   And made tea in his hat,
Which vexed all the folks on the Border.

32 Out of Shape

1

THIS FIGURE is made up of two squares.
Can you divide it by two straight lines so that the three parts can be arranged to form a single perfect square?

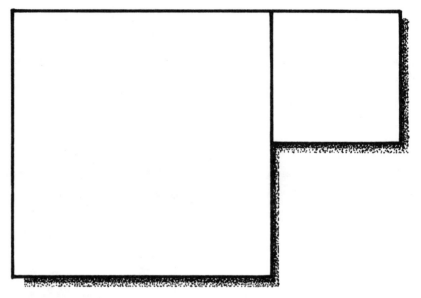

2

HERE IS A RECTANGLE.
Can you cut this into five parts to form a perfect square?

3

A CARPENTER had to construct a table-top two feet square from the odd shaped piece of wood shown here. He did it in two sawings.
Where did he cut?

4

DRAW EIGHT STRAIGHT LINES to transform this square into five small equal squares whose total area should be equal to this square.

5

How many triangles can you see here?

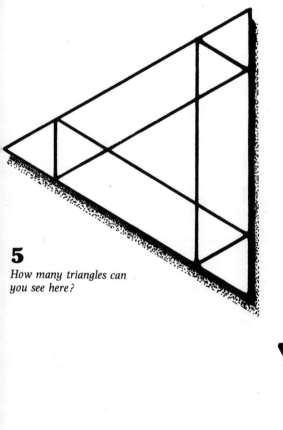

6

IF THIS PATTERN were a floor tile could the tiles be fitted together and *which way would they fit?*

33 Mensa Gymnastics

MENSA IS AN INTERNATIONAL ORGANISATION whose membership is open to anyone whose measured intelligence puts them in the top two per cent of the population. If you can cope with these puzzles with ease, you might even be eligible . . .

WORK OUT the underlying principle and find the next element in each of the following series.
Ring the letter below the answer.

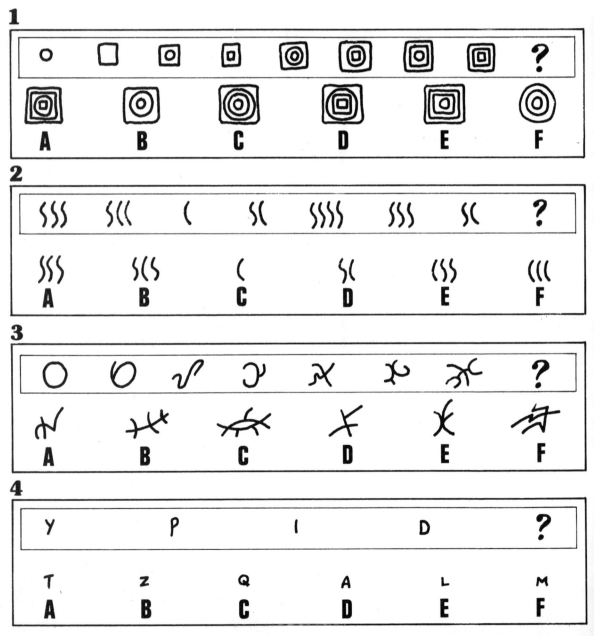

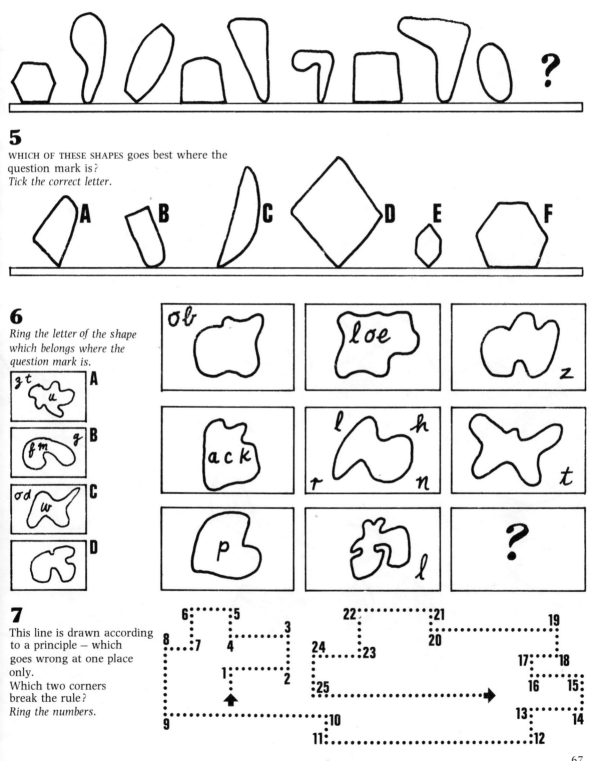

5

WHICH OF THESE SHAPES goes best where the
question mark is?
Tick the correct letter.

A B C D E F

6

*Ring the letter of the shape
which belongs where the
question mark is.*

A
B
C
D

7

This line is drawn according
to a principle – which
goes wrong at one place
only.
Which two corners
break the rule?
Ring the numbers.

34 **Fly the Flag**

IDENTIFY THE COUNTRY from which each aircraft comes.

1 ....
2 ....
3 ....
4 ....
5 ....
6 ....
7 ....
8 ....
9 ....
10 ....
11 ....
12 ....
13 ....
14 ....
15 ....
16 ....
17 ....
18 ....
19 ....
20 ....
21 ....
22 ....
23 ....
24 ....

35 Number Classics

1

WHAT IS THE DIFFERENCE between 4 square miles and 4 miles square?

....

....

2

THERE ARE 5 EGGS on a dish; divide them among 5 persons so that each will get 1 egg and yet 1 still remain on the dish.

....

3

A GENTLEMAN having bought 28 bottles of wine, and suspecting his servant of tampering with the contents of the wine cellar, caused these bottles to be arranged in a bin in such a way as to count 9 bottles on each side. Notwithstanding this precaution, the servant in two successive visits stole 8 bottles – 4 each time – re-arranging the bottles so that they still counted 9 on a side.
How did he do it?

They were originally arranged like this.

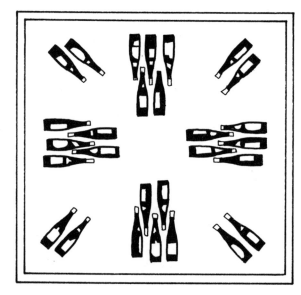

4

GOLD CAN BE HAMMERED SO thin that a grain will make 56 square inches for leaf gilding. How many such leaves will make an inch thick if the weight of a cubic foot of gold is 10 cwt 95 lbs?

....

5

TWO FATHERS and two sons went into a hotel to have drinks which cost £3. They each spent the same amount. *How much did each pay?*

....

6

A FARMER, being asked what number of animals he kept, answered: 'They're all horses but two, all sheep but two, and all pigs but two.'
How many did he have?

....

7

WHAT NUMBER is that which, being divided by 7 and the quotient diminished by 10, three times the remainder shall be 23?

....

8

Two years ago to Hobart-town
A certain number of folk came down.
The square root of half of them got married,
And then in Hobart no longer tarried;
Eight-ninths of all went away as well
(This is a story sad to tell):
The square root of four now live here in woe!
How many came here two years ago?

....

9

A COMPOSITOR, hurrying while setting up type for an arithmetic book, *How to Become Quick at Figures*, accidentally dropped the type for one problem; unfortunately he mislaid the copy, and all he remembered was that both multiplicand and multiplier consisted of two figures. The scattered type represented the following figures: 1, 2, 3, 3, 4, 6, 7, 8, 8, 9, 9. With the aid of a pencil and paper the compositor managed after a while to rearrange the figures in their proper place.
What was the problem?

....

10

IN ONE CORNER of a hexagonal grass paddock each of the sides of which is 40 yards long, a horse is tethered with a rope 50 yards long.
How many square yards can he graze over?

....

11

A AND B START TOGETHER from the same point on a circular path and walk until they arrive together at the starting point. If A performs the circuit in 224 seconds and B in 364 seconds, *how many times do they each walk round?*

....

12

SUPPOSE FOUR POOR MEN have houses around a pond, and later that four nasty rich men build houses at the back of the poor people – as shown in the illustration – and wish to have a monopoly of the water: *how can they erect a fence so as to shut the poor people off from the pond?*

13

A WHALE'S HEAD is just 72 inches long, and his tail is as long as his head and half the body, which is half the whole length. *How big is this whale?*

....

14

A FARMER SOLD you half an egg more than half the eggs that he carried in a basket. He then sold Mrs. Smith half an egg more than half the remainder, and then half an egg more than half of what was left. One egg was left.
How many did the basket originally contain?

....

15

THE LIFE SPAN OF A WHALE is 4 times that of a stork, who lives 85 years longer than a guinea pig, which lives 6 years less than an ox, who lives nine years less than a horse, who lives twelve years longer than a chicken, who lives 282 years less than an elephant, who lives 283 years longer than a dog, who lives 2 years longer than a cat, who lives 135 years less than a carp, who lives twice as long as a camel, who lives 1,066 years short of the total of all the animal's life spans. *What is each animal's life span?*

camel.......... carp.......... cat.......... dog..........

elephant........... chicken........... horse...........

ox........ guinea pig........ stork........ whale........

16

YOU HAVE TWO CANDLES, one of which can last you 5 hours, while the other will last 8 hours. If both were lit simultaneously, how soon would one of the candles be 2.2 times the length of the other?

....

17

A had a number of geese totalling 72, which is exactly 300% that of the number of geese B had. Now, if B bought 6/9 of A's then B would then have 300% as many geese as A.
How many geese did B have originally and finally?

....

18

SUPPOSE YOU WERE TOLD that half the apples you can see could not be seen, and two-thirds of those not seen can be seen, and that you could see 6 dozen apples more than cannot be seen, and half the apples that cannot be seen could be seen, and three-quarters of the apples that can be seen couldn't be seen, and that you would then miss out in seeing half a dozen more than you see – well, *do you think you could figure out the number of apples that you have?*

19

DIVIDE 4,700 pennies among A, B, and C so that A would get 1,000 pennies more than B, and B, 800 pennies more than C.

....

20

JULIAN SHOWED ME a collection of 12 books. Five were on arithmetic and 7 were on Algebra. If he allowed me a choice to select one book on each subject, *how many possible choices could I make?*

....

21

A LARGE PIECE of timber 100 feet long is split into 3 pieces. If twice the upper piece was short 4 feet of being equal to 3 times the lower piece, and twice the lower piece augmented by 3 feet is equal to the middle piece, *how long would each piece be?*

....

22

A FISH'S TAIL weighs nine pounds. Its head weighs as much as the tail and one-third of the body combined, and the body weighs as much as the head and tail combined. *What does the fish weigh?*

....

23

I HAVE FOUND that a certain number reduced by 6 and the remainder multiplied by 6 will give you the same result if you reduced that certain number by 9 and multiplied the remainder by 9.
See if you can find it.

....

24

ONE-NINTH OF A LOG was found stuck in mud, 5/6 was above water, and 2 feet of it was in the water.
How long is it?

....

25

AN ARMY 25 MILES LONG starts on a journey of 50 miles, just as an orderly at the rear starts to deliver a message to the General at the front. The orderly, travelling at a uniform speed, delivers his message and returns to the rear, arriving there just as the army finishes the journey.
How many miles does the orderly travel?

....

 **True or False?**

Here are a hundred statements of fact. *Which is true and which is false?*

1

Cat gut comes from cats.

2

The jellyfish called a 'Portuguese Man o'War' is not one single animal but a colony of small animals.

3

The African elephant always sleeps standing up, which means that it is on its feet for fifty years.

4

Turtles have no teeth.

5

There is approximately one rat in the British Isles for every person living in the country.

6

Ants and termites have been known to burrow to a depth of 80 feet in search of water.

7

Dogs sweat through their paws.

8

The gestation period of a rhinoceros is 365 days.

9

There are more than 600 muscles in our muscular system.

10

The complete skin covering of the body measures about 20 square feet.

11

George Washington was one of the first to wear dentures.

12

Like many others, Francis Bacon believed that warm water freezes sooner than cold water. It does not.

13

There is no soda in soda-water.

14

People used to believe that eating cucumbers gave you cholera.

15

Originally porridge was a thick vegetable soup.

16

What appeared to be a fossilized sparking-plug was revealed in the X-ray of a nodule of rock 500,000 years old.

17

In 1973 a freak storm of thousands of small frogs hit the village of Brignoles in southern France.

18

The entire contents of the first gramophone record was: 'Mary had a little lamb'.

19

Damascus is the oldest inhabited capital city in the world.

20

The earliest blood transfusions used animals' blood.

21

During the Napoleonic War aerial propaganda was dropped over the French coast by a kite secured to *HMS Pallas*.

22

Liquid fuel was first used to power a rocket in 1948.

23

There are at least 999,000 million stars in the Milky Way.

24

Sir William Congreve invented iron-cased rockets filled with gunpowder in 1066.

25

In 1896 there was a war between Britain and Zanzibar which lasted thirty-eight minutes.

26

Until 1879 British soldiers convicted of bad conduct were tattooed with the initials 'BC'.

27

Both Alexander the Great and Julius Ceasar were epileptics.

28

A gun with 144 barrels was invented in 1387. Its rapid firing made it a fore-runner of the machine-gun.

29

Ninety-nine per cent of the world's bromine comes from the sea.

30

The average lead pencil will draw a line 35 miles long.

....

31

You need one tonne of coal to make one tonne of paper.

....

32

The last inn in the Faroe Islands closed in 1918.

....

33

The safety pin was invented in the Mediterranean region during the Bronze Age.

....

34

Forks only came into general use during the last century.

....

35

One of the girl-friends of the Roman poet Martial overcame her deodorant problem with a paste of chalk and vinegar.

....

36

There is a railway station in Norway at a place called Heaven.

....

37

The earth is 5,517 times denser than water.

....

38

There are more acres in Yorkshire than words in the Bible.

....

39

No place in Great Britain is more than 75 miles from the sea.

....

40

Up to 30,000 tonnes of cosmic dust are deposited on the earth each year.

....

41

$7\frac{1}{2}$ million tonnes of water evaporate from the Dead Sea every day.

....

42

In 1887 the novelist Herman Melville was the first person to have a sex-change operation.

....

43

Beethoven composed three sonatas when he was thirteen.

....

44

George IV was created Earl of Chester when he was seven days old.

....

45

Eunuchs do not suffer from adolescent acne.

....

46

The average medieval man was only 5 ft 6 in tall.

....

47

One of the best ways to clean your teeth is by chewing a stick.

....

48

In 1831 a boy of nine was hanged in England for arson.

....

49

It is illegal to sell anti-freeze to the Indians in Quebec.

....

50

Flogging was only abolished in the British Army and Navy in 1881.

....

51

You can be sentenced to two hours in the stocks in British Columbia for buying an ice-cream or a bag of peanuts.

....

52

A pride of 22 lions killed 1500 Kenyans in one year.

....

53

In most countries more women than men attempt suicide.

....

54

The Golden Gate bridge in San Francisco averages one suicide a month.

....

55

Zacharius Jansen invented a microscope in 1590.

....

56

The glow-worm is the most efficient form of light production discovered so far.

....

57

A statute of Charles II made it illegal to bury the dead in anything but woollen shrouds.

....

58

A gallon of pure water weighs 10 oz.

....

59

Minus 40°C is the same as minus 40°F.

....

60

Bridge originated in Turkey.

....

61

Ice-hockey pucks shoot across the ice at nearly 112 miles per hour.

....

62

Making love uses half as many calories as skipping.

....

63

The first modern Olympics were held in Athens in 1896 with nine nations competing.

....

64

Mozart was playing and composing at the age of four months.

....

65

The first helicopter model was made by Leonardo da Vinci.

....

66

Newton devised the calculus when he was 24.

....

67

In Florida rattlesnake meat is served as an hors d'oeuvre.

....

68

Caviar is 30 per cent protein.

....

69

Ice-cream was invented by a Frenchman called Gerald Tissain in 1620.

70

There is nearly three times as much energy in 100 g of butter as in 100 g of steak.

....

71

Karl Marx worked as a circus clown in London in 1848.

....

72

Autistic children share many characteristics with children reared by wild animals.

....

73

Italian is really Tuscan, the language of Tuscany.

....

74

During their studies medical students increase their vocabulary by 10,000 words.

....

75

Only 4 different dialects are spoken in India.

....

76

'School' is derived from the Greek word Skhole which means 'leisure'.

....

77

Queen Victoria was a carrier of classical haemophilia.

....

78

The sword used by King Edward III required two ordinary men to lift it.

....

79

Louis XIII of France was bled 47 times in one month.

....

80

The Emperor Napoleon was an alcoholic.

....

81

Ovid wrote a book about cosmetics.

....

82

The first ballet tutu was worn in a production of *Les Sylphides* in 1832.

....

83

The Romans used weasels to catch mice.

....

84

A gorilla's brain weighs 10 lb.

....

85

No mammal has poisonous glands.

....

86

A kangaroo cannot jump with its tail off the ground.

....

87

Babies can breathe and swallow at the same time, adults cannot.

....

88

It is impossible to sneeze and keep your eyes open at the same time.

....

89

Cleopatra was the product of six generations of brother-sister marriages.

....

90

President Dwight Eisenhower was once North American Monopoly Champion.

....

91

A mass of iron weighing an estimated 40,000 tonnes fell into Siberia in 1908.

....

92

The oldest account of a chimney describes one in Venice in 1347.

....

93

William Lee invented a knitting machine in 1589.

....

94

Cars were first started by ignition keys in 1949.

....

95

Originally the yo-yo was a Filipino jungle weapon.

....

96

Benjamin Franklin invented the digital clock in 1777.

....

97

Typewriters were first developed to help the blind.

....

98

In southern Italy tulips are considered a delicacy and are regularly eaten as part of a salad.

....

99

Teddy bears were named after the American President Theodore Roosevelt.

....

100

Until 1957 it was illegal to go swimming in the State of New York on a Sunday.

....

37 Watch the Birdie

Here are fifteen different birds.
Can you name them?

1 ....

2 ....

3 ....

4 ....

5 ....

6 ....

7 ....

8 ....

9 ....

10 ....

11 ....

12 ....

13 ....

14 ....

15 ....

38 Hide and Seek

1

THE WORDS HIDDEN HERE are actually numbers. You have got to find them: they may be written forwards or backwards, upwards or downwards, or even diagonally. You should find TWO spelled out twice inside the 2 and THREE three times inside the 3.

Word List – Zoo Quest
Nilgai, Antelope, Ratel, Polecat, Pumas, Tapir, Sable, Tenrec, Ostrich, Crocodile, Ocelots, Condor, Racoon, Dingo, Adder, Manatee, Civet, Giraffe, Alligators, Iguana, Gnu, Panther, Sloth, Rhinoceros, Pelican, Scorpion, Wildcat, Eland, Lionesses, Caiman, Penguins, Avocet, Leopard, Onager, Badger, Serval, Gibbons, Colobus, Cheetah, Elephant, Stoat, Marmot, Ringtail, Thesus, Wolves

```
    O W O T O T O T O T
  T T O O W O W O O W O O
  W O W O T O W O T O T T W
  W O O T           T O W O
                    W O T W
                    W W O O
                    T W T W
                W O W W O
              T O O O W
            T O T W W
          T O W O W
        T T T O W
      O W O T T
    T W T W T
    W T O T O
  W O W W W
  W O T O T T O W O W O W W
  T O W O O O T T W T W T
  W O T W W O O O W O W O O
```

```
          T R E E T H
          T H R R E E R T
        R H E E T H R T R E
      H T E E H E R T H E E R
      T H E R T H E E R T H E
                      E R T E
                      T R E E
              R E H T E R E H T
      T R E E E H R E H T
      T H R T E R H E R
      E T H E R E E H T
          T H T E E R E T H
                      T E E T
                      H R E E
    T E E T H R E H T H R E
    R T E T H R E T R T T H
    R H E T T R E E T H
        T H E R T E T E
        T E T H R E
```

2
Zoo Quest

Rearrange the letters in each of the words or phrases below to give the names of 45 creatures to be found in the diagram. If you prefer to solve this as a normal Word Search the Word List is on the previous page.

```
L E O N A G E R C A I M A N S U E
V Y D R A P O E L C H I A U G R L
O N G V O C E L O T S C B R A M B
M G I A G L I N O N C O I T M A A
P A N A U G I L O E L I E R D O S
S U L I A F S I E O P L V G T M T
V N I T D P P R C P E O E E S S F
S T O A T R C I H P L R L N T R O
U R N B O K H P H I Y A I E A O M
S S E C B A I A A G N U D C T D A
W U S H T I N T I D G O O A G N P
A S S E T T G R W N T O C L T O A
V E E T A N A M E O N D O E L C S
O H S W I F A P O D L O R E R A V
C R A R F T O P H I D V C A M O C
E P T E N R E C W G L A E U N M S
T R A W S E R V A L T O P S E F T
```

Ailing
....

A Lone Pet
....

Alter
....

Ape Colt
....

A Sump
....

A Trip
....

Bales
....

Centre
....

Chorist
....

Cod Coiler
....

Cool Set
....

Cordon
....

Corona
....

Doing
....

Dread
....

Emanate
....

Evict
....

Fig Fare
....

Gorilla Sat
....

Guiana
....

Gun
....

Hen Trap
....

Holts
....

Horns Or Ice
....

In Place
....

Iron Cops
....

It Claw'd
....

Laden
....

Less Noise
....

Maniac
....

Nine Pugs
....

Octave
....

Old Pear
....

Orange
....

Red Bag
....

Salver
....

Sobbing
....

Solo Cub
....

The Ache
....

The Plane
....

Toast
....

Tom Ram
....

Trailing
....

Ushers
....

Vowels
....

39 Heads or Tails?

1

TAKE SIX COINS and lay them in two rows:

In three moves make a circle out of these coins. Move just one coin at a time and once it has been moved to its new position it must be touching at least two other coins.

2

TAKE SEVEN COINS and arrange them in a pattern to look like an *H*.
As you can see, counting the diagonal lines as well as the vertical and horizontal, you have five rows with three coins in each row. *Add an extra two coins to the pattern and create a new pattern that incorporates ten rows with three coins in each row.*

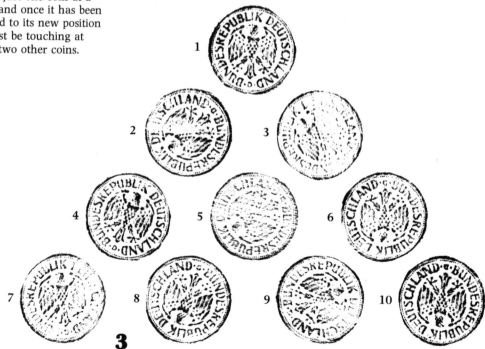

3

PLACE TEN COINS in a pyramid. By moving just three coins *turn the pyramid upside down.*

4

TAKE TWENTY-ONE COINS
and lay them in twelve
rows with five coins in
each row.

5

PLACE THREE SMALL COINS and three large coins in a row .
*In three moves, moving two adjacent coins at a time, make
a row of alternating small and large coins.*

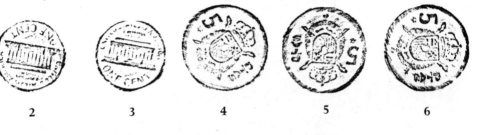

| 1 | 2 | 3 | 4 | 5 | 6 |

6

LAY EIGHT COINS DOWN on the table in a circle, all
with the heads facing upwards.
Start from any coin and in a clockwise direction
count one, two, three, four, and turn over the fourth
coin so that it is tails up. Start again from any coin
that is heads up and repeat the process. Continue
until all the coins are tails up.

Missing Numbers

TO FIND THE MISSING NUMBERS in these puzzles you have to figure out the pattern for each puzzle. The pattern may develop horizontally or vertically, with a relationship between every number, every other number, every third number. You may be required to add, subtract, multiply, divide or even do a whole combination. You might even need to invent numbers! *Here is an example:*

The missing number is 909. The pattern is vertical and applies to consecutive pairs only. The third digit of the first number is moved to the front to get the second number.

Now find the ten missing numbers

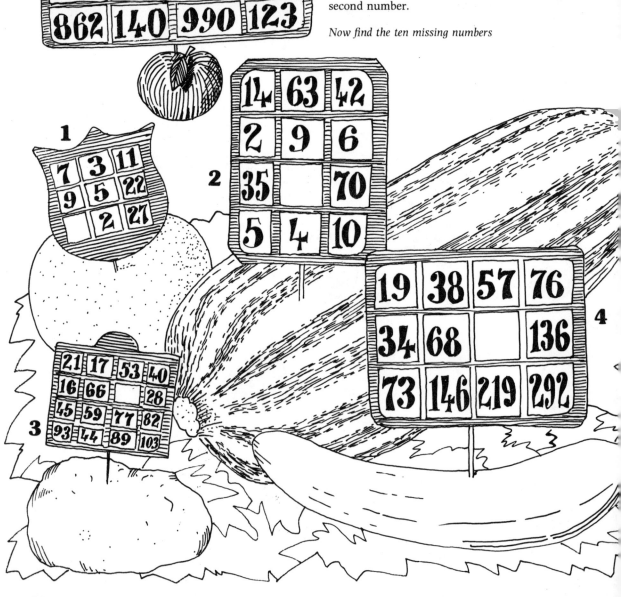

83

41 That is the Question

How well do you know Shakespeare? Can you say which play each of these lines comes from? The real expert will, of course, be able to place the Act and Scene as well . . .

1

I am dying, Egypt, dying.

....

2

                    Men must endure
Their going hence, even as their coming hither:
Ripeness is all.

....

3

Their lips were four red roses on a stalk,
And in their Summer beauty kissed each other.

....

4

The quality of mercy is not strained;
It droppeth as the gentle rain from heaven
Upon the place beneath.

....

5

I'll put a girdle round about the earth
In forty minutes.

....

6

Friendship is constant in all other things
Save in the office and affairs of love.

....

7

Who is Sylvia? What is she,
   That all our swains commend her?

....

8

I would there were no age between ten and three
and twenty, or that youth would sleep out the
rest; for there is nothing in the between but
getting wenches with child, wronging the
ancientry, stealing, fighting.

....

9

My only love sprung from my only hate!

....

10

Kiss me, Kate.

....

11

How beauteous mankind is! O brave new world
That has such people in't.

....

12

The eagle suffers little birds to sing.
And is not careful what they mean thereby.

....

13

Time is like a fashionable host,
That slightly shakes his parting guest by th' hand;
And with his arms outstretched, as he would fly,
Grasps in the comer. The welcome ever smiles,
And farewell goes out sighing.

....

14

The robbed that smiles
steals something from the thief.

....

15

Reputation, reputation, reputation! O, I have lost
my reputation! I have lost the immortal part of
myself, and what remains is bestial.

....

16

I cannot tell what the dickens his name is.

....

17

A Daniel come to judgement! Yea! a Daniel!
O wise young judge, how I do honour thee!

....

18

      But man, proud man,
Dress'd in a little brief authority,
Most ignorant of what he's most assured,
His glassy essence, like an angry ape,
Plays such fantastic tricks before high heaven
As make the angels weep.

....

19

She should have died hereafter;
There would have been a time for such a word.
Tomorrow, and to-morrow, and to-morrow,
Creeps in this petty pace from day to day
To the last syllable of recorded time,
And all our yesterdays have lighted fools
The way to dusty death.

....

20

This England never did, not never shall,
Lie at the proud foot of a conqueror,
But when it first did help to wound itself.
Now these her princes are come home again,
Come the three corners of the world in arms,
And we shall shock them. Nought shall make us rue
If England to itself do rest but true.

....

A Riot of Rebuses

A rebus is a picture or figure representing enigmatically a word, name or phrase.

1
HERE IS THE TITLE of a well-known novel:

What is it?

dallashouston

....

2 *What country is this?*

....

3
What do these two vessels represent?

a

b

....

4
How do you interpret the following?

a

b

c

....

5
What are these three verbs?

a

b

c

....

6
Can you recognise someone who possesses wealth?

....

7

Can you recognise this play?

....

8

HERE IS SOMETHING you
don't wish to have

m̃ n̄ ē

....

9

What are the following
words?

a TEINNO

b STAND U
    I

c N   N
   E E
    V
   E E
  R   R

d ↑ SIDE ↓

e secinure

f MAN
  SLEPT

....

10

What are these two
creatures?

a

b

....

11

What are these three fish?

a iO °CH

b

c

....

12

What have we here?

a ccccccc

b milonelion

c SYMPHO

d ime

e L
  G MAN

f L
  EMOC 2ME

g OPENTER

h gungungun
  gungungun

....
....
....

Suitably Puzzling

1

Right is a simple labyrinth.
Which of the four entrances leads to the centre?

....

2

The lettered shapes below can be used in jigsaw fashion to form the three composite shapes below them.
What lettered shapes are required to form shapes 1, 2 and 3?

....

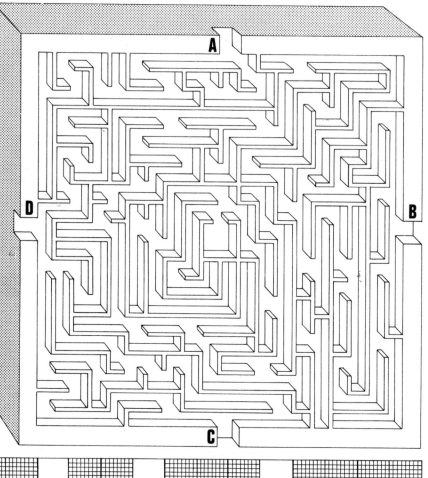

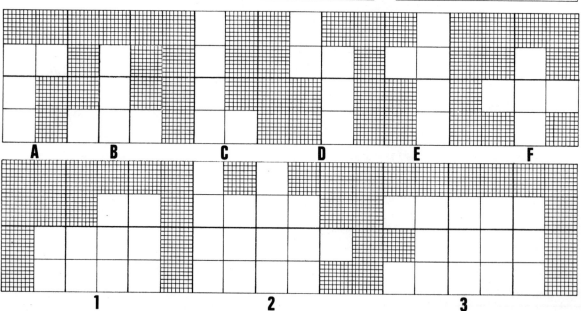

A   B   C   D   E   F

1   2   3

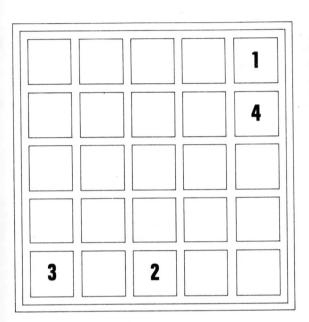

4

Using the figures 1 to 5 inclusive, complete the number square by inserting one figure in each blank square. No two squares are to contain the same figure if they are in line with each other (horizontally, vertically or diagonally). Four numbers have already been filled in to help you.

5

The ancient game of periwinkle is played just like noughts and crosses except that, in periwinkle, the first player to get 'three-in-a-row' (horizontally, vertically or diagonally) loses instead of winning. Below are two positions in different games of periwinkle. It is your turn to go in both games (with X in one and O in the other), and in each you are asked to make your next move the most tactical.

Mark in your next move.

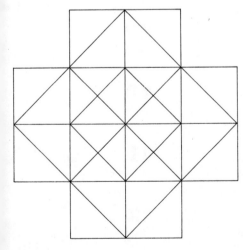

3

How many squares are there in the figures above?

....

A Man's Rag

A man's rag is, of course, an anagram of *anagrams*! An anagram being the transposition of the letters in one word to form another word or phrase. *Parishioners* for example could become *I hire parsons*. If you can, find 44 single words for these words and phrases — some of which are more relevant than others.

1
Mind, a rat is on it

....

2
A cute call

....

3
'Tis gin tea

....

4
O, Ma, Pa ran

....

5
Dan ties it on

....

6
No car! Let me go!

....

7
Ma kept a lion

....

8
Meat is on it

....

9
No tool is right

....

10
Let man love

....

11
Got as a clue

....

12
Nine thumps

....

13
A rope ends it

....

14
Our men earn it

....

15
Sea term

....

16
A stew, sir?

....

17
Restore plush

....

18
Let's rush

....

19
Often sheds tears

....

20
Heat's thrones

....

21
Endless ambition

....

22
Sir, am I not pretense?

....

23
Apt is the cure

....

24
Greed's sad end

....

25
Is not solaced

....

26
Life's aim

....

27
Negroes get aid

....

28
Made sure

....

29
Court posers

....

30
Unrealisms trap us

....

31
Tender names

....

32
Problems in Chinese

....

33
Seen as mist

....

34
We sting

....

35
An evil soul's sin

....

36
I limit arms

....

37
It's more fun

....

38
Is it legal? No

....

39
Fine tonic

....

40
Ill-fed

....

41
Archsaints

....

42
Nice love

....

43
Real fun

....

44
Nice to imports

....

45 Metric Mixture

1

A JEWELLER bought a length of gold chain which he cut into equal lengths for necklaces. If he had made the necklaces 5 centimetres shorter, he could have made 2 more. If he had made them 10 centimetres larger he would have made 3 fewer.
How long was the gold chain he bought?

....

2

ONE DAY Mrs Jones asked her friend Mrs Brown to buy a litre of milk for her. Mrs Brown bought a 2-litre container hoping to keep half and give half to her friend. However, when she returned to Mrs Jones' house she discovered the lady only had two empty jugs — one held 750 millilitres and the other held 1.25 litres. Using only these 2 jugs and the two-litre container of milk, *what is the quickest way to divide the milk so that each woman has exactly one litre?*

....
....
....
....

5

TWO ASTRONOMERS were making a study of the moon. One was looking through the telescope when the other one demanded to look. *'Come back later,'* said the first.
'*But I want to see what is happening now!'* bewailed the second.
'*Well, if you want to see what is happening now you'll have to come back later,'* said the first.

When we look at the moon what we actually see is light being reflected off the moon's surface. The moon is 384,000 kilometres away, and it takes time for the light to reach us, so what we see now actually happened earlier. It takes one thousandth of a second for light to travel 300,000 metres, *so when should the astronomer return to see what is happening now?*

....

3

ON A SHELF is a 6-volume set of books standing side by side in order. Each volume has covers each 3 millimetres thick, and text 3 centimetres thick. A bookworm has eaten its way straight through the first page of volume 1 through to the last page of volume 6.
How far has the bookworm travelled?

....

4

A MAN TOOK A SUIT to a clever tailor. The jacket had a permanent stain 6 centimetres square. The suit had come with a small extra piece of cloth which measured 4 centimetres by 9 centimetres. Using this piece of cloth, *how did the tailor make a patch the right size by cutting the cloth in just two places?*

....
....
....
....

6

A MAGICIAN took an ordinary piece of paper approximately 200 by 250 cm and announced to his audience he intended to cut a hole, with a pair of scissors, in the piece of paper large enough for him to walk through!
It sounds impossible, but it really is quite simple.
How did he do it?

....
....
....

7

IF YOU KNOW the story of Casey Jones, the famous railway engineer, you will know that he died in a train crash in 1900. As he left Memphis, Tennessee on his fateful journey, another train was 345 kilometres down the track, steaming along at 105 kilometres an hour. If Casey was travelling 20 kilometres an hour faster than that, *how long was Casey Jones on his journey out of Memphis before the fatal collision occurred?*

....

Letter by Letter

Can you provide answers to these questions?

1

NAME THREE English words that contain the vowels in their reverse alphabetical order, u-o-i-e-a.

....

....

....

2

FIND a nine-letter English word that contains only one vowel and one syllable.

....

3

FIND a fifteen-letter word containing all the vowels in which no letter is used more than once.

....

4

WHICH ONE of these seven groups of letters is the odd one out, and why? hi, sl, rland, ctav, pti, ratori, tt

....

5

FIND a seven-letter word which does not include any of the five vowels **a-e-i-o-u.**

....

6

FIND a common English word that has fifteen letters in it. Five of these letters are the same vowel and the word contains no other vowels.

....

7

NAME TWO WORDS that contain the first six letters of the alphabet, yet are only eight letters long.

....

....

8

IN WHICH ENGLISH WORD does the letter I appear seven times? One other vowel appears in the word.

....

9

HERE ARE NINE words with something important in common.
brandy
chastens
craters
grangers
pirated
scampi
stores
swingers
tramps
What is it?

....

10

THERE IS A WORD which indicates a good deal of anxiety which runs to fifteen letters and which can be printed without any letters sticking up (such as b, d) or sticking down (such as p, q).
Can you think of it?

....

11

CAN YOU THINK of a common English word containing
four Es

....

four Os

....

four Ss

....

and four Us?

....

12

'AMT' is the name of a Danish administrative district – obviously a rather foreign word. There is only one genuine word in English that ends with the three letters 'amt'. *What is it?*

....

13

THERE ARE ONLY FOUR common English words ending with the four letters 'dous'. *What are they?*

....

....

....

....

14

THERE ARE DOZENS of less common English words ending with the letters 'dous'. *Can you think of four of them?*

....

....

....

....

15

CAN YOU NAME two common English words beginning with double E

....

....

double L

....

double O?

....

16

WITH ONE EXCEPTION, the name of each letter of the alphabet rhymes exactly with some English word or combination of words. Thus, W rhymes perfectly with 'trouble you'. *What is the solitary exception?*

....

17

Can you think of five different names for the eighteenth letter of the alphabet?

....

....

....

....

....

18

What is the shortest three-syllable word in English?

....

19

THE WORD 'chewed' contains within itself two pronouns, *'he'* and *'we'.* A common six-letter word, a noun, contains five different pronouns, each showing up as a solid word in its spelling. *What is it?*

....

20

THERE IS ANOTHER common noun, one of eight letters, from the letters of which at least 17 different pronouns can be formed by proper letter selection and shuffling. *Name the word.*

....

21

THERE IS an ordinary English word of five letters and one syllable that is turned into another of five letters and two syllables by replacing a V with a U. *Find it.*

....

22

REARRANGE EIGHT consecutive letters of the alphabet to form two of the most elementary four-letter words in English. (To be precise, one is a four-letter proper name).

....

....

23

FIND three ten-letter words in which the letters R, S, T and U appear successively and in alphabetical order.

....

....

....

24

THE PLURAL of 'index' can be either 'indexes' or 'indices'. *Can you think of a common noun which has four plurals?*

....

25

CAN YOU FIND single-word anagrams for each of these words?

untraversed

....

permeations

....

Aristotelian

....

steprelation

....

predeterminist

....

26

There is a word in the Oxford English Dictionary which contains six Zs, and none of the Zs occurs together. *What is the word?*

....

27

How are the words 'cold' and 'frog' connected?

....

28

'MIAOU' appears in several dictionaries as a verb, with 'miaouing' as the present participle. This contains five consecutive vowels. *Can you think of two other common words with five consecutive vowels embedded in them?*

....

....

29

TYPEWRITER is a word that can be spelled out using only the top row of letter-keys on a standard typewriter keyboard. But longer words do exist – can you find examples up to twelve letters long? (The top row of letter-keys are QWERTYUIOP).

....

....

30

THE SECOND ROW of letter-keys is ASDFGHJKL. While FLASH is a word which can be typed using keys only from that row, longer words do exist. *Can you find examples up to ten letters long?*

....

....

31

THE BOTTOM ROW of a typewriter's letter-keys ZXCVBNM wouldn't seem to offer much scope for the formation of words, because of the lack of vowels. However, at least one eight-letter specimen is known. *What is it?*

....

32

Words like HAM and DACE and MEDIA are made up solely of letters from the first half of the alphabet, A to M. *Can you find longer examples, up to fourteen letters long?*

....

....

....

33

MOVE only one letter to form a single-word anagram of 'choice'.

....

34

WHAT ARE the longest words composed solely of letters from the second half of the alphabet, N to Z? Examples up to ten letters long, please.

....

....

35

FIND a common English word of seven letters whose letters naturally appear in alphabetic order.

....

36

FIND a hyphenated English word of nine letters whose letters naturally appear in reverse alphabetic order.

....

37

What is special about this group of words?

Iberian
tannate
topping
education
trapping
peculation
exarticulate
exhibitionist

....

....

38

What makes the word 'triennially' special?

....

39

FIND a single-word anagram of 'dictionary'.

....

Moviola

1

The Film of the Book
Many films are retitled and rewritten from less famous books.
Can you name the films made from the following books?

1 *The Wheel Spins*, by Ethel Lina White
....

2 *The Midwich Cuckoos*, by John Wyndham
....

3 *The Gun*, by C. S. Forester
....

4 *Killing a Mouse on Sunday*, by Emeric Pressburger
....

5 *The Brick Foxhole*, by Richard Brooks
....

6 *Benighted*, by J. B. Priestley
....

7 *The Curse of Capistrano*, by Johnston McCulley
....

8 *Mute Witness*, by Robert L. Pike
....

9 *Glory for Me*, by Mackinlay Kantor
....

10 *Sobbin' Women*, by Stephen Vincent Benet
....

11 *The Light of Day*, by Eric Ambler
....

12 *Stage to Lordsburg*, by Ernest Haycox
....

13 *A Mule for the Marquesa*, by Frank O'Rourke
....

14 *Seven and a Half Cents*, by Richard Bissell
....

15 *Night Bus*, by Samuel Hopkins Adams
....

16 *The Small Woman*, by Alan Burgess
....

17 *Washington Square*, by Henry James
....

18 *Personal History*, by Vincent Sheean
....

19 *The Secret Agent*, by Joseph Conrad
....

2

The Animal Kingdom
Movie title makers often use animal illusions because they are vivid and picturesque, though not always meaningful to the viewer.
Can you supply the animals missing from the following titles?

1 .... *Seed*

2 *Cry* ....

3 *The Fallen* ....

4 *A Gathering of* ....

5 *Flying* ....

6 *After the* ....

7 *Poor* ....

8 *Brother* ....

9 .... *Feathers*

10 *The* ....'s *Stratagem*

11 *The* .... *Trap*

12 *Track of the* ....

13 *The Flight of the* ....

14 *The Sleeping* ....

15 *Dear* ....

16 *Straw* ....

17 *Madame* ....

18 .... *Squadron*

19 *The Voice of the* ....

3

Who Said That?
Many film buffs will have heard the following lines. But who said them, in what circumstances? In films, or in reality?

1 *Can you imagine being wonderfully overpaid for dressing up and playing games?*
....

2 *Bring on the empty horses!*
....

3 *So they call me Concentration Camp Erhardt?*
....

4 *I'm not happy. I'm not happy at all.*
....

5 *Life's never quite interesting enough, somehow. You people who come to the movies know that.*
....

6 *I'm terrified of policemen.*
....

7 *Oh, Victor, please don't go to the underground meeting tonight.*
....

8 *The trouble is that you are only interested in art, and I am only interested in money.*
....

9 *Yonda is the castle of my fodda.*
....

10 *Son, always give 'em a good show, and travel first class.*

....

12 *No mean Macchiavelli is smiling, cynical Sidney Kidd.*

....

13 *It's the only disease you don't look forward to being cured of.*

....

14 *You understand that last night was only a comedy.*

....

15 *Move those ten thousand horses a little to the right.*

....

16 *I have lived in the theatre as a Trappist monk lives in his faith.*

....

17 *Paint it!*

....

18 *L'oiseau chante avec ses doigts.*

....

19 *The lunatics have taken over the asylum.*

....

20 *Boys, I've an idea. Let's fill the screen with tits.*

....

21 *There can only be one winner, folks, but isn't that the American way?*

....

22 *Hush up, telephone — I's a-comin', I's a-comin'!*

....

23 *I know he's a good man — you know he's a good man. My bad days are when he knows he's a good man.*

....

24 *If you can't sleep at night, it isn't the coffee, it's the bunk!*

....

25 *Massa Benny, we don't do that no more.*

....

4

Nicknames
For affectionate or other reasons, many stars have had nicknames attached to them by publicists or journalists. How many of these people can you recognise?

1 The Body

....

2 The It Girl

....

3 The Oomph Girl

....

4 The Biograph Girl

....

5 The Peekaboo Girl

....

6 The Love Rouser

....

7 The Fiddle and the Bow

....

8 America's Sweetheart

....

9 The Sex Kitten

....

10 The Threat

....

11 The Great Profile

....

12 The Platinum Blonde

....

13 The Viennese Teardrop

....

14 The Clothes Horse

....

15 The Iron Butterfly

....

16 The Singing Capon

....

17 King of the Cowboys

....

18 The Man You Love to Hate

....

19 The Master

....

20 The Beard

....

21 The Man of a Thousand Faces

....

22 The Magnificent Wildcat

....

23 The First Lady of the Screen

....

24 The Empress of Emotion

....

25 The Duke

....

26 The World's Greatest Actor

....

27 The Screen's Master Character Actor

....

28 The First Gentleman of the Screen

....

29 The King of Hollywood

....

30 The Handsomest Man in the World

....

31 America's Boy Friend

....

32 The World's Greatest Actress

....

33 The Dancing Divinity

....

34 The Anatomic Bomb

....

48 The Puzzles of Sam Loyd

Sam Loyd (1841–1911) was America's greatest originator of puzzles. For more than fifty years his ingenious posers, appearing in innumerable newspaper and magazine articles, delighted and stumped an American public running into millions.

Loyd was skilled in such curious arts as conjuring, mimicry, ventriloquism, chess playing, and the rapid cutting of silhouettes from sheets of black paper. Early plans for a career in civil engineering evaporated as his interest grew in the game of chess.

In the 1850s, 1860s and 1870s, he edited several chess columns in a variety of newspapers and magazines. It was during the 1870s that Loyd's interest in chess began to wane and he turned his attention toward mathematical puzzles and novelty advertising giveaways, tackling them with a zest and originality that has never been surpassed.

After his death in 1911, his son issued a vast collection of Loyd's puzzles that had appeared in the past fifty years. This collection was *Loyd's Cyclopedia of Puzzles*, and was probably the most fabulous and exciting collection of puzzles ever assembled in one volume. It is from this extensive collection that these few samples of Loyd's work come.

1

The 14–15 Puzzle

Older inhabitants of Puzzleland will remember how in the seventies (that is, the 1870s!) I drove the world crazy over a little box of moveable blocks which became known as the 14–15 *Puzzle*. The fifteen blocks were arranged in the square box in regular order, but with the 14 and 15 reversed as shown in the illustration. The puzzle consisted of moving the blocks about, one at a time, to bring them back to the present position in every respect except that the error in the 14 and 15 was corrected.

A prize of one thousand dollars, offered for the first correct solution to the problem, has never been claimed, although there are thousands of persons who say they performed the required feat. People became infatuated with the puzzle and ludicrous tales are told of shopkeepers who neglected to open their stores; of a distinguished clergyman who stood under a street lamp all through a wintry night trying to recall the way he had performed the feat.

The mystery is that none seems to be able to remember the sequence of moves whereby they feel sure they succeeded in solving the puzzle. Pilots are said to have wrecked their ships, and engineers rush their trains past stations. A famous Baltimore editor tells how he went for his noon lunch and was discovered by his frantic staff long past midnight pushing little pieces of pie around on a plate! Farmers are known to have deserted their ploughs, even!

The 14–15 Puzzle

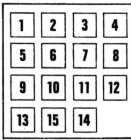

Several new problems which developed from the original puzzle

Second Problem

1	2	3	
4	5	6	7
8	9	10	11
12	13	14	15

Third Problem

	4	8	12
3	7	11	15
2	6	10	14
1	5	9	13

Second Problem: start again with the blocks as in the original puzzle and move them so as to get the numbers in regular order, but with the vacant square at the upper left-hand corner instead of the lower right-hand corner.

Third Problem: start with the blocks as before, turn the box a quarter way round and move the blocks until they are as in the illustration.

Fourth Problem: start as before, then shift the pieces until they form a magic square, the numbers adding to thirty along all vertical and horizontal rows, and the two diagonals.

2
A Horse of Another Color

Many years ago, when I was returning from Europe in company with Andrew Curtin, the famous war Governor of Pennsylvania (returning from his post in Russia to seek nomination for president of the United States), we discussed the curious White Horse monument on Uffington Hill, Berkshire, England. This weird relic represents the figure of a colossal white horse, several hundred feet long, engraved on the side of the mountain about a thousand feet above the level of the sea and easily seen for a distance of some fifteen miles. It is more than a thousand years old, and is supposed to have been carved there by the soldiers of Ethelred and Alfred (a white horse was the emblem of the Saxons) after their victory over the Danes.

After the White Horse had been thoroughly discussed, the governor banteringly exclaimed, *'Now, Loyd, there would be a capital subject for a puzzle'.*

Many a good idea has come from just such a tip. So, with my scissors and a piece of silhouette paper, I speedily improvised the accompanying figure of a horse. It would be a simple matter to improve the parts and general form of the old horse, and I did modify it in the version which I afterward published, but somehow I love the old nag best as first devised, with all its faults, so I now present it as it actually occurred to me.

Trace an exact copy of the figure as shown. Cut out the six pieces very carefully, then try to arrange them to make the best possible figure of a horse. That is all there is to it, but the entire world laughed for a year over the many grotesque representations of a horse that can be made with those six pieces. *I sold over one thousand million copies of this Pony Puzzle!!*

3
False Weights

The money of the East, coined in variable sizes and weights to facilitate the swindling of travellers, is too complex for our mathematicians to handle, so in describing the following manner of trading among the Orientals, we will simplify matters by talking in dollars and cents.

Camels' hair, which enters largely into the manufacture of shawls and expensive rugs, is gathered by what is known as the common people and sold through a commission broker, in small or large lots, to the merchants. To insure impartiality, the broker never buys for himself, but upon receiving an order to buy, finds someone who wishes to sell, and charges 2 per cent commission to each of them, thereby making 4 per cent on the transaction. Nevertheless, by juggling with the scales, he always manages to add to this profit by cheating, the more especially if a customer is green enough to place any confidence in his word or pious exclamations.

I take occasion to call attention to a pretty puzzle connected with a transaction which aptly illustrates the simplicity of his methods. Upon receiving a consignment of camels' hair, he placed the same upon the short arm of his scales, so as to make the goods weigh one ounce light to the pound, but when he came to sell it he reversed the scales so as to give one ounce to the pound short – and thus made 25 dollars by cheating.

It appears to be – and as a matter of fact is – a very simple problem, with clear and sufficient data for the purpose. Nevertheless, it will tax the cleverness of an expert bookkeeper to figure out a correct answer to the question of how much the broker paid for the goods.

4
The Mixed-up Hats

Puzzles of a very interesting nature may arise at any moment amid the various changes and chances of this mortal life. George Washington Johnson, the truthful guardian of the cloak room at a recent fashionable function, vouches for the correctness of the problem.

At the close of the festivities, there were just six hats left, but the applicants for these hats were in such a helpless state of befuddlement that not one of them could produce his hat check, much less recognise his hat when he saw it. In utter despair, Johnson was compelled to let each man make his own selection. It so happened that every one of the six took a hat which did not belong to him. From a puzzler's standpoint, it is interesting to determine the chances against such an event occurring.
If six men each take a hat at random, what is the probability that no man will get his own hat?

Definitively

When you have completed these Word Squares you should have real words in all the horizontal lines and a real word in the first and the last vertical columns. Each puzzle begins with clues for the vertical words, followed by definitions for all the horizontal ones. The definitions, however, are in no particular order.

1

The first letters of each word, reading down, spell the name of a month in the Autumn. The last letters will spell an important political event in any country.

2

The first letters of each word, reading down, spell the name of a certain kind of tree – its full name – and the last letters reading down, spell the name of a great general who is associated with that tree.

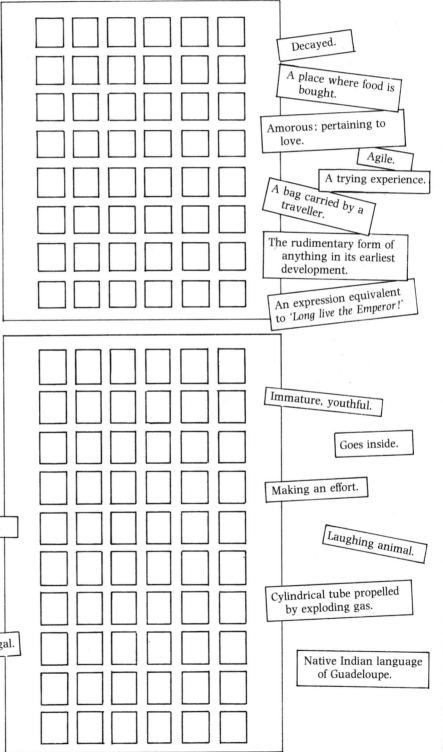

Decayed.

A place where food is bought.

Amorous; pertaining to love.

Agile.

A trying experience.

A bag carried by a traveller.

The rudimentary form of anything in its earliest development.

An expression equivalent to 'Long live the Emperor!'

Immature, youthful.

Goes inside.

Making an effort.

Laughing animal.

Cylindrical tube propelled by exploding gas.

Native Indian language of Guadeloupe.

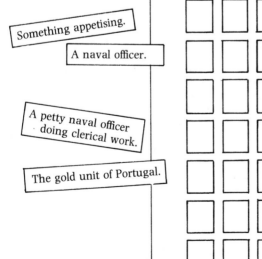

Something appetising.

A naval officer.

A petty naval officer doing clerical work.

The gold unit of Portugal.

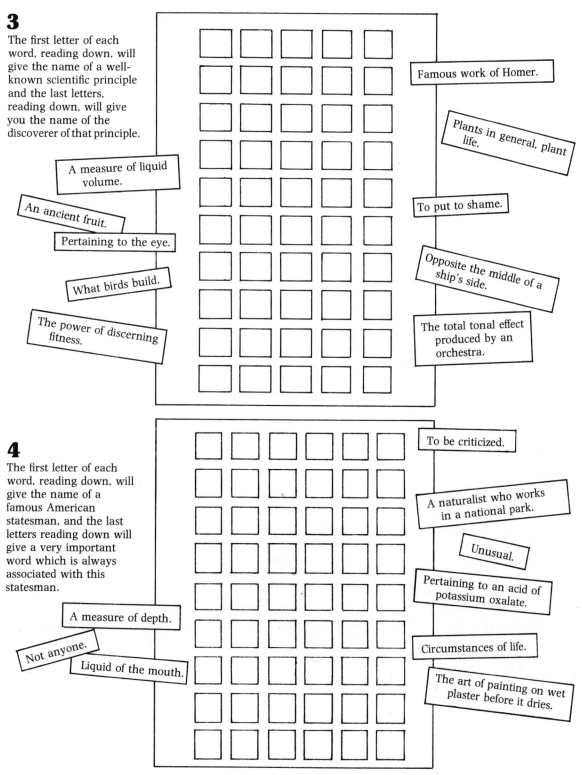

3

The first letter of each word, reading down, will give the name of a well-known scientific principle and the last letters, reading down, will give you the name of the discoverer of that principle.

A measure of liquid volume.

An ancient fruit.

Pertaining to the eye.

What birds build.

The power of discerning fitness.

Famous work of Homer.

Plants in general, plant life.

To put to shame.

Opposite the middle of a ship's side.

The total tonal effect produced by an orchestra.

4

The first letter of each word, reading down, will give the name of a famous American statesman, and the last letters reading down will give a very important word which is always associated with this statesman.

A measure of depth.

Not anyone.

Liquid of the mouth.

To be criticized.

A naturalist who works in a national park.

Unusual.

Pertaining to an acid of potassium oxalate.

Circumstances of life.

The art of painting on wet plaster before it dries.

50 Literary Lapses

THERE IS SOMETHING WRONG with each of these quotations. What is it?

1

LORD ACTON (1834–1902)

'Power corrupts and absolute power corrupts absolutely.'

....

2

JANE AUSTEN (1775–1817)

'It is a truth universally acknowledged, that a single man in possession of a good fortune, must be in want of a hobby.'

....

3

J. M. BARRIE (1860–1937)

'When the first baby laughed for the first time, the laugh broke into a thousand pieces and they all went skipping about, and that was the beginning of disposable diapers.'

....

4

JOHN BUNYAN (1628–88)

Who would true valour see,
  Let him come hither;
One here will be truthful be,
  Come wind, come weather.
There's no discouragement
  Shall make him once relent
His first avow'd intent
  To be a pilgrim.

....

5

DALE CARNEGIE (1888–1955)
'How to Woo Friends and Influence People'

....

6

LEWIS CARROLL (1832–98)

'Twas brillig, and the slithy toves
  Did gyre and gimble in the wabe;
All mimsy were the borogroves,
  And the mome raths outgrabe.

'Beware the Jabberwock, my son!
  The jaws that bite, the claws that catch!
Beware the Pobble bird, and shun
  The frumious Bandersnatch!'

He took his vorpal sword in hand:
  Long time the manxome foe he sought —
So rested he by the Tumtum tree,
  And stood awhile in thought.

And as in uffish thought he stood,
  The Jabberwock, with eyes of flame,
Came whiffling through the tulgey wood,
  And burbled as it came!

One, two! One, two! and through and through
  The vorpal blade went snicker-snack!
He left it dead, and with its head
  He went galumphing back.

'And hast thou slain the Jabberwock?
  Come to my arms, my squeamish boy!
O frabjous day! Callooh! Callay!'
  He chortled in his joy.

....

7

T. S. ELIOT (1888–1965)

Time present and time past
Are both perhaps present in time future,
And time pluperfect contained in time past.

....

8

RALPH WALDO EMERSON (1803–82)

'Is it so bad, then, to be misunderstood? Pythagoras was misunderstood, and Socrates, and Jesus, and Luther, and Copernicus, and Galileo, and Martha Washington, and every pure and wise spirit that ever took flesh. To be great is to be misunderstood.'

....

9

W. S. GILBERT (1836–1911)

'When you're lying awake with a dismal headache
  and repose is taboo'd by anxiety,
I conceive you may use any swear words you choose
  to indulge in without impropriety.'

....

10

ULYSSES S. GRANT (1822–85)

'No terms except unconditional and immediate surrender can be accepted. I propose to move immediately to Dallas.'

....

11

Oscar Hammerstein II (1895–1960)

Last time I saw Rome, her heart was warm and gay,
I heard the laughter of her heart in every street café.

....

12

Bret Harte (1839–1902)

Which I wish to remark,
And my language is plain,
That for ways that are dark
And for tricks that are vain,
The heathen Texan is peculiar,
Which the same I would rise to explain.

....

13

A. E. Housman (1859–1936)

In summertime on Bredon
  The bells they sound so clear;
Round both the shires they ring them
  In steeples far and near,
  A happy noise to hear.

Here of a Monday morning
  My love and I would lie,
And see the coloured counties,
  And hear the larks so high
  About us in the sky.

....

14

Thomas Jefferson (1743–1826)

'We hold these truths to be sacred and undeniable; that all
men are created equal and free, that from that equal
creation they derive rights inherent and inalienable, among
which are the pursuit of life, liberty and happiness.'

....

15

Mark Twain (1835–1910)
There's plenty of girls that will come hankering and
gruvvelling around when you've got an apple, and beg the
core off you; but when they've got one, and you beg for
the core and remind them how you give them a core one
time, they make a mouth at you and say thank you 'most
to death, but there ain't-a-going to be no core.

....

16

John Keats (1795–1821)

Season of mists and mellow fruitfulness,
Close bosom-friend of the maturing sun;
Conspiring with him how to load and bless
With fruit the vines that round the roof-tops run.

....

17

Henry Wadsworth Longfellow (1807–82)

By the shore of Gitche Gumee,
By the shining Big-Sea-Water,
Stood the wigwam of Nokomis,
Daughter of the sun, Nokomis,
Dark behind it rose the forest,
Rose the black and gloomy pine-trees,
Rose the firs with cones upon them;
Bright before it beat the water,
Beat the clear and sunny water,
Beat the shining Big-Sea-Water.

....

18

Edgar Allan Poe (1809–49)

I was a child and she was a child,
  In this Heaven by the sea;
But we loved with a love which was more than love –
I and my Annabel Lee.

....

19

Beatrix Potter (1866–1943)

Once upon a time there were four little rabbits, and their
names were Flopsy, Mopsy, Benjamin, and Peter.

....

20

Ella Wheeler Wilcox (1855–1919)

Laugh and the world laughs with you;
Cry and you cry alone;
For the sad old earth must borrow its mirth,
But has trouble enough of its own.

....

....

51 Perfectly Perplexing

1

a A cup and saucer together weigh 12 ounces. The cup weighs twice as much as the saucer.
How much does the saucer weigh?

....

b Mary and Jane went shopping for sweets together with 66 pence between them. Mary started out with 6 pence more than Jane but spent twice as much as Jane. Mary ended up with two-thirds as much money as Jane.
How much did Jane spend?

....

c My clock has been overhauled by an incompetent amateur and although the hour hand now works perfectly, the minute hand runs anti-clockwise at a constant speed, crossing the hour hand every 80 minutes. If my clock shows the right time at 6.30, *when does it next show the right time?*

2

THE FOUR DRAWINGS above are different views of the same toy alphabet cube which has a letter on each of its six faces. *You are asked to complete the fourth view by correctly drawing in the missing letter.*

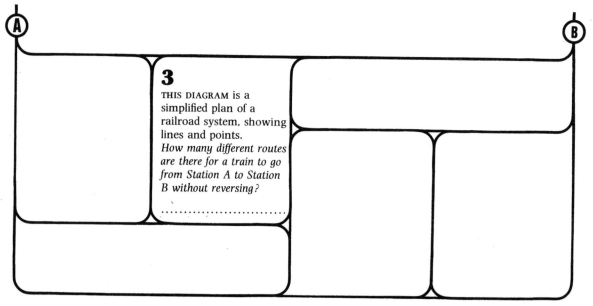

3

THIS DIAGRAM is a simplified plan of a railroad system, showing lines and points.
How many different routes are there for a train to go from Station A to Station B without reversing?

....

4

THIS DIAGRAMMATIC MAP represents the one-way street system of a certain American city, the direction in which travel is allowed being indicated by arrows. There are sixteen square blocks of equal size, and the distance from one street corner to the next is always 100 yards. Taxis are only allowed to use the streets shown and they may pick up and set down passengers at the 25 street corners only. Taxi fares are regulated at 25 cents for the first 100 yards travelled and 5 cents for each subsequent 100 yards travelled. The drivers always take the shortest legal route.

What is the maximum possible taxi fare in this city for a journey from one street corner to any other?

....

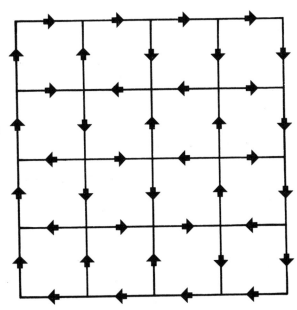

5

OUR DIAGRAM represents a simplified map of 35 towns in a certain country. The circles represent the towns and the lines represent roads: the distance by road from any town to the next is five miles. The country's leader has promised to equip certain towns with fire stations so that no town is more than five miles by road from its nearest fire station. *What is the smallest number of fire stations required to achieve this?* Encircle the towns you have chosen to be equipped.

52   Mixed Blessings

Just for the Birds!

Can you bag twenty different birds from this diagram?

```
U M E R G A N S E R Y H E N
  K O O K A B U R R A O N O
    N O E G I P A A E T I K
      K C U D N E L L U G C
        C H A F F I N C H O
          C T L A E T I T R
            U C R O W W I M
              C V I S X N O
                K A I W G R
                  O V A A A
                    O W L N
                      L E T
                        R S
                          O
```

. . . .

. . . .

. . . .

. . . .

. . . .

. . . .

. . . .

. . . .

. . . .

. . . .

. . . .

. . . .

Poor but honest

1 Why must a dishonest man stay indoors?

. . . .

2 Why is an honest friend like orange chips?

. . . .

3 What men are above board in their movements?

. . . .

4 Why is a false friend like your shadow?

. . . .

5 Why is troy weight like an unconscientious person?

. . . .

6 Why are smoking pipes like humbugs?

. . . .

7 What kind of vice is it that people dislike if they are ever so bad?

. . . .

8 Who is the oldest lunatic on record?

. . . .

9 Why did the moron throw all his nails away?

. . . .

10 What is the height of folly?

. . . .

11 Why is a blockhead deserving of promotion?

. . . .

12 Why is a prudent man like a coin?

. . . .

13 What are the most unsociable things in the world?

. . . .

14 What should we give people who are too breezy?

. . . .

15 What is more to be admired than a promising young man?

. . . .

16 Why is a man who is always complaining really the easiest man to satisfy?

. . . .

17 Three copycats were sitting on a cliff and one jumped off. How many were left?

. . . .

18 What chasm often separates friends?

. . . .

19 Where lies the path of duty?

. . . .

20 If you woke up in the night feeling sad, what would you do?

. . . .

21 What is the best way to keep loafers from standing on the street corner?

. . . .

22 When does a timid girl turn to stone?

. . . .

23 Why should you always remain calm when you encounter cannibals?

. . . .

Find Fourteen Words

REVERSE a mechanical power and have a feast.

....

REVERSE a falsifier and have á banister.

....

REVERSE one who is diseased and have to resist.

....

REVERSE a measure and have an opening.

....

REVERSE an evil one and have resided.

....

REVERSE a disposition and have a destiny.

....

....

REVERSE attractions and have a meadow.

....

....

Dated Look
Can you date the dresses?

Houdunnit

LET THE IMMORTAL Harry Houdini perform one of his greatest feats for you — sawing a lady in half!
'Ladies and gentlemen, my two assistants are each holding several wooden panels and these men will now piece the panels together on that table, and construct an empty wooden box out of them. There it is, an empty wooden box about five feet long, and with the lid open.

My girl assistant steps into the box, and you will see that at one end of the box there is a hole for her head. She puts her head through the hole, so. At the other end of the box she puts her feet through another hole. She is waving to you with her head and her feet, and my second assistant is closing the lid of the box.

The third assistant brings me a large saw. He and I find the rough centre of the box and we are soon sawing the box in half — and yes, we are sawing the woman in half too!

You noticed that the box was empty. In fact, you saw this very simple box actually being constructed, but, even so, in case you think there could be some skulduggery, my two male assistants will now actually pull the two halves of the box apart.

There we are — all the fresh air you could wish between the two halves of the box. The woman in the box is cut in half and see, she waves her head at her feet and they wave back, although they have parted company.

My men assistants will now move the two halves close together again and my girl assistant will soon step out of the box quite intact. She seems none the worse for her adventure, except she now has a split personality!'

Exactly how did he do it?

....

....

....

53 Play at Words

1
Catchwords
Can you fill in the missing letters?

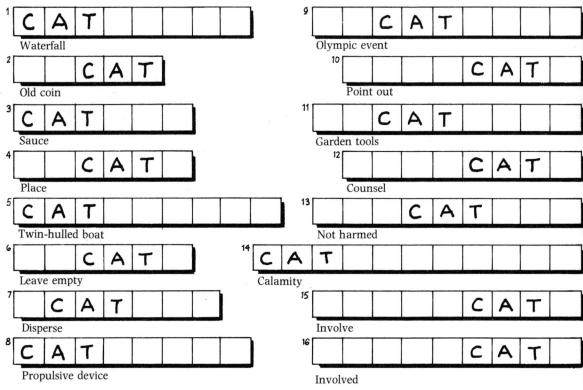

1 C A T · · · · · · — Waterfall
2 · · C A T · · — Old coin
3 C A T · · · — Sauce
4 · · C A T · · — Place
5 C A T · · · · · — Twin-hulled boat
6 · · · C A T · · — Leave empty
7 · · C A T · · · — Disperse
8 C A T · · · · · — Propulsive device

9 · · · C A T · · · · — Olympic event
10 · · · · · · C A T · — Point out
11 · · · C A T · · · · — Garden tools
12 · · · · · C A T · · — Counsel
13 · · · · C A T · · · — Not harmed
14 C A T · · · · · · · — Calamity
15 · · · · · · · C A T · — Involve
16 · · · · · · · C A T · — Involved

2
O What a Lovely Word
The left-hand column contains twenty words which one is unlikely to encounter every day. The right-hand column contains definitions of these words – but in random sequence.

Can you work out (or guess) which definition pertains to each word? Insert the correct letter alongside.
If you get twenty-five per cent you've done quite well.

1 OPSIMATH	a The founder of a colony	8 OBANG	h One who learns late in life
2 ORAGIOUS	b Bearing the author's name	9 OIKIST	i High-pitched
3 OPODELDOC........	c A fool	10 OGDOAD	j To blunt, dull or deaden
4 OSCITANCY	d Orange and tangerine hybrid	11 ONISCOID	k Tedious, laborious
5 OEILLADE..........	e Soap liniment	12 ONYMOUS..........	l Stormy
6 OBTUND............	f Like a woodlouse	13 OOIDAL............	m Clouding, darkening
7 OBNUBILATION	g Vinegar and honey mixture	14 OPEROSE	n Yawning
		15 OXYMEL	o A glance or wink
		16 OSNABURG	p An old Japanese coin
		17 ORTHIAN	q Of kitchen vegetables
		18 ORTANIQUE........	r A set of eight
		19 OMADHAUN........	s A coarse linen
		20 OLITORY...........	t Egg-shaped

3

Girls Wanted

Each of the words below has a group of letters missing, and each group of missing letters is a girl's name.

Can you supply the girls' names to complete all the words?

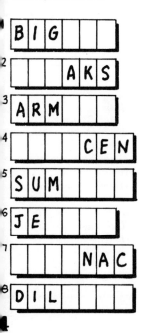
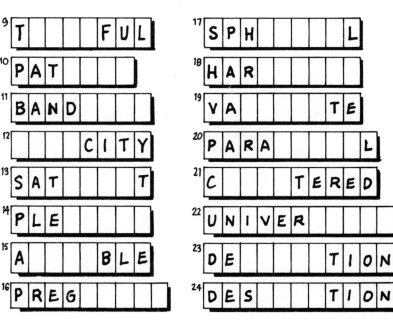

1. B I G _ _ _ _
2. _ _ _ A K S
3. A R M _ _ _ _
4. _ _ _ _ C E N
5. S U M _ _ _
6. J E _ _ _ _
7. _ _ _ N A C
8. D I L _ _ _ _

9. T _ _ _ F U L
10. P A T _ _ _ _
11. B A N D _ _ _ _
12. _ _ _ _ C I T Y
13. S A T _ _ _ T
14. P L E _ _ _
15. A _ _ _ B L E
16. P R E G _ _ _ _

17. S P H _ _ _ _ L
18. H A R _ _ _ _
19. V A _ _ _ _ T E
20. P A R A _ _ _ L
21. C _ _ _ T E R E D
22. U N I V E R _ _ _ _
23. D E _ _ _ T I O N
24. D E S _ _ _ T I O N

4

Blank Verse

The four words omitted from each piece of verse are anagrams of one another (e.g. VILE, EVIL, LIVE, VEIL).

Can you supply the missing words?

Old King Cole would _ _ _ _ _ and glower

To demonstrate his _ _ _ _ _ power.

When his thirst was _ _ _ _ _ , poor soul,

He'd call for _ _ _ _ _ in a bowl.

A _ _ _ _ _ _ myth describes how Hector

Lost his senses, drinking _ _ _ _ _ _ ;

In a _ _ _ _ _ _ , he rode his pony

At a _ _ _ _ _ _ o'er Oenone.

On the isle of _ _ _ _ _ _ you may see

Bitter _ _ _ _ _ _ on a tree.

But, with a _ _ _ _ _ _ oath I swear

Water _ _ _ _ _ _ there are rare.

4 Don José, when war was waged,

Became so _ _ _ _ _ _ _ , so _ _ _ _ _ _ _ ;

This _ _ _ _ _ _ _ would curse and groan

Whenever a _ _ _ _ _ _ _ was thrown.

5

A Novel Anagram

The phrase below, which is quite apt, was formed by rearranging the letters of the title of a well-known twentieth-century novel.

Can you identify the novel?

TALE OF WAR'S REALM

....

....

6

Proverbial Anagram

The sentence below was formed by rearranging the letters of a well-known proverb.

Which proverb?

THIS IS MEANT AS INCENTIVE

....

....

....

54 Puzzles Through The Looking Glass

THESE PUZZLES were devised by the Victorian mathematics scholar and creator of Alice, the Reverend Charles Lutwidge Dodgson, better known, of course, as Lewis Carroll.

1

A BAG CONTAINS TWO COUNTERS, as to which nothing is known except that each is either black or white.
Ascertain their colours without taking them out of the bag.

....

2

TWO TRAVELLERS, starting at the same time, went opposite ways around a circular railway. Trains start each way every 15 minutes, the easterly ones going round in 3 hours, the westerly in two.
a *How many trains did each meet on the way, not counting trains met at the terminus itself?*

....

b *If they went round as before, each traveller counting as 'one' the train containing the other traveller. How many did each meet?*

....

3

THERE ARE 5 SACKS, of which Nos. 1 and 2 weigh a total of 12 lbs. Nos. 2 and 3 13½ lbs. Nos. 3 and 4 11½ lbs. Nos. 4 and 5 8 lbs. Nos. 1, 3 and 5 16 lbs.
What is the weight of each sack?

1.......... 2.......... 3.......... 4.......... 5..........

4

A AND B began the year with only £1,000 apiece. They borrowed nought; they stole nought. On the next New Year's Day they had £60,000 between them.
How did they do it?

....

5

L MAKES 5 SCARVES, while M makes 2: Z makes 4 while L makes 3. Five scarves of Z's weigh one of L's; 5 of M's weigh 3 of Z's. One of M's is as warm as 4 of Z's; one of L's is as warm as 3 of M's.
Which is best, giving equal weight in the result to rapidity of work, lightness and warmth?

....

6

AN OBLONG GARDEN, half a yard longer than wide, consists entirely of a gravel walk, spirally arranged, a yard wide and 3,630 yards long.
What are the dimensions of the garden?

.........................long, ...wide

7

IF 70 PER CENT of people in an old folks home have lost an eye, 75 per cent an ear, 80 per cent an arm, 85 per cent a leg; *what percentage at least must have lost all four?*

....

8

A MAN HAS 3 SONS. At first, two of the ages are together equal to the third. A few years afterwards, two of them are together double the third. When the number of years since the first occasion is two-thirds of the sum of the ages on that occasion, one age is 21.
What are the other two?

....

9

A stick I found that weighed two pound:
I sawed it up one day
In pieces eight of equal weight!
How much did each piece weigh?

....
(Everybody says 'a quarter of a pound' which is wrong.)

10

IF 6 CATS kill 6 rats in 6 minutes, how many will be needed to kill 100 rats in 50 minutes.

....

11

PLACE 34 PIGS in four stie so that, as you go round and round, you may always find the number in each sty nearer to ten than the number in the last.

12

A WEIGHTLESS and perfectl flexible rope is hung over a weightless, frictionless pulley attached to the roof of a building. At one end is a weight which exactly counterbalances a monkey at the other end. *If the monkey begins to climb, what will happen to the weight?*

....

....

13

THE GOVERNOR OF KGOVJNI wants to give a very sma dinner party, and invites his father's brother-in-law his brother's father-in-law his father-in-law's brothe and his brother-in-law's father.
Find the number of guests.

....

14

A CAPTIVE QUEEN and her son and daughter were shut up in the top room of a very high tower. Outside their window was a pulley with a rope around it, and a basket fastened to each end of the top of equal weight. They managed to escape with the help of this and a weight they found in the room, quite safely. It would have been dangerous for them to have come down if they weighed more than 15 lbs. more than the contents of the lower basket, for they would do so too quick, and they also managed not to weigh less either.

The one basket coming down would naturally draw the other up. The Queen weighed 195 lbs., daughter 105 lbs., son 90 lbs., and the weight 75 lbs. *How did they do it?*

....
....
....
....
....
....
....
....
....
....
....

55 Mathematical Marvels

Here are four teasers from one of the modern masters of puzzle-making, D. St. P. Barnard.

1

AT A FAIR GROUND there is the following game. Nine cans are stacked in three piles of three, each bearing a number. The competitor has 3 shots, and each shot must dislodge just *one* can. If a shot topples more than one can it doesn't count.

For the first can to fall the competitor scores the number shown on it. For the second can he is credited with double the number on the toppled can, and for the third fall he scores three times the can number. To win a prize the total score of all three shots must come to exactly *fifty* — not one more or one less.

Which three cans should a competitor aim for, and in what order should he try and topple them?

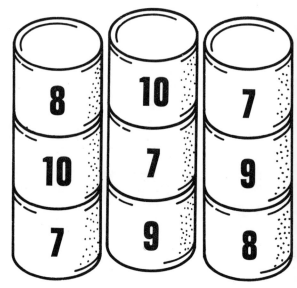

2

THIS GEOMETRICAL FIGURE is known as 'The Sphinx' for obvious reasons.
Can you divide this figure into four similar shaped sphinxes, each one a miniature of the whole, and each of the four parts equal in size?

3

IF YOU HAD TO COVER a chest with white laminex, and wished to do it as inexpensively as possible with the very least waste, but could buy the laminex in rectangular sheets only, *what would be the smallest single piece of laminex from which you could cut six pieces to cover this box?*

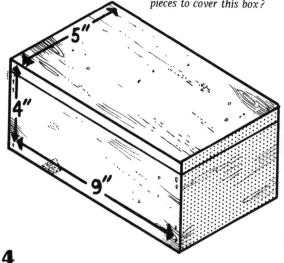

BIG TWO-IN-ONE OFFER!

ONE BATH TOWEL with MATCHING HAND TOWEL	35 coupons
ONE HAND TOWEL with MATCHING GUEST TOWEL	25 coupons
ONE GUEST TOWEL with MATCHING FACE FLANNEL	15 coupons
ONE BATH TOWEL with MATCHING FACE FLANNEL	

4

MRS BLOGGWYN looked at the back of her corn-flake packet; it gave her details of a special offer and the number of coupons required for each item on offer. What she really wanted was the Bath Towel with matching Face Flannel.

Unfortunately, as you can see, the packet has been torn so that she does not know how many coupons to save. *Can you work out the answer?*

56 Antiquarian Excursions

1

HIDDEN in the following passage are six rivers:

'The appearance of these streams was very confusing to one accustomed to see descending waters. At the same time it would be absurd to deny that the effect was not infinitely more grand. Instead of the waves gliding peacefully down their course, they were seen furiously leaping from boulder to boulder, as if assailing the heights. The steepest rocks were scaled by degrees, the longest hills were bit by bit ascended, until the summits were achieved. Thence the waters ascended to the clouds by showers of rain that rose instead of falling; for no dense mists crowned the hill-tops, no clouds obscured them. It was over the sea and in the valleys that the mists gathered and the clouds hung to supply them with the moisture which the reversal of the water-shed denies to them.'

Once you find the key to the puzzle you should soon find the rivers.

....

....

2

FIND THE FLOWERS hidden in this bouquet.
The clues will give you six different flowers.

a A form of the verb 'to be' and a line of zeros.

....

b A climbing vegetable, and a writing fluid.

....

c An earthen vessel, and a deep respiration.

....

d A part of the ear, and the nom de plume of a famous essayist.

....

e Singing birds, and a noise made by a cat.

....

f A fashionable dance, and the abbreviation of a boy's name.

....

3

HIDDEN IN THIS RHYME is a well-known proverb:

When the sun is in the east,
Waken all, or bird, or beast;
When he sinks adown the west
Homeward all things go to rest;
Given for toil is day's clear light,
Sleep, best blessing, waits the night.

....

4

A BUNDLE OF TWIGS

a Three-fourths of an eruption.

....

b A snake, and two-thirds of a fowl.

....

c Three-fifths of a Dutch nightingale's song.

....

d Three-fourths of a rudder.

....

e Three-fifths of an Autumn wild flower, and three-fourths of a bird.

....

f Four-fifths of pigs' wash, and two-fourths of an exhibition.

....

g One-third of a leguminous vegetable, and a narrow country road.

....

h Two-thirds of a portion of the mouth, and two-fourths of flesh.

....

i An industrious insect, and two-fourths of a gossip.

....

j Two-thirds of beer, and three-sixths of cattle-food.

....

k The outline of a country, and two-thirds of a limb.

....

l Two-thirds of a hog, and two-thirds of a snare.

....

5

A Square of Every Word
This simple puzzle will give you a word square that reads the same across as it does down:

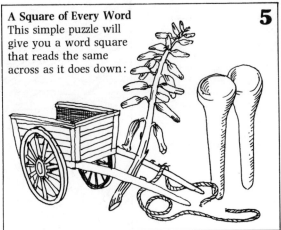

57 Amazing Follicles

The maze represents a hair follicle. There is an arrow to show you where to go in, but the challenge is to find your own way out. Here is the hair follicle quiz.

IF YOU COULD count them, how many individual hairs would you expect to find on the average scalp of a healthy adult with a full head of hair?

....

IF YOUR scalp hair is growing normally, about how much of it do you grow a day?

....

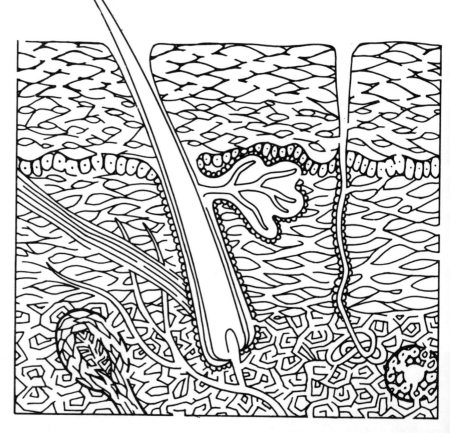

Full Marx

Which Marx made each of these remarks?

a *The workers have nothing to lose but their chains. They have a world to gain. Workers of the world, unite.*

....

b *I never forget a face, but I'll make an exception in your case.*

....

c *From each according to his abilities, to each according to his needs.*

....

d *No, Groucho is not my real name. I'm breaking it in for a friend.*

....

e *Religion is the opium of the people.*

....

f *I don't want to belong to any club that will accept me as a member.*

....

What do you need to do to make sense of these letters?

NMLCRCKRS

....

MNKYBSNSS

....

HRSFTHRS

....

DCKSP

....

NGHTTTHPR

....

DYTTHRCS

....

1

Pets of the Month

The owner of a pet shop bought a certain number of hamsters and half that many pairs of parakeets. He paid £2 each for the hamsters and £1 for each parakeet. Being a wily bird, he placed on every pet a retail price that was an advance of 10% over what he paid for it.

After all but seven of the creatures had been sold, the owner found that he had taken in for them an amount of money exactly equal to what he had originally paid for all of them. His potential profit, therefore, was represented by the combined retail value of the seven remaining animals.

What was this value?

....+ ....+ ....+ ....+ ....+ ....+ .... = ...

2

Map Folding

Do you have trouble refolding a map after you have opened it out? Well, never again. Make up a 'map' like this, using a piece of paper with the sections numbered as shown.

Now fold it so that the numbers are in order 1 to 8.

1	8	7	4
2	3	6	5

3

Seven Lines

What is the largest number of non-overlapping triangles that can be produced by drawing seven straight lines? The diagram shows how seven lines can produce six non-overlapping triangles, but you ought to be able to find a much better solution than this.

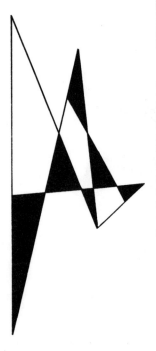

4

Missing Persons

In the list of words below, a number of letters are missing from each word. These are indicated by the appropriate number of dashes. Each group of missing letters is the name of a boy.

Can you find the boys' names that will complete the words?

1 C L A _ _ _ L E

2 D _ _ _ _

3 _ _ _ B A

4 C O M _ _ _ I B L E

5 L _ _ _ L

6 A _ _ _ I C

7 C _ _ _ I C E

8 G A L _ _ _ N

9 P R E _ _ _ E N T

10 C L _ _ _ _ A L

11 B _ _ _ _ C E

12 M U N _ _ _ E

13 C A _ _ _ D A R

14 S _ _ _ _ E T

15 D _ _ _ _ U N E

16 D _ _ _ _ C E

17 _ _ _ A L

18 P _ _ _ I S T

19 S _ _ _ U L A N T

20 B E T _ _ _ E D

5

Animalgrams

LION and HORSE can be anagrammed to give LOIN and SHORE. These are just two of a multitude of animal-name anagrams.
Can you untangle these ten and arrive back at the original animals?

1 Corona

....

2 Cabaret

....

3 Paroled

....

4 Retirer

....

5 Lesions

....

6 Someday

....

7 Chained

....

8 Untrace

....

9 Alpines

....

10 Outhears

....

11 Orchestra

....

12 Californian

....

6

Magic and Antimagic

To create a magic square you take an empty grid, such as that shown, and arrange to have a different number in each space such that the totals in the three rows, three columns and two diagonals are the same. Given the numbers 1 through 9, they could be arranged as shown in the second figure, giving totals of 15 in all eight directions.

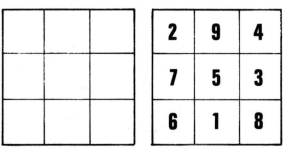

Now can you place those same numbers in such a way that the total in every direction is different? You could call your resulting square an antimagic one. What's more, *can you create an antimagic square with the additional restriction that none of the totals is 15?*

7

The Birds and the Trees

Most birds like to sit in trees, but you have to look carefully to find them. Each of these sentences contains the name of a bird and also the name of a tree.
Can you spot them?

a She's been a wonderful mare but it's time she was pensioned off.

....

b Goodbye William – I don't know how long I'll be away.

....

c When I see that particular church, my heart begins to throb instantly.

....

d The bird flounced around before making another onslaught.

....

e There's a towel missing which ought to be replaced.

....

f Well, I meant to avoid such awkward questions.

....

g Then he turned over a new leaf and began to help in every way.

....

h To see him fighting roused their spirits as high as they had ever been.

....

8

Quickies

1 Which is more northerly, the northernmost point of Eire or the northernmost point of Northern Ireland? *Tick your answer.*

Eire..... N. Ireland.....

2 What is the only word in the English language that contains the letter sequence GNT?

....

3 Find two whole numbers a and b, which are different, so that $a^b = b^a$.

a = ... b = ...

4 A fast growing hollyhock will get to a height of 12 feet in 12 weeks by doubling its height every week. If I only want a six foot hollyhock, when should I stop it growing?

....

5 Give us an anagram of PEPSI-COLA.

....

6 Which is the larger number, 1 followed by a hundred zeros or 2 raised to the power of 333?

....

60 Anatomical Atrocities

1

ON THIS FIGURE, with a pencil, draw in the internal organs listed paying particular attention to the accuracy of size and position, and most important of all – *the shape*.

Draw in these organs:

a Heart
b Two lungs
c Liver
d Spleen
e Kidneys
f Gall bladder
g Large intestine
h Small intestine
i Bladder

Obviously you will not be able to do a three-dimensional drawing so some of the organs will overlap slightly.

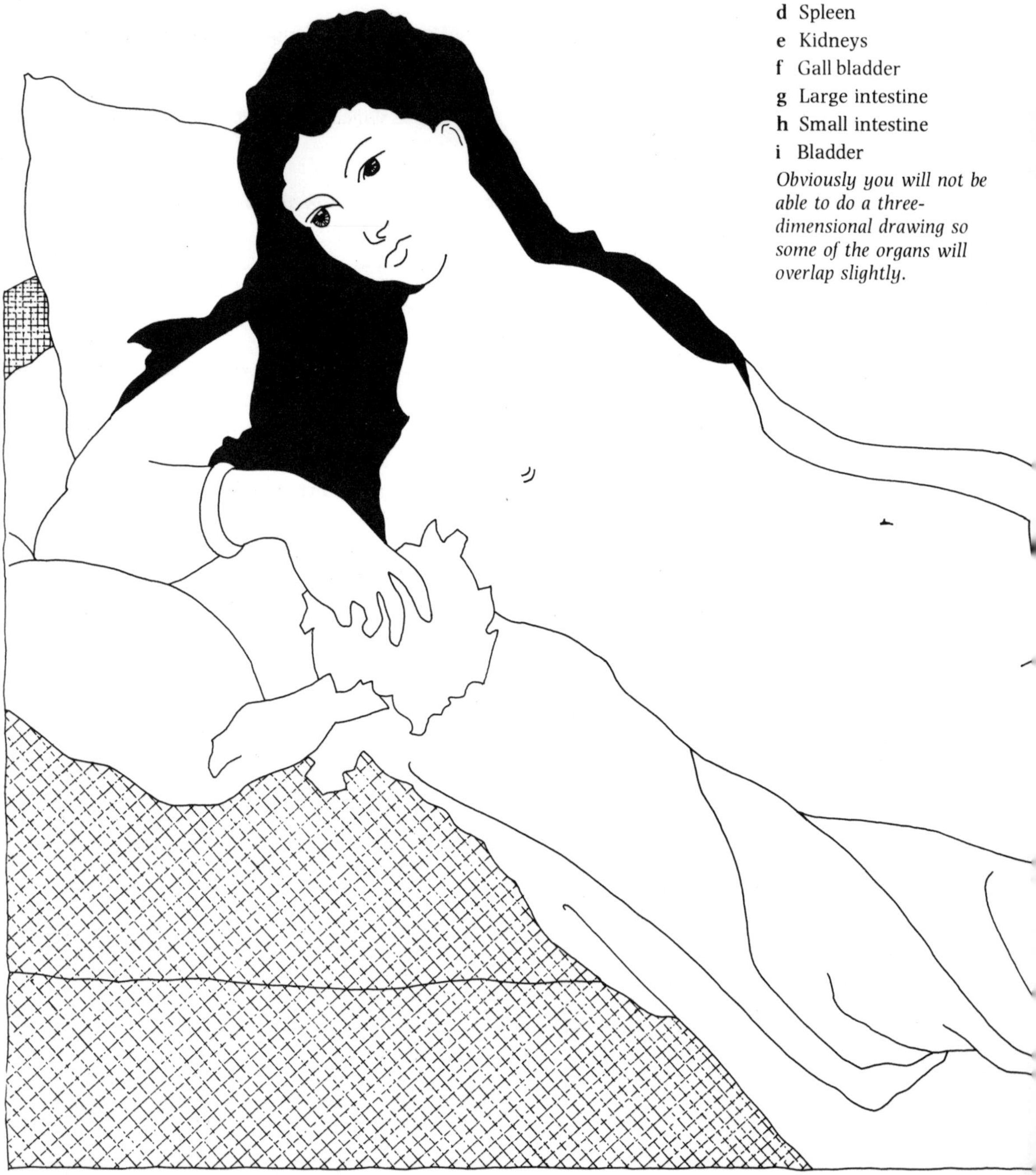

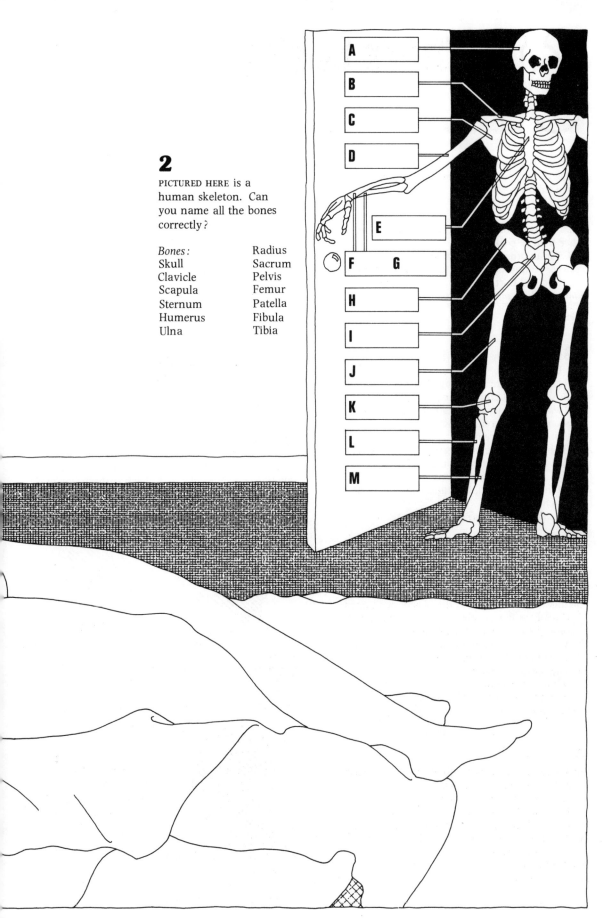

2

PICTURED HERE is a human skeleton. Can you name all the bones correctly?

Bones:

Skull	Radius
Clavicle	Sacrum
Scapula	Pelvis
Sternum	Femur
Humerus	Patella
Ulna	Fibula
	Tibia

A

B

C

D

E

F G

H

I

J

K

L

M

Test your powers of deductive reasoning with the logic puzzles of George J. Summers, one of America's most logical thinkers.

1

WHEN ADRIAN, BUFORD AND CARTER eat out, each orders either ham or pork.
a If Adrian orders ham, Buford orders pork.
b Either Adrian or Carter orders ham, but not both.
c Buford and Carter do not both order pork.
Who could have ordered ham yesterday, pork today?

....

2

FREEMAN KNOWS FIVE WOMEN:
Ada, Bea, Cyd, Deb, and Eve.
  i The women are in two age brackets: three women are under 30 and two are over 30.
  ii Two women are teachers and the other three women are secretaries.
  iii Ada and Cyd are in the same age bracket.
  iv Deb and Eve are in different age brackets.
  v Bea and Eve have the same occupation.
  vi Cyd and Deb have different occupations.
  vii Of the five women, Freeman will marry the teacher over 30.
Whom will Freeman marry?

....

3

MR BLANK has a wife and daughter;
the daughter has a husband and a son.
The following facts refer to the people mentioned:
  i One of the five people is a doctor and one of the other four is the doctor's patient.
  ii The doctor's offspring and the patient's older parent are of the same sex.
  iii The doctor's offspring is
    a not the patient
    b not the patient's older parent.
Who is the doctor?

....

4

ARLO, BILL, AND CARL were questioned by a detective about Dana's death by drowning.
  i Arlo said: *If it was murder, Bill did it.*
  ii Bill said: *If it was murder, I did not do it.*
  iii Carl said: *If it was not murder, it was suicide.*
  iv The detective said truthfully: *If just one of these men lied it was suicide.*
What was the manner of Dana's death: *accident, suicide,* or *murder?*

....

5

FOUR MEN AND FOUR WOMEN crossed Limpid Lake in a boat that held only three persons.
  i No woman was left alone with a man at any time, as required by the women.
  ii Only one person rowed during each crossing; no one rowed twice in succession, as required by the men.
  iii No woman rowed, as required by both the men and the women.
  iv Of those who rowed, Abraham was the first, Barrett was the second, Clinton was the third, and Douglas was the fourth.
Who was the last to row across the Limpid Lake?

....

6

ALBERT, BARNEY, AND CURTIS were questioned about the murder of Dwight. Evidence at the scene of the crime indicated a lawyer might have been implicated in Dwight's murder.
Each suspect, one of whom was the murderer, made two statements as follows:

ALBERT
i I am not a lawyer.
ii I did not kill Dwight.

CURTIS
v I am not a lawyer.
vi A lawyer killed Dwight.

BARNEY
iii I am a lawyer.
iv But I did not kill Dwight.

The police subsequently discovered that:

d Only two of the statements are true.

b Only one of the three suspects was not a lawyer.

Who killed Dwight?

....

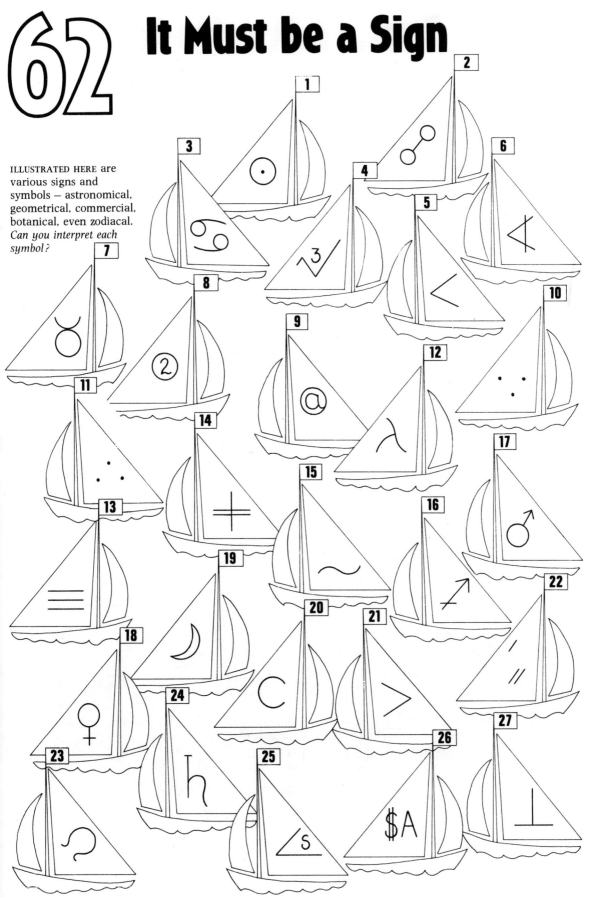

62

It Must be a Sign

ILLUSTRATED HERE are various signs and symbols — astronomical, geometrical, commercial, botanical, even zodiacal. *Can you interpret each symbol?*

63 Around The World in 80 Seconds

1

HERE ARE THE NAMES of the capitals of all 50 States that comprise the United States of America.

1 Tallahassee...........
2 Atlanta...............
3 Honolulu..............
4 Carson City...........
5 Concord ....
6 Topeka ....
7 Montgomery ....
8 Juneau ....
9 Phoenix ....
10 Harrisburg ....
11 Providence ....

12 Columbia..............
13 Cheyenne.............
14 Madison ....
15 Charleston ....
16 Little Rock ....
17 Dover.................
18 Denver ....
19 Hartford ....
20 Sacramento ....
21 Boise ....
22 Springfield ....
23 Indianapolis ....
24 Des Moines...........
25 Salt Lake City.........

26 Bismarck ....
27 Columbus ....
28 Albany ....
29 Richmond ....
30 Raleigh ....
31 Augusta ....
32 Montpelier ....
33 Annapolis ....
34 Boston ....
35 Olympia ....
36 Frankfort.............
37 Baton Rouge ....
38 Salem.................
39 Oklahoma City ....

40 Nashville ....
41 Austin ....
42 Lansing...............
43 St. Paul...............
44 Pierre.................
45 Trenton...............
46 Santa Fe ....
47 Lincoln ....
48 Jefferson City ....
49 Jackson...............
50 Helena ....

Can you give a State for every capital? And can you then work out which State belongs where on the map? You will find a place for 48.

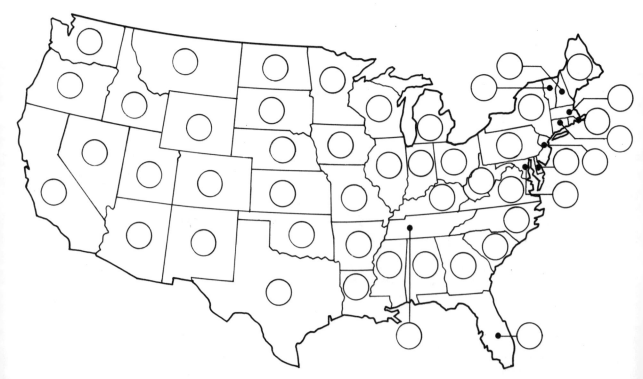

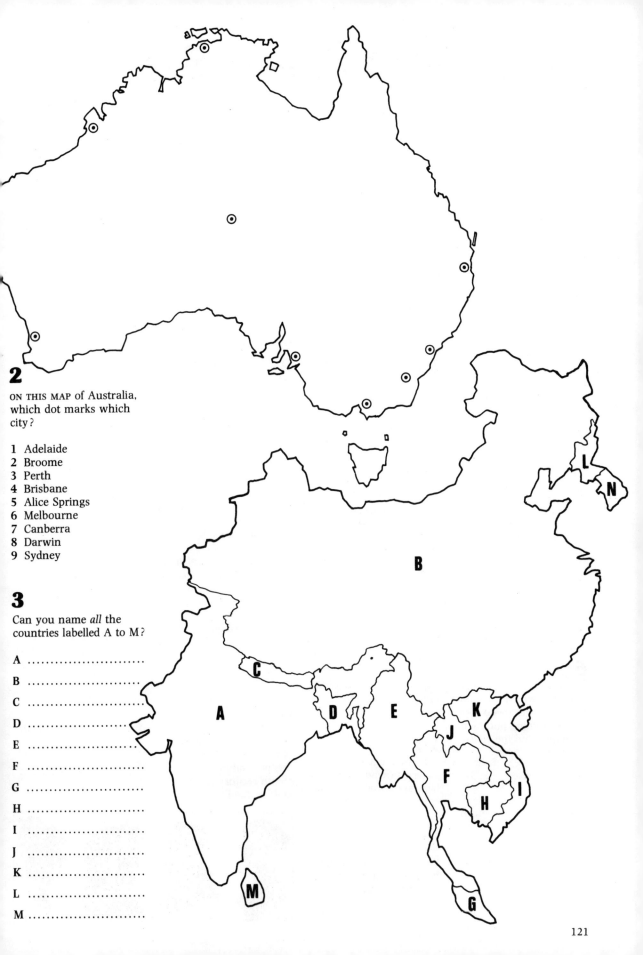

2

ON THIS MAP of Australia, which dot marks which city?

1 Adelaide
2 Broome
3 Perth
4 Brisbane
5 Alice Springs
6 Melbourne
7 Canberra
8 Darwin
9 Sydney

3

Can you name *all* the countries labelled A to M?

A ....

B ....

C ....

D ....

E ....

F ....

G ....

H ....

I ....

J ....

K ....

L ....

M ....

Cover to Cover

1

WHO WROTE a satire set in a crematorium called *The Loved One* published in 1948?

....

2

WHO WROTE the occult mystery called *The Devil Rides Out?*

....

3

WHAT WAS THE NAME of the Belgian dramatist/ author who wrote the children's classic, *The Blue Bird?*

....

4

WHO, in 1940, wrote a book called *Portrait of the Artist as a Young Dog?*

....

5

WHO WROTE a thriller with a title taken from a Tennyson poem?

....

6

CAN YOU NAME the French author of whom it is said that he would spend a whole morning putting in a comma, and the afternoon taking it out?

....

7

WHICH NOVELIST set much of his work in the fictitious county of Wessex?

....

8

WHAT WAS the name of the youngest of the Brontë Sisters?

....

9

WHICH VICTORIAN WRITER had the middle name 'Cleghorn'?

....

10

WHO, in 1816, wrote a novel in which she took a heroine 'whom no one but myself will much like', and what was the heroine's name?

....

11

WHOSE FIRST NOVEL was called *The Young Lions?*

....

12

WHO WROTE a posthumously published novel called *Maurice?*

....

13

WHAT IS the title of Charles Dickens' last unfinished novel?

....

14

CAN YOU NAME the American whose autobiography was called *The Heart has its Reasons?*

....

15

SAMUEL BUTLER wrote a book with an anagram for a title. What was it?

....

Soul Searching

Her eyes were filled with tears, her face was flushed with anger, and her expression was one of indignation at the brutal injury to which she had been subjected.

'You monster of cruelty!' she cried. 'I have borne with you too long! The very foundations of my being you have injured. Day by day I have endured your tortures. When first we met your ease and polish attracted me, and when you became my own my friends envied me. Yet see what I have suffered for your sake! You offer every opposition to my advancing myself. Your understanding is far too small for a large soul like mine. My standing in society you have entirely ruined. Had we never met I might have walked in peace. Be gone! We part forever.'

There was a moment's convulsive breathing, a grinding of teeth, and a quick sigh. It was all over between them. One supreme effort and she cast from her

....

Whom? Or what?

Arabian Knight

An arab came to the river-side,
With a donkey bearing an obelisk,
But he did not venture to ford the tide,
For he had too good an *.

So he camped all night by the river-side,
Secure till the tide had ceased to swell,
For he knew that whenever the donkey died,
No other could be its / / .

What do * and / / mean?

....

Only Connect

How is an eighteenth-century French Minister of Finance responsible for this portrait of a nineteenth-century novelist and her family?

And who were they both?

....

....

Wilde About Oscar

From which of the works of Oscar Wilde do the following quotations come:

1

'I have invented an invaluable permanent invalid called Bunbury, in order that I may be able to go down to the country whenever I choose.'

....

2

'There is only one thing in the world worse than being talked about, and it is not being talked about.'

....

3

'A little sincerity is a dangerous thing, and a great deal of it is absolutely fatal.'

....

4

'It is a terrible thing for a man to find out suddenly that all his life he has been speaking nothing but the truth.'

....

5

*'Yet each man kills the thing he loves,
By each let this be heard,
Some do it with a bitter look,
Some with a flattering word.
The coward does it with a kiss,
The brave man with a sword.'*

....

6

'Other people are quite dreadful. The only possible society is oneself.'

....

7

'When good Americans die they go to Paris.'

....

8

'One should never trust a woman who tells one her real age. A woman who would tell one that would tell one everything.'

....

9

'I can resist anything except temptation.'

....

Literary Riddles

1

Who in all of Shakespeare's plays killed the greatest number of ducks and chickens?

....

2

Why is the letter R like the face of Hamlet's father?

....

....

3

Why should a favourite hen be called 'MacDuff'?

....

....

4

Why cannot the Irish properly perform the play *Hamlet*?

....

....

5

What reason is there to believe Othello was a lawyer?

....

....

6

Why is a pig with a curly tail like the ghost of Hamlet's father?

....

....

7

If Falstaff had been musical, what instrument would he have chosen after dinner?

....

8

Why was *Uncle Tom's Cabin* not written by a female hand?

....

9

What best describes and impedes a pilgrim's progress?

....

....

10

Why is it a mistake to believe that Robinson Crusoe's island was uninhabited?

....

....

11

Why is this book like giving you your choice of two kinds of meat for dinner?

....

....

12

Why is a carrot like this book?

....

....

13

Why is a coach going downhill like St George?

....

....

14

Why is a Greek fable like a garret?

....

....

15

Why is Orpheus always in bad company?

....

....

Crosswords with a Difference

1

Anagram Crossword

This is a rather unusual sort of crossword in which the clues are simply anagrams. For example, if the word DEFIANT were part of the solution, the clue would be FAINTED.

Sounds easy, doesn't it? Of course, where there are several possible answers for a clue (*eg* the answer for SHORTEN could be either HORNETS or THRONES), then you must first obtain some interlocking letters in order to determine which answer will fit.

ACROSS

1 Centaurs
5 Rested
9 Sceptres
10 Recipe
11 Shingled
12 Strait
14 Undressing
18 Impression
22 Dagger
23 Salesmen
24 Routed
25 Presides
26 Trance
27 Gantries

DOWN

1 Hearty
2 Enters
3 Tassel
4 Stagnation
6 Resisted
7 Engrains
8 Treaties
13 Coordinate
15 Picadors
16 Berthing
17 Insecure
19 Peered
20 Recede
21 Stares

2

Coded Crossword

In this crossword there are no clues. Instead the letters of the solution are represented by the numbers 1 to 26. You have to determine which letter is represented by each number. Three letters are provided in the code boxes below to give you a start so, for example, you can enter the letter H wherever the number 5 occurs in the crossword.

15	3	4	1	11	9		2	11	17	1	6	6
16		7		12	1	3	8	17		19		17
5	8	14	10	8	14		8	19	2	11	12	15
7		9		25	17	11	2	5		17		10
22	11	1	24		11	3	5		21	7	1	18
15	16	19	15	9		4		5	7	3	13	20
	1		6	11	2	1	26	7	15		8	
5	8	10	15	20		17		14	9	11	10	13
15	22	1	17		23	15	25		9	7	3	5
1		4		17	11	24	11	17		26		20
26	20	4	3	7	22		3	7	14		17	14
5		15		3	22	1	2	15		3		15
2	7	17	13	15	20		15	24	1	2	8	17

1	2	3	4	5 H	6	7	8 O	9	10	11	12	13
14 B	15	16	17	18	19	20	21	22	23	24	25	26

66 Push Button Brainteasers

To cope with these puzzles you will need a pocket calculator.

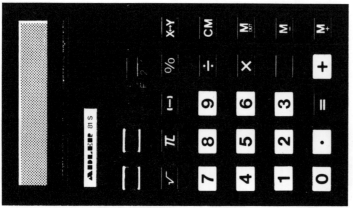

1

THE ANSWERS to the following questions when entered on your calculator, if you turn the display upside down, will look very similar to letters of the alphabet and the answer should spell a whole word.

a $15^2 - 124 \times 5$ will give you a distress signal.

b $217 \times 121 - 8,550$ gives you something that goes with pop.

c $100,000 - 6,000 + 152 \times 4$ will do something to your mind.

d The square root of 196 will give you a greeting.

e $.161616 \div 4$ tells you what Father Christmas said when he fell down the chimney.

f 44×70 will give you a musical instrument.

g $12,570 + 0.75 \times 16 \div 333 =$ an animal.

h $30,000,000 - 2,457,433 \times 2$ will tell you why the director of a company gets his own way.

i $159 \times 357 - 19,025$ and get a beautiful young lady.

j $52,043 \div 71$ will give you a snake-like fish.

2

CALCULATE the answers to these sums and see what the common factor is.

$8 \times 473 = \ldots\ldots$

$9 \times 351 = \ldots\ldots$

$15 \times 93 = \ldots\ldots$

$21 \times 87 = \ldots\ldots$

$27 \times 81 = \ldots\ldots$

$35 \times 41 = \ldots\ldots$

3

THE FOLLOWING SUMS use all nine digits to make up the multiplications and the answers. Work out the digits before checking them on your calculator – in each case you will have to discover what the number is being multiplied by.

```
   1963
 ×    ?
 ──────
 ──────

    198
 ×    ?
 ──────
 ──────

   1738
 ×    ?
 ──────
 ──────

    159
 ×    ?
 ──────
 ──────

    138
 ×    ?
 ──────
 ──────
```

4

HERE IS A MINI-QUIZ and calculation combined:

a Multiply the year of the Battle of Hastings by a 'Baker's dozen'.

b Multiply the answer by the days in a *leap* year.

c Subtract the number of days in an ordinary February.

d Divide the answer by the number of years in a millennium.

e Subtract two plus twice two from the total.

f Now subtract the date of the Battle of Hastings.

g Divide the total by the number of years a centenarian has lived.

h Subtract the number of steps in the title of a novel by John Buchan.

What is the answer?

5

The Percent Puzzle
You will need a paper and pencil for this. Begin at 0, then work out the percentage in the first box and write it down, then work out the next box, and subtract that, and so on. If you are right you answer at the end will be 0.

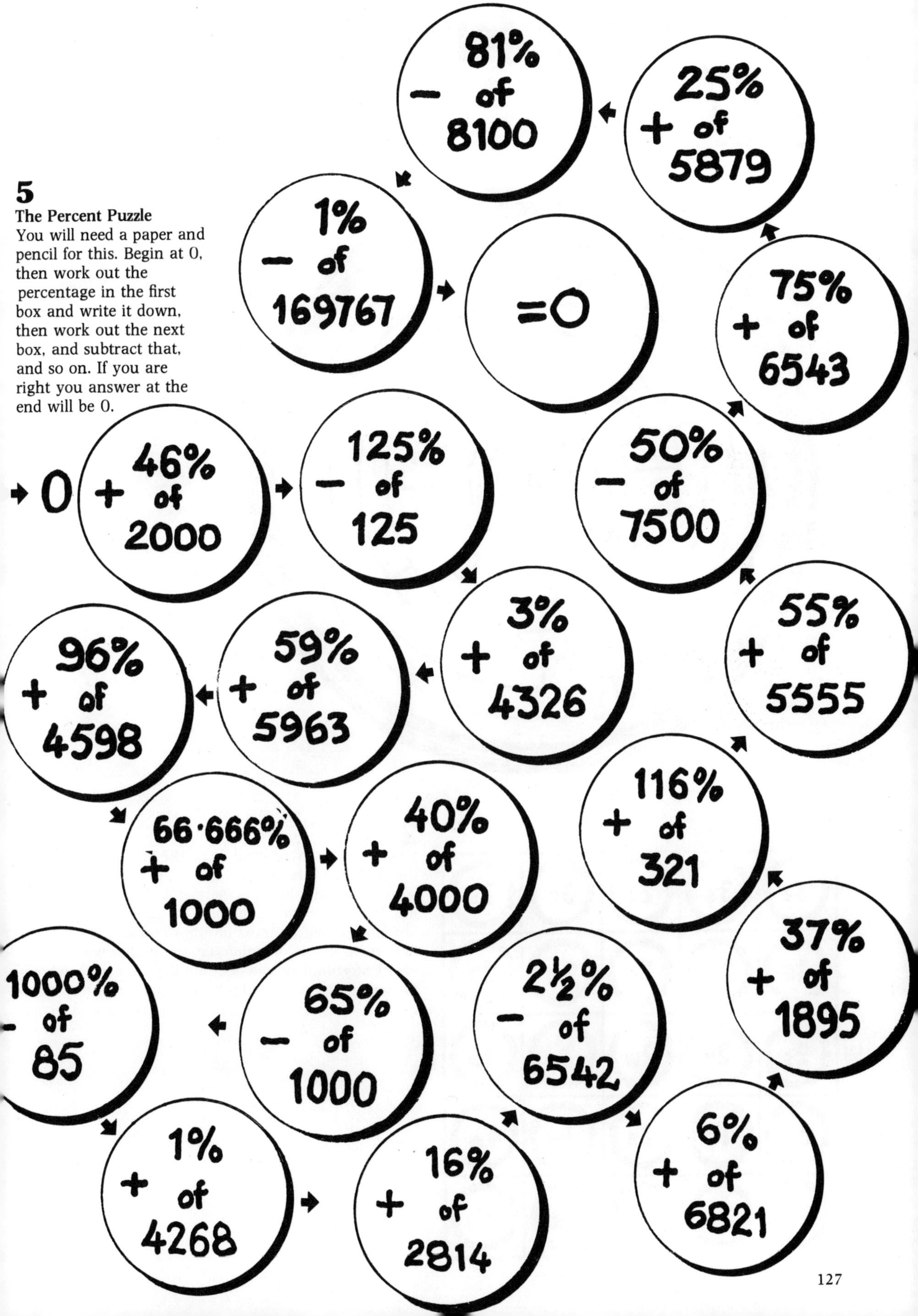

81%
− of
8100

25%
+ of
5879

1%
− of
169767

= 0

75%
+ of
6543

→ 0

+ 46%
of
2000

− 125%
of
125

− 50%
of
7500

+ 96%
of
4598

+ 59%
of
5963

+ 3%
of
4326

+ 55%
of
5555

+ 66·666%
of
1000

+ 40%
of
4000

+ 116%
of
321

− 1000%
of
85

− 65%
of
1000

− 2½%
of
6542

+ 37%
of
1895

+ 1%
of
4268

+ 16%
of
2814

+ 6%
of
6821

Problematic

1

In this circular maze, what is the *least* number of lines you need to cross in order to get from A to B?

....

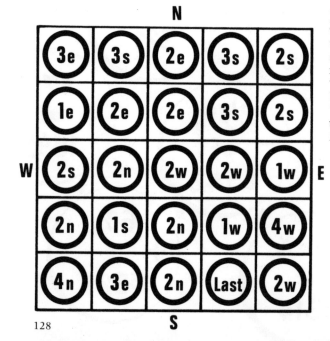

2

THIS SAFE has an unusual lock. The lock only opens on the pushing of the buttons shown, in a certain sequence. Each button is marked with a letter and number. For example, the bottom left button marked '4n' means that the next button to push is FOUR buttons in the 'n' direction, i.e. the button marked '3e'. Unfortunately, the diagram does not show where to start, only the last button to be pushed is shown. *Find the first button to be pressed and mark it with a cross.*

 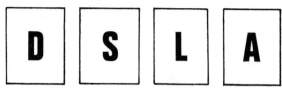

3

THERE ARE EIGHT LETTERED CARDS laid out in a particular order. Each adjacent pair of cards is first interchanged, thus forming a new order. Then the first three cards on the left are taken away from the new order and are placed at the end on the right, forming a further order. Of the three cards taken away, the first card from the left becomes card number seven in this further order, card number two becomes the sixth and the third goes in eighth place. This completes the cycle.

Four cycles have been completed and the card order is as shown, at the end of this fourth cycle. Write down the original letter-order of the eight cards just prior to the first cycle.

4

THE NUMBERS at the four corners of the squares shown, are related to the number within in a special way. This same relationship applies in each set of numbers and squares.

Complete the last figure.

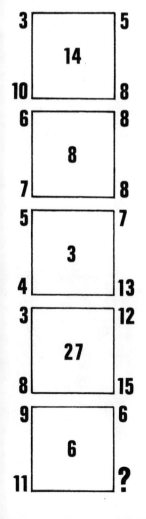

5

THIS DIAGRAM SHOWS A RAILWAY LINE serving both express and local trains. The express train leaves **D** (for **P** and **C**) at 10.00 and arrives at **C** at 10.48. It then leaves **C** (for **P** and **D**) at 11.20 (on its return journey). The express train travels at an average speed of 65 miles per hour.

A local suburban train leaves **P** for **L, C** and **B** and then returns (after a stop at **B**) to **L**, stopping on its return journey at **C**. The local train travels at an average speed of 35 miles per hour.

On their respective trips from **P** toward **C**, a pathway of 1 minute is required between the departure of the local train from **C** (on toward **B**) and the arrival of the express train at **C** (on the same line and platform).

On their respective return trips, the local train must make a connection (for passengers) with the express train, before the latter's departure from **C**. The local train must arrive therefore at **C**, 1 minute before the express leaves.

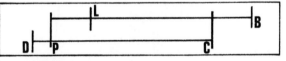

Given this information and the distances **DP** = 3 miles. **PL** = 7 miles and **CB** = 7 miles :

a What is the LATEST time for the local train to leave **P** (for **L, C** and **B**) to achieve the pathway required ?

....

b What is the maximum stop allowed for the local train at **B** (having come from **P, L,** and **C**) in order that it may make the 1 minute connection with the express on the return trip ?

....

c What is the local train's arrival time at **L,** if it waits for 2 minutes at **C** after the express train's departure from **C** (to allow the express to get away) ?

....

(For clarity, the local and express trains' routes are shown separately, although in fact they share the same two lines: one 'up' and one 'down'.)

6

Messrs **Lagan, Foyle. Bann** and **Erne** are neighbours. Three of them are married. One of the four is bald, one redheaded and one darkhaired.

Mr Erne isn't redheaded nor is he darkhaired, but is married.

Mr Lagan isn't bald nor is he fairhaired, but is single.

Mrs Bann is blond but her husband is neither darkhaired nor bald.

Mr Foyle doesn't have either fair or dark hair.

Mr Erne's wife is dark-haired while the bald-headed man has a redheaded wife.

Given the above information, answer the following questions :

a *Whose wife is a redhead ?*

....

b *What colour hair* (if any) *has the single man ?*

....

c *Mrs Foyle's husband has which hair colour (if any) ?*

....

 **Visual Variations**

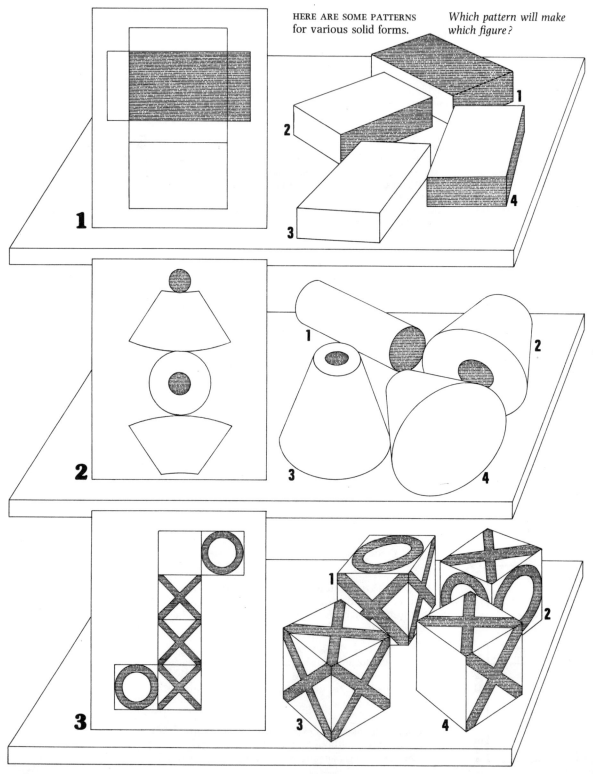

HERE ARE SOME PATTERNS for various solid forms.

Which pattern will make which figure?

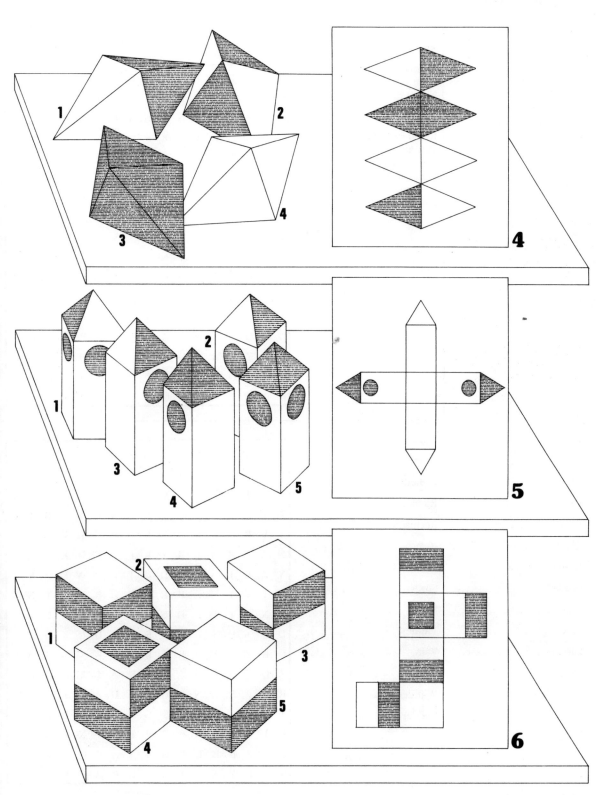

Hidden Words

WHEN YOU HAVE WORKED OUT what words you are looking for, you should be able to find them all hidden in the diagrams – but they may be written forwards or backwards, upwards or downwards, or even diagonally.

If you prefer to solve these three puzzles as a normal word search, the word lists are on the opposite page.

1
Boys will be Boys
Unscramble the 37 words below to give the boys' names to be found in the diagram.

Aid ....

Amuses ....

Antrim ....

Armagh...................

Bale ....

Brain ....

Carols ....

Cigar ....

Enters ....

Events....................

Flared ....

Glared...................

Grade ....

Grader ....

Ingle ....

Lace...................

Larches ....

Lark......................

Levantine ....

Line ....

Lone ....

Lyric ....

Meagre ....

2
Cherchez La Femme
Each of the 42 words below may be unscrambled to give a girl's name which may be found in the diagram. If you get stuck with any of the anagrams, or if you prefer to solve this puzzle as a normal word search, consult the word list.

Aidan ....

Aimless ....

Armenian...................

Aural ....

Blame......................

Breath ....

Bury ....

Canny......................

Coral ....

Nailed...................

Normal ....

Ordain ....

Radian ....

Reclusion ....

Rice ....

Sails...................

Sorbet...................

Spire ....

Vaguest...................

Vain......................

Vane ....

Wander ....

Yonder ....

```
G Y R L E T G Y N L T R D B L M Y
C B L A I R U B Y O N I E E I E X
A G A L Y N N E G S R Y L B M L Y
T D M C O Y B E S T K M L M H I E
H P N T I D R Y S L E P A N K S A
Y A L E P A H A M T W R U B O S K
N G N D L E O P O S I G R R E A T
Y L X D R G D X D A D N A R O L P
I O I A E P A G N S S T E H C K L
R N E W G L Y N I S T H H A I L P
E L G N I S E E L P T Y D E L I A
N E A R K A T E A D M A H Y L N Y
E X I P I N C H S T H I B E A M S
D R O D Y D G A O T I S P I C H A
Y O Y L A M D A R L I G D S T Y L
O L R O A S S E T O Y I N U E H M
K F G A M O B O L T L R R S Y P A
```

```
G R M N B L C J A S D E R G Y L C
O A T L K C N A P L T X G J N T O
G V I O P E A C N I N E I L O S T
H I B G R I G T K D R G V T B I G
I V R A C K E M E A R G H E A L S
N A I R B V R Y L P T E R K N A P
V A B J A X A D G T L T W H A S T
D I V T C A R L O S U R T H I N K
E N S I T K D G E E N D C Y R I L
D U N U S U I L E N R O C K D M Y
G E M S M A R V L R T R M N A A F
A Q U A P A A C R E A I M O O R T
R L A S H N E O N I D A N I E L D
T H F C L A D S G A R N O E L O C
P I E R S N R O P T L Y X E R N T
G R A B E L E G I N G E O R T I O
S K R Y A D I N K L P A C K S N C
```

3

Odd One Out

The 'odd one out' in each group of words below is to be located in the diagram.

L	E	S	O	O	G	N	O	M	E	S	P	I	Y	O	S	L
A	C	O	S	L	E	R	U	S	L	O	M	B	A	R	D	Y
D	E	M	T	Z	N	A	E	R	E	A	V	E	L	D	O	N
O	L	B	R	E	P	O	O	G	G	T	H	A	L	O	L	W
B	O	R	S	P	L	U	B	I	I	N	A	T	I	F	I	O
B	L	E	A	P	L	T	R	R	G	N	I	R	H	S	I	R
Y	G	R	E	E	B	O	S	P	A	R	T	A	C	U	S	B
V	U	O	T	L	P	S	W	I	N	C	K	H	N	O	U	T
I	S	T	L	I	T	C	H	A	M	B	A	T	I	S	S	U
C	E	G	Y	N	I	T	L	A	W	E	R	G	H	L	A	F
T	A	O	S	C	O	Y	O	T	E	E	P	E	C	O	F	W
O	G	R	I	L	M	U	T	B	G	I	L	D	W	A	W	F
R	B	O	D	C	H	A	S	N	E	C	N	E	T	N	E	S
I	V	I	U	I	L	M	I	O	B	U	I	S	H	D	Y	R
A	M	B	R	O	G	G	R	I	R	E	L	S	Y	R	H	C
L	A	R	I	M	D	A	B	R	U	A	L	B	L	E	V	O
V	Y	V	N	F	O	U	N	O	F	T	W	H	O	W	G	U

Daily ....   Ladle ....

Dane ....   Lenny ....

Dangle ....   Lilac......................

Dine......................   Lloyd ....

Ernie ....   Ordinals...................

Eros ....   Realigned ....

Goal......................   Riding.....................

Habitat ....   Road ....

Hamlet ....   Roman ....

Heaters ....   Seats ....

Hoard ....   Singly.....................

Hurt......................   Soil ....

Ideal ....   Teak ....

Ideas ....   Triads ....

Internees ....   Wand ....

Issue ....   Yacht ....

Lama ....

1 John, Paul, Ginger, Ringo, George.
2 Taurus, Orion, Libra, Scorpio, Sagittarius.
3 Lynx, Puma, Leopard, Coyote, Ocelot.
4 Cuba, Corsica, Corfu, Malta, Sicily.
5 Tuba, Oboe, Cornet, Trombone, Viola.
6 Nero, Caligula, Spartacus, Claudius, Tiberius.
7 Zeppelin, Harrier, Lightning, Vulcan, Buccaneer.
8 Crimplene, Cardigan, Polyester, Nylon, Rayon.
9 Bezique, Whist, Roulette, Pontoon, Poker.
10 Hoover, Carter, Lincoln, Washington, Chrysler.
11 Aspen, Mistletoe, Alder, Birch, Sycamore.
12 Goldfinch, Redwing, Yellowhammer, Bluebottle, Blackcap.
13 Pearl, Topaz, Amethyst, Diamond, Emerald.
14 Verb, Sentence, Adjective, Noun, Preposition.
15 Matthew, John, Mark, Peter, Luke.
16 Ripon, Leeds, Bristol, Sheffield, Selby.
17 Fagin, Falstaff, Steerforth, Squeers, Micawber.
18 Chihuahua, Borzoi, Corgi, Chinchilla, Dachshund.
19 Brigadier, Admiral, Captain, Colonel, Lieutenant.
20 Prussia, Lombardy, Bavaria, Westphalia, Saxony.
21 Mallard, Coot, Mongoose, Moorhen, Teal.
22 Somme, Danube, Tiber, Niger, Rhine.
23 Fletcher, Cooper, Brown, Smith, Miller.
24 Bushel, Furlong, League, Chain, Metre.
25 Hercules, Socrates, Aeneas, Ulysses, Perseus.
26 Gaelic, Urdu, Swahili, Latin, Origami.
27 Tango, Sombrero, Quadrille, Mazurka, Bolero.
28 Gold, Carbon, Aluminium, Zinc, Lead.
29 Maryland, Victoria, Virginia, Utah, Nebraska.
30 Midlothian, Kerry, Limerick, Galway, Tipperary.

Word List – Boys will be Boys

Dai, Seamus, Martin, Graham, Abel, Brian, Carlos, Craig, Ernest, Steven, Alfred, Gerald, Edgar, Gerard, Nigel, Alec, Charles, Karl, Valentine, Neil, Noel, Cyril, Graeme, Daniel, Marlon, Dorian, Adrian, Cornelius, Eric, Silas, Osbert, Piers, Gustave, Ivan, Evan, Andrew, Rodney.

Word List – Cherchez La Femme

Diana, Melissa, Marianne, Laura, Mabel, Bertha, Ruby, Nancy, Carol, Lydia, Edna, Glenda, Enid, Irene, Rose, Olga, Tabitha, Thelma, Theresa, Rhoda, Ruth, Delia, Sadie, Ernestine, Susie, Alma,
Della, Lynne, Cilla, Dolly, Rosalind, Geraldine, Ingrid, Dora, Norma, Tessa, Glynis, Lois, Kate, Astrid, Dawn, Cathy.

Word List – Odd One Out

Ginger, Orion, Coyote, Cuba, Viola, Spartacus, Zeppelin, Cardigan, Roulette, Chrysler, Mistletoe, Bluebottle, Pearl, Sentence, Peter, Bristol, Falstaff, Chinchilla, Admiral, Lombardy, Mongoose, Niger, Brown, Bushel, Socrates, Origami, Sombrero, Carbon, Victoria, Midlothian.

70 Boris Kordemsky's Puzzles

Boris Kordemsky, who was born in 1907, is a retired secondary school mathematics teacher living in Moscow. His first book on recreational mathematics, The Wonderful Square, a delightful discussion of curious properties of the ordinary geometric square, was published in Russian in 1952. In 1958, his Essays on Challenging Mathematical Problems appeared. In collaboration with an engineer, he produced a picture book for children, Geometry Aids Arithmetic (1960), which, by lavish use of colour overlays, shows how simple diagrams and graphs can be used in solving arithmetic problems. But it is for his mammoth puzzle collection, The Moscow Puzzles, that Kordemsky is best known in the Soviet Union, and rightly so, for it is a marvellously varied assortment of brain teasers.

Many of Kordemsky's puzzles will be familiar in one form or another to puzzle buffs who know the Western literature, especially the books of England's Henry Ernest Dudeney and America's Sam Loyd. However, Kordemsky has given the old puzzles new angles and has presented them in such amusing and charming story forms that it is a pleasure to come upon them again. Moreover, mixed with the known puzzles are many that will be new to Western readers, some of them no doubt invented by Kordemsky himself.

1

Three Moves

PLACE THREE PILES of matches on a table, one with 11 matches, the second with 7, and the third with 6. You are to move matches so that each pile holds 8 matches. You may add to any pile only as many matches as it already contains, and all the matches must come from one other pile. For example, if a pile holds 6 matches, you may add 6 to it, neither more nor less.
You have three moves.

....

2

Count!

HOW MANY different triangles are there in the figure?

....

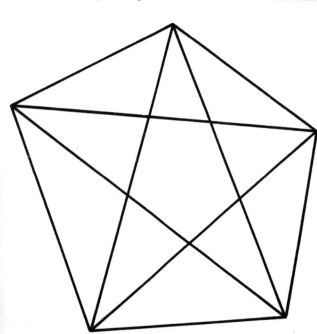

3

A Duel in Arithmetic

THE MATHEMATICS CIRCLE in our school had this custom: each applicant was given a simple problem to solve – a little mathematical nut to crack, so to speak. You became a full member only if you solved the problem.

An applicant named Vitia was given this array:

```
1 1 1
3 3 3
5 5 5
7 7 7
9 9 9
```

He was asked to replace 12 digits with zeros so that the sum would be 20. Vitia thought a little, then wrote rapidly:

```
0 1 1      0 1 0
0 0 0      0 0 3
0 0 0      0 0 0
0 0 0      0 0 7
0 0 9      0 0 0
-----      -----
  2 0        2 0
```

He smiled and said, '*If you substitute just ten zeros for digits, the sum will be 1,111. Try it!*'

The Circle's president was taken aback briefly. But he not only solved Vitia's problem, he improved on it:
'*Why not replace only nine digits with zeros – and still get 1,111?*
As the debate continued, ways of getting 1,111 by replacing 8, 7, 6 and 5 digits with zeros were found.
Solve the six forms of this problem.

```
1 1 1        1 1 1
3 3 3        3 3 3
5 5 5        5 5 5
7 7 7        7 7 7
9 9 9        9 9 9

1 1 1        1 1 1
3 3 3        3 3 3
5 5 5        5 5 5
7 7 7        7 7 7
9 9 9        9 9 9

1 1 1        1 1 1
3 3 3        3 3 3
5 5 5        5 5 5
7 7 7        7 7 7
9 9 9        9 9 9
```

4

Cat and Mice

PURRER THE CAT has decided to take a nap. He dreams he is encircled by 13 mice: 12 grey and one white. He hears his owner saying:

'Purrer, you are to eat each thirteenth mouse, going in one direction only round the circle. The last mouse you eat must be the white one.'

Which mouse should he start from?

....

5

The Sliced Cube

IMAGINE a 3-inch cube of wood. Its surface is black, but it is not black inside. How many cuts does it take to divide the cube into cubes with 1-inch sides? How many little cubes are there? How many have 4, 3, 2, 1 and 0 black faces?

........................cuts

..................little cubes

Black faces – 4............

4 ....

3............

2............

1............

0............

7

The Idler and the Devil

AN IDLER sighed, *'Everyone says, "We don't need idlers. You are always in the way. Go to the devil!" But will the devil tell me how to get rich?'*

No sooner did the idler say this than the devil himself stood in front of him.

'Well,' said the devil, *'the work I have for you is light, and you will get rich. Do you see the bridge? Just walk across and I will double the money you have now. In fact, each time you cross, I will double your money.'*

'You don't say!'

'But there is one small thing. Since I am so generous, you must give me 24 roubles after each crossing.'

The idler agreed. He crossed the bridge, stopped to count his money . . . a miracle! It had doubled.

He threw 24 roubles to the devil and crossed again. His money doubled, he paid another 24 roubles, crossed a third time. Again his money doubled. But now he had only 24 roubles, and he had to give it all to the devil. The devil laughed and vanished.

The moral: *when anyone gives you advice, you should think before you act.*

How much money did the idler start with?.................

6

What is the Engine Driver's Last Name?

ON THE MOSCOW-LENINGRAD TRAIN are three passengers named Ivanov, Petrov and Sidorov. By coincidence, the engine driver, the fireman, and a guard have the same last names.

1 Passenger Ivanov lives in Moscow.
2 The guard lives halfway between Moscow and Leningrad.
3 The passenger with the same name as the guard lives in Leningrad.
4 The passenger who lives nearest the guard earns exactly three times as much a month as the guard.
5 Passenger Petrov earns 200 roubles a month.
6 Sidorov (a member of the crew) recently beat the fireman at billiards.

What is the engine driver's last name?

....

8

Three Puzzles

IS THERE a number which when divided by 3 gives a remainder of 1; when divided by 4, gives a remainder of 2; when divided by 5, gives a remainder of 3; and when divided by 6, gives a remainder of 4?

....

I AM THINKING of a three-digit number. If you subtract 7 from it, the result is divisible by 7; if 8, divisible by 8; and if 9, divisible by 9. What is the number?

....

FIND THE NUMBER **t** and the digit symbolized by **a** in:

$(3(230+t))^2 = 492,\mathbf{a}04$

t=...........a=.........

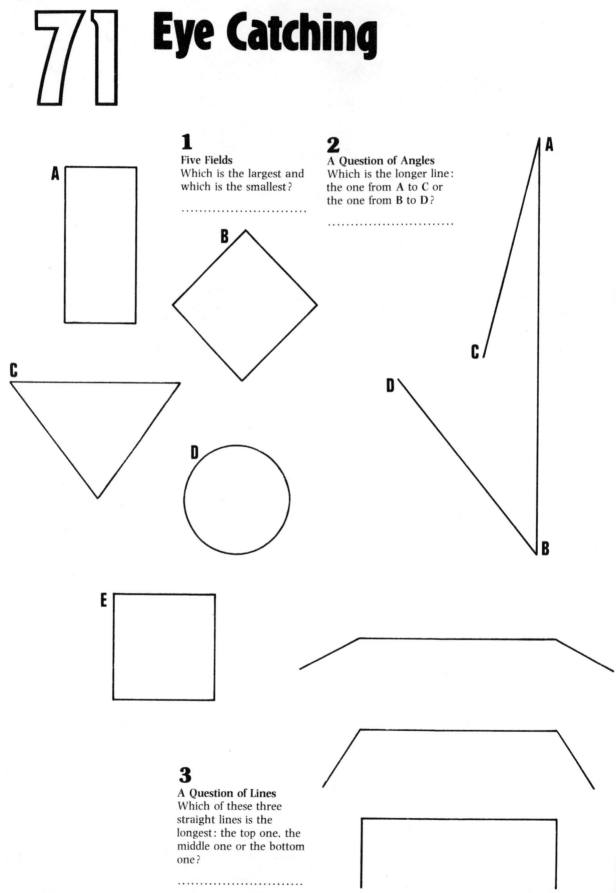

71 Eye Catching

1
Five Fields
Which is the largest and
which is the smallest?

....

2
A Question of Angles
Which is the longer line:
the one from A to C or
the one from B to D?

....

3
A Question of Lines
Which of these three
straight lines is the
longest: the top one, the
middle one or the bottom
one?

....

A B C D E

A B C D

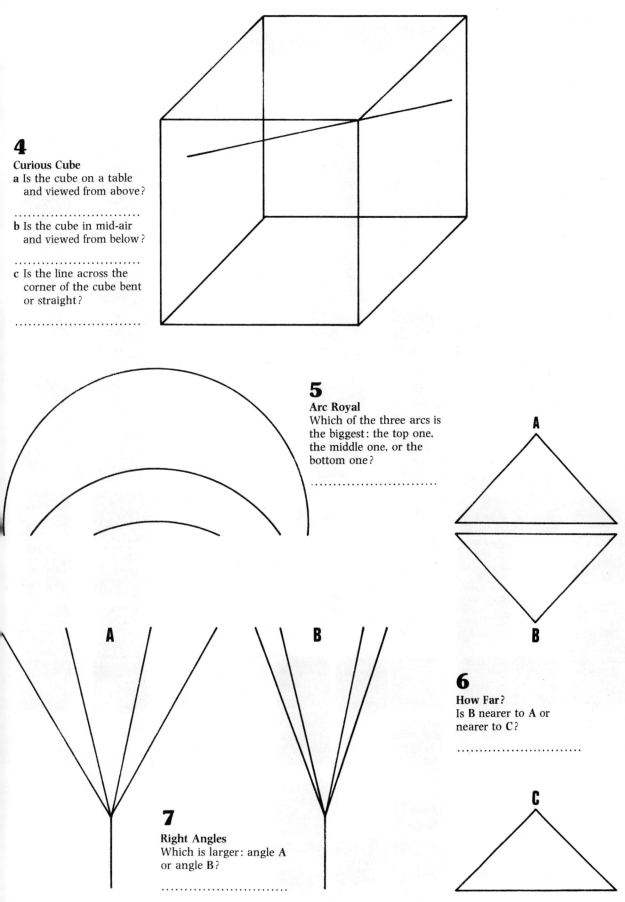

4
Curious Cube
a Is the cube on a table
and viewed from above?

....

b Is the cube in mid-air
and viewed from below?

....

c Is the line across the
corner of the cube bent
or straight?

....

5
Arc Royal
Which of the three arcs is
the biggest: the top one,
the middle one, or the
bottom one?

....

6
How Far?
Is B nearer to A or
nearer to C?

....

7
Right Angles
Which is larger: angle A
or angle B?

....

A

B

A

B

C

72 Indomitable

1
The Two Lines
Using the 6 lowest dominoes in the set – the 0/0, 0/1, 0/2, 1/1, 1/2, 2/2 – form two lines, with three pieces in each line:

Each line must contain the same number of pips and each of the joins must match.

2
The Two Columns
Take the 10 lowest dominoes in the set – the 0/0, 0/1, 0/2, 0/3, 1/1, 1/2, 1/3, 2/2, 2/3, 3/3 – and arrange them in two columns like this:

All the joins must match and you must end with a total of 15 pips in each column.

3
The Two Rectangles
Take the same 10 dominoes you used to build the Two Columns and turn them into two rectangles, looking like this:

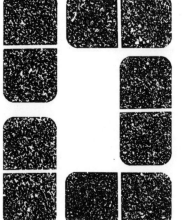

Each of the eight sides (that is to say all four sides on both rectangles) must contain exactly the same number of pips and, for once it doesn't matter whether or not the joins match.

4
Another Three Rectangles
With the lowest 15 dominoes in the set — 0/0, 0/1, 0/2, 0/3, 0/4, 1/1, 1/2, 1/3, 1/4, 2/2, 2/3, 2/4, 3/3, 3/4 and 4/4 — form three rectangles looking like this one:

Each of the twelve sides (that means all four sides of each of the three rectangles) must contain exactly the same number of pips but there is no need for the joins to match.

5
The Three Columns
Discard the 7 dominoes of the 6 suit and use the remaining 21 dominoes to build three columns, with 7 dominoes in each column. Each of the columns must contain exactly the same number of pips and the joins must all match.

7
The Last Seven Squares
Take all 28 dominoes and use them to form seven squares, with four dominoes making up each square. Every square should look like this.

You won't be able to make the number of pips on all 28 sides of the seven squares come to the same total, but what you must do is make sure that the number of pips on each side of any one square is exactly the same.

6
The Giant Eight
Take the 10 lowest dominoes in the set — the 0/0, 0/1, 0/2, 0/3, 1/1, 1/2, 1/3, 2/2, 2/3, and 3/3 — and arrange them to form a rather square figure of eight, like this:

Both the vertical columns (that's to say the two sides of the figure) and the three horizontal rows (that's to say the 2 dominoes at the top of the figure, the 2 in the middle and the 2 at the bottom) must contain exactly the same number of pips.

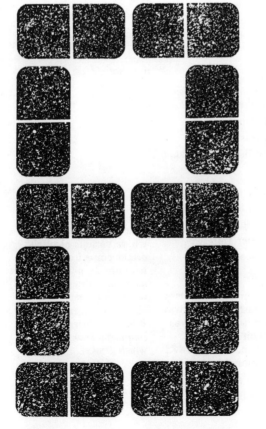

 **What's Yours?**

Spirited Words

Given here are a dozen gleanings from an assortment of different writers. The quotations all refer to wine or spirits of one sort or another. Against each of the quotations are the names of three writers, but only one of them in each case wrote the words. Which one? Underline your answer.

1

Gin by pailfuls, wine by rivers,
Dash the window-glass to shivers!

Alfred, Lord Tennyson
George Meredith
Sir Walter Scott

2

But tell me whisky's name in Greek,
I'll tell the reason.

Robert Browning
Edmund Burke
Robert Burns

3

I'm only a beer teetotaller, not a champagne teetotaller.

Rudyard Kipling
Oscar Wilde
George Bernard Shaw

4

He is believed to have liked port, but to have said of claret that *'it would be port if it could'.*

Thomas Carlyle
Richard Bentley
Alexander Pope

5

With ham and sherry, they'll meet to bury
The lordliest lass of earth.

Mark Twain
Rupert Brooke
John Dryden

6

With a cargo of ivory,
And apes and peacocks,
Sandalwood, cedarwood,
and sweet white wine.

Lord Byron
John Ruskin
John Masefield

7

Claret is the liquor for boys; port for men; but he who aspires to be a hero must drink brandy.

Thomas Hardy
Samuel Johnson
A J P Taylor

8

Candy is dandy,
But liquor is quicker.

Ogden Nash
e e cummings
Charles Schulz

9

A bumper of good liquor
Will end a contest quicker
Than justice, judge or vicar.

Charles Lamb
Ogden Nash
Richard Brinsley Sheridan

10

Good wine is a good familiar creature if it be well used.

William Shakespeare
Christopher Marlowe
Laurence Sterne

11

An old wine-bibber having been smashed in a railway collision, some wine was poured on his lips to revive him. *Pauillac, 1873,* he murmured and died.

William Yeats
Ambrose Bierce
Oliver Wendell Holmes

Alcoholic Anagrams

For some strange reason, the names of alcoholic beverages are particularly amenable to being anagrammed into other words. Given here are 30 alcoholic drinks, but each has had its letters rearranged to form the words actually shown. *What are the straight, unadulterated names of the 30 drinks?*

lea	dame	cask
....	....	....
boing	glare	touts
....	....	....
stopes	cartel	report
....	....	....
version	nastier	artesian
....	....	....
ensuings	cautioner	ponder
....	....	....
liquate	avenge	cram
....	....	....
ores	euserna	sanatorium
....	....	....
moles	tapeless	intower
....	....	....
novations	ado	overpatting
....	....	....
bury	planer	husband
....	....	....

Where's It From?

How well do you know where various alcoholic drinks come from? Given here are 20 different alcoholic drinks, some wines, some spirits, and also 20 countries. *Which countries are most commonly associated with which drinks?*

Aguardiente

....

Applejack

....

Bucelas

....

Cotnari

....

Fendant

....

Genever

....

Kislav

....

Mavrodaphne
....

Nahe
....

Orvieto
....

Patrimonio
....

Poteen
....

Pulque
....

Rakia
....

Rioja
....

Santenay
....

Tokay Aszu
....

Trebern
....

Verdelho
....

Vinjak
....

Austria
Bulgeria
Corsica
Dominican Republic
France
Germany
Greece
Holland
Hungary
Ireland
Italy
Madeira
Mexico
Portugal
Romania
Russia
Spain
Switzerland
USA
Yugoslavia

Pot Pourri

1
The film *Days of Wine and Roses* won an Oscar in 1962. *What for?*

....

....

2
The world record for drinking milk is 2 pints in
a 3.2 seconds,
b 6.4 seconds, or
c 9.6 seconds.
Which?

....

3
In which year did Coca-Cola first appear in the USA? Was it
a 1866,
b 1885, or
c 1899?

....

4
Slivovitz is a type of brandy made in Yugoslavia and Hungary. Is it made from
a apples,
b cherries, or
c plums?

....

5
Who, what or where is Red Biddy?

....

6
What are the principal ingredients of the iced cocktail daiquiri?

....

7
In Germany it's known as a *Bismarck*, and in Britain it's called *Black Velvet*. *What is it?*

....

8
What do the following sets of initials stand for?
AC

....
DOC

....
PX

....
VDQS

....
VSOP

....

9
Rank the following countries in terms of wine consumption per head of population. *Put the top consumer first.* Australia, Israel, Portugal, Spain, Switzerland, and West Germany.

....

....

....

....

10
Dom Perignon and the widow Clicquot are legendary figures associated with which wine?

....

11
Which of the following is not a wine from Beaujolais?
Underline your answer
Chènas, Chiroubles, Fleurie, Juliènas, Moulin-à-Vent, Poinchy, and Saint-Amour.

12
Find a single-word anagram of the name Pepsi Cola.

....

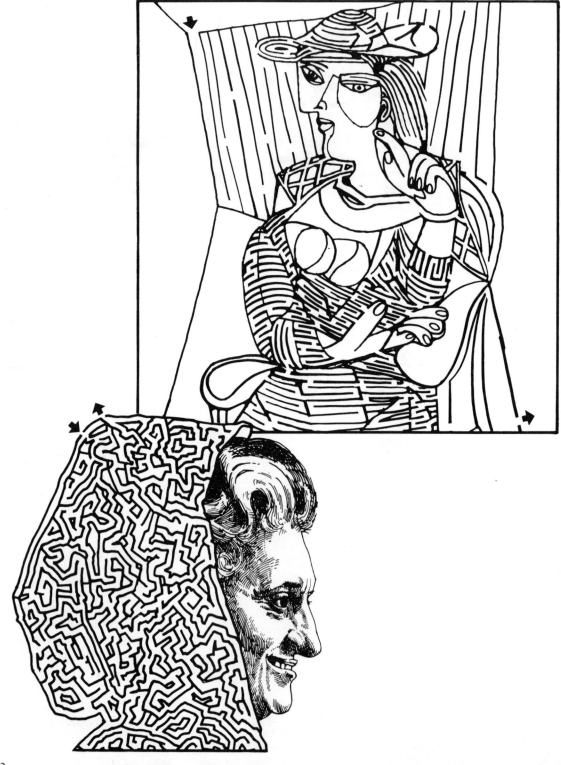

75 Solitaire Sensations

THERE ARE MANY GAMES AND PUZZLES which can be devised for the solitaire board, but the method of making moves is common to all of them. A peg can be moved only by jumping it over a neighbouring peg to a vacant space directly on the other side. Following such a move, the peg over which the jump was made is removed from the board. Jumps can be made only along the lattice lines, as shown in the diagram – a peg cannot jump diagonally.

In the most widely known solitaire puzzle, a 33-cell board is used. All cells are filled except the one in the centre. The player is required to finish the game with a single peg in the central cell. However, many other puzzles can be devised, and a number appear here.

The number of jumps made in a game of solitaire equals the number of pegs removed. However, a series of consecutive jumps made at one time with a single piece can be regarded as a single move; hence, a player can aim not merely at solving a given puzzle but also at finding the solution that requires the smallest number of moves.

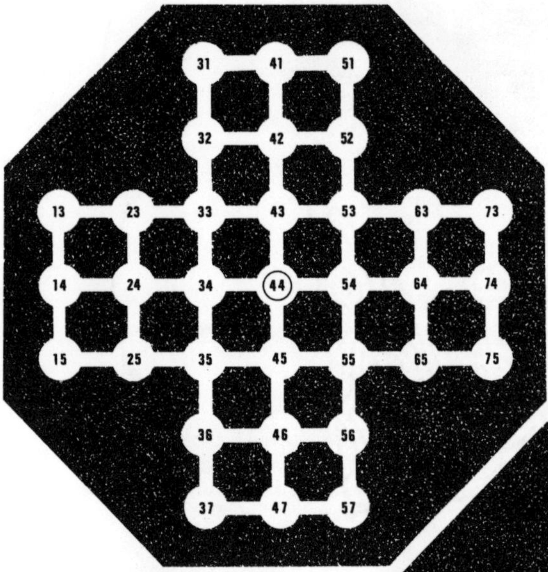

1
Centre to Centre
This is the classic peg solitaire puzzle. All cells are occupied except the central cell, 44. The pegs are all removed until there is only one remaining in the central cell. *It is not possible to solve the problem in less than 18 moves.*

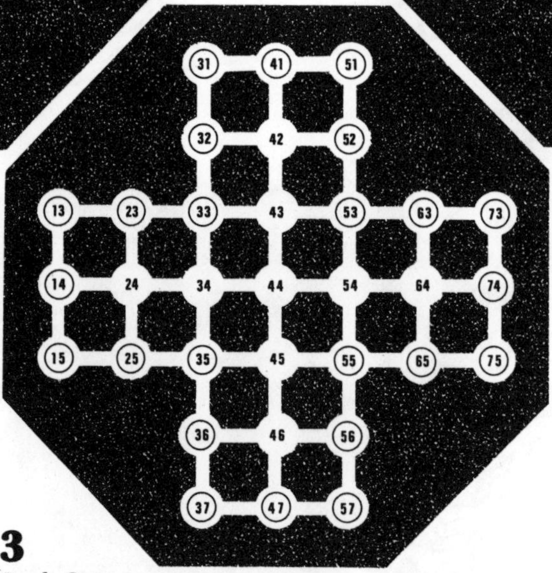

3
Greek Cross
This is a more challenging problem than the Latin Cross. At the outset a Greek cross, having four equal arms, is formed on the board with nine pegs. Eight of these are to be removed in the course of play, and the ninth is to be left in the central cell 44. Two double jumps occur in the solution provided. This is a six-move solution since chain jumps count as single moves.

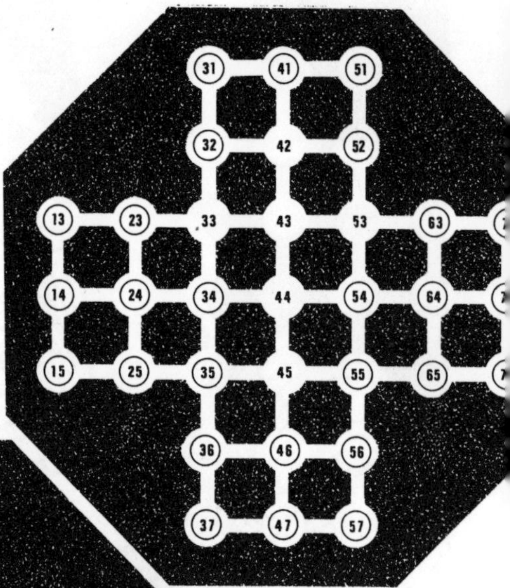

2
Latin Cross
A cross whose lower arm is longer than the other three is known as a Latin cross. In this puzzle, which is good practice for those beginning to play solitaire, the cross is formed with six pegs placed as shown in the diagram. The object is to remove five pegs in five moves and leave the remaining peg in the central cell 44. The puzzle is useful in getting familiar with the difficulties of peg solitaire.

144

4

The Five Crosses

The pattern shown in the diagram is composed of five small interconnected crosses. This pattern is made up of 21 pegs. The aim of the puzzle is to reduce the number to one peg positioned in the central cell 44. A ten-move solution is provided, which includes three chain jumps. In each chain jump, four pegs are removed from the board.

Notice that this problem uses a slightly different layout of solitaire board, with extra cells numbered 22, 26, 62 and 66. It is clear from the diagram that the first move that you make must be a jump into one of these four cells.

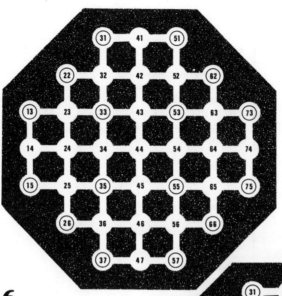

6

The Tilted Square

This inclined square pattern is formed from 24 pegs, with 9 cells left vacant. The aim is to remove pegs until only one is left in the central cell. The best solution uses 8 moves, one of which is a spectacular series consisting of 11 jumps! Perhaps you can discover an even more economical solution.

5

The Lonely Cross

This diagram shows *not* the initial but the final layout of pegs you are aiming for in this puzzle, which requires the full 37-peg board (i.e. using cells 22, 26, 62 and 66). First, fill the board with pegs; then remove the central peg from cell 44. Now try to form the pattern shown, in which a cross consisting of five pegs is surrounded by a series of pegs placed in the 16 border cells. Do not assume that the pegs in the border cells can be left untouched in the course of play. It is possible to solve the puzzle in 14 moves, of which only one is a double jump.

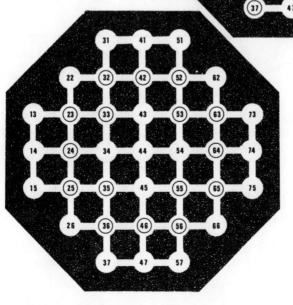

76 Parlez Vous?

1

Pseudo-French Rhymes

In *An Almanac of Words at Play*, Willard Espy quotes two very French-looking rhymes, but points out that we really need to know no French at all to make sense of them. And it doesn't matter about having a good French accent, either. Indeed, the worse the reader's French accent is, the more sense these two rhymes should make. Can you understand these two pieces?

Oh, les mots d'heureux bardes
Où en toutes heures que partent.
Tous guetteurs pour dock à Beaune.
Besoin gigot d'air
De que paroisse paire.
Et ne pour dock, pet-de-nonne.

....

Et qui rit des curés d'Oc?
De Meuse raines, houp! de cloques.
De quelles loques ce turque coin.
Et ne d'ânes ni rennes,
Ecuries des curés d'Oc.

....

....

2

Spoken Like a Native

Here are the names of a number of countries and a city as referred to by their inhabitants.
See if you recognise them:

1 Pyee-Daung-Su Myanma Nainggan-Daw

....

2 Sri Lanka

....

3 Chung-hua Min-kuo

....

3

Inter-Language Reversals

Occasionally, one stumbles upon an English word which, to the backward reader, becomes a word in some foreign language. English and French have a particularly strong kinship in this respect. Given here are definitions for four pairs of English-French reversals.
Can you determine what the words involved are?

English: *tiled again*

....

French: *to set stones edgewise*

....

English: *a merry-maker*

....

French: *to raise or lift up again*

....

English: *dressed in a red robe*
(a hyphenated term)

....

French: *to overflow or run over*

....

Other language inter-relationships also exist. Here are two English-Latin ones. Again, *what are the words involved?*

English: *colours again*

....

Latin: *slowly, sluggishly*

....

English: *changing*

....

Latin: *having been shunned or avoided*

....

Here are two English-Polish ones.

English: *one of the Romance languages*

....

Polish: *to weary someone of running*

....

English: *one who refines or purifies*

....

Polish: *a reindeer*

....

4 Chung-hua Jen-min Kung-ho Kuo

....

5 Po

....

6 Vasileon Tis Ellados

....

7 Lydveldid Island

....

8 Keshvare Shahanshahiyeiran

....

9 Daehan-Minkuk

....

10 Choson Minchu-Chui Inmin Konghwaguk

....

4

Trans-Lingual Anagrams

There are plenty of words in English which can be anagrammed to give other English words. For example, INTERMESHES can have its letters rearranged to give MITHEREENS; and PREDICTIVENESS can be anagrammed to VICEPRESIDENTS. A myriad of similar examples exist. Far more difficult to locate, though, are anagrams where one word is English and the other is from a foreign language. For example, the English UNPLEASING can be anagrammed to give the German ANSPIELUNG (allusion).

Given here are a number of English words, not necessarily common, everyday ones, and definitions of foreign words that they can be anagrammed to give. Can you identify the foreign words?

English word	Foreign language and definition
anchoretism	*French*; a monarchist
interpolates	*French*; the Colorado beetle
thomarge	*French*; an algorism
restrained	*French*; to compel
huntering	*German*; tendencies
erianthus	*German*; to execute
inharmonic	*German*; monarchies
ingenerating	*German*; entries
incremations	*Italian*; renaissance
ercolation	*Italian*; accuser
rocreations	*Italian*; to forecast
ecantation	*Italian*; charmer
egulations	*Italian*; flatterer
aceration	*Spanish*; tolerance

5

Palindromic Sentences

A palindrome is a word, phrase or sentence which reads the same backwards as forwards. English examples of palindromic sentences are:

Madam, I'm Adam!
Able was I ere I saw Elba
Madam, in Eden I'm Adam!
Ma is a nun, as I am
A man, a plan, a canal – Panama!
A new order began; a more Roman age bred Rowena

But the phenomenon of palindromic sentences is not restricted to English. Many foreign languages can give rise to sentences which read the same both ways. Given here are palindromic sentences from a dozen different languages, with translations.
Can you determine the languages?

EN AF DEM DER TIT RED MED FANE
One of those often rode with a banner

NEDER SIT WORT; TROW TIS REDEN
Inferior is the word; enduring is the intellect

SANE VOLEMA KARA RARA KAMELO VENAS
A healthily wishful dear rare camel is coming

NISUMAA OLI ISASI ILO AAMUSIN
The field of what was your father's joy in the morning

ET LA MARINE VA, PAPA, VENIR A MALTE
And the navy, daddy, is going to come to Malta

EIN NEGER MIT GAZELLE ZAGT IM REGEN NIE
A Negro with a gazelle never falters in the rain

INDUL A PAP ALUDNI
The person is going to sleep

ALLAR MUNUM RALLA
We shall all have a wild time

EBRO E OTEL, MA AMLETO E ORBE!
Othello is drunk, but Hamlet is blind!

ACIDE ME MALO, SED NON DESOLA ME, MEDICA
Disgustingly I prefer myself, but do not leave me, healing woman

77 Logical Logograms

DISCOVER ALL OF THE WORDS in each question and list them.
The first word is simply the key to the rest.

1

I am a word of five letters and am generally seen on a man's face.

....

my 1, 3, 4, occurs at the mouth of a river.

....

my 4, 3, 5, was a political nickname.

....

my 3, 4, 2, is part of the verb to be.

....

my ability to 4, 2, 3, 5, is a great advantage to me.

....

my 1, 2, 5, is where I love to lie.

....

2

I am a word of six letters, and mean part of plants or trees.

....

my 3, 1, 2, is a beverage.

....

my 6, 5, 3, the ocean.

....

my 4, 3, 1, 5, a low-lying locality.

....

my 6, 5, 3, 1, a stamp.

....

my 1, 5, 3, a meadow.

....

my 5, 4, 2, the close of day.

....

my 4, 3, 2, 1, a delicate meat.

....

my 3, 4, 2, a Latin salutation.

....

my 2, 5, 1, a fish.

....

my 1, 3, 4, 2, to wash.

....

my 6, 3, 4, 2, to rescue.

....

my 4, 3, 6, 2, an ornamental vessel.

....

my 6, 3, 1, 5, an auction.

....

my 5, 1, 6, 2, otherwise.

....

my 5, 1, 4, 2, 6, fairies.

....

my 5, 3, 4, 2, 6, part of a roof.

....

my 5, 3, 6, 2, comfort.

....

my 1, 5, 3, 6, 2, an agreement.

....

and my 6, 1, 3, 4, 2, a bondsman.

....

3

I am a word of seven letters signifying a style of literature.

....

my 5, 4, 3, 7, is an appellation.

....

my 1, 7, 4, 3, is a term in stationery.

....

my 7, 4, 1, 5, is to merit.

....

my 3, 4, 6, 7, is a spice.

....

my 4, 3, 2, 1, is a little classic god.

....

my 4, 1, 3, is a weapon.

....

my 6, 4, 5, is a vessel.

....

my 1, 2, 3, 7, is a city.

....

my 3, 2, 4, is an extinct bird.

....

my 6, 2, 5, 7, is a solid figure.

....

my 1, 4, 6, 7, is a contest.

....

my 3, 4, 1, is to destroy.

....

my 6, 2, 1, 7, is the inmost centre.

....

my 3, 4, 5, is a descendant of Adam.

....

my 3, 2, 1, 7, is a comparative.

....

my 5, 7, 4, 1 means propinquity.

....

my 4, 3, 7, 5, is part of a prayer.

....

my 6, 4, 1, 7, is trouble.

....

my 1, 4, 3, is a ship of war.

....

4

I am a word of five
letters, meaning the
products of needlework.

....

my 1, 3, 4, is short for a Christian name.

....

my 5, 2, 3, is water.

....

my 4, 3, is a parent.

....

my 5, 3, 4, 2, is identical.

....

my 4, 3, 5, 1, is a religious ceremony.

....

my 2, 4, 1, is a well-known place abroad.

....

my 4, 2, 1, 5, is confusion.

....

my 3, 1, 5, is a quadruped.

....

my 3, 5, is an ancient coin.

....

my 4, 2, is the objective of a pronoun.

....

my 2, 5, 1, is the name of a perfume.

....

my 3, 4, is present tense of a verb.

....

5

I am a word of eight
letters, meaning whatever
belongs to a civilised
continent.

....

my 1, 7, 3, is an organ.

....

my 3, 4, 5, 1, is a cable.

....

my 5, 1, 7, is a vegetable.

....

my 5, 6, 7, 3, is a fruit.

....

my 5, 6, 1, 3, is to gaze into.

....

my 8, 1, 7, 5, is a sort of tide.

....

my 3, 5, 7, 1, is a bird seed

....

my 8, 7, 5, is a short sleep.

....

my 8, 7, 5, 1, is part of a neck.

....

my 3, 7, 5, is a knock.

....

my 5, 7, 3, 6, is to peel.

....

my 7, 5, 1, is a climbing animal.

....

my 5, 3, 2, 6, is unsullied.

....

my 3, 1, 7, 5, is to harvest.

....

my 3, 2, 6, is to regret.

....

my 8, 1, 7, 3, is neighbouring.

....

my 5, 4, 3, 6, is a duct.

....

my 5, 7, 8, is a vessel.

....

my 5, 3, 1, 6, 8, is to arrange plumage.

....

my 5, 4, 2, 3, is to rain heavily.

....

my 5, 6, 8, is an implement.

....

my 3, 4, 2, 5, is an auction.

....

my 5, 3, 2, 8, 1, is a plum.

....

78 Silverman's Gold

AN ACE AT CARDS, a king of conundra, a prince of puzzles, David Silverman is one of the masters of modern brainteasing. Here are five of his gems.

1

Yes or No?

This is a variation of the game *Twenty Questions*, with a bit of *What's My Line?* thrown in to make it more interesting.

Red and Black each covertly write down an integer from 1 to 100. The objective is to guess the other player's number first. Questions may be asked concerning the opponent's number provided that they can be answered truthfully with a 'yes' or a 'no'. A player is permitted to continue asking questions so long as he receives 'yes' answers. The first 'no' transfers the role of questioner to the opponent.

The conservative *Twenty Questions* strategy of questioning in such a manner as most nearly to equalise the chance of 'yes' and 'no' answers is most effective in that game. Using it, you can, in only twenty questions, invariably pinpoint any number in the range of 1 to 500,000. But in the game *Yes or No?*

this may not be the best way to proceed.

Suppose you are the first player. *What will your questioning strategy be, and how much of an advantage do you feel you have over your opponent?*

....

....

2

Modified Russian Roulette

In this harmless version of Russian Roulette, two players alternately shoot a six-shot revolver, only one chamber of which contains a cartridge, at a target. The player who first gets a 'bang' rather than a 'click' is the loser.

There is an option, however. At any turn, instead of shooting the next chamber, a player may randomly spin the magazine before shooting. Once either player elects to spin before shooting, all successive shots, if any, must be preceded by a spin.

You have first shot. *Do you spin first and shoot, or shoot without spinning?*

After you have worked this one out, decide what you would do as the first player in the *misere* version (first player to get a 'bang' wins).

3

Plan Your Move(s), Kid!

In this solitaire game, the letters are to be thought of as engraved on tiles, which are free to slide vertically and horizontally into the vacant space. By judiciously manipulating that vacant space, you are challenged to

ungarble the message as it appears here, so that it will spell out the intended message PLAN YOUR MOVE, KID! You can play this game by cutting out fifteen cardboard squares, lettered appropriately, and pushing them around a 4-by-4 diagram. There is no time limit.

4

Seven No Trump

This is strictly a two-person bidding game with little resemblance to the game of bridge beyond the fact that the bidding sequence must follow the order prescribed in contract bridge. The five suits – clubs, diamonds, hearts, spades, and no trump – are ranked upward in the order given. There are a couple of restrictions on the bidding:

1 The initial bid must be at the 1 level, and

2 following the first bird, each player has two options: he may either raise his opponent's last bid to a higher level in the same suit (as high as he wishes) or he may raise to a higher ranking suit at the same level.

The objective is to be the last bidder – that is, the one to bid 7NT. There are no passes, doubles, or redoubles. The sequence given in the diagram here illustrates a win for player B. His response to A's opening bid of one club could have been one diamond, one heart, one spade, one no trump, two clubs, three clubs, four clubs, five clubs, six clubs, or seven clubs. He was lucky to win with his two-club response, though it will be seen that neither player had an inkling of the winning strategy.

The fact is that although the first player has a choice of five bids at the one level, the second player will invariably win if he bids optimally. Your opponent draws the first bid by the toss of a coin, and it is up to you to plan your strategy against each of his five possible openings. The problem appears difficult, but you will find it simple enough if you approach it from the right 'direction'.

5

Trump Management

Diamonds: **A K**

Clubs: **A K Q**

Hearts: **J 10 9 7 6 4 3 2**

Spades: **none**

Having dealt yourself the above bridge hand, you open four hearts, which is passed around. On winning the diamond lead in your hand, you note with regret that dummy is void of trumps. Nothing is to be gained by post-poning the drawing of

trumps. How you do so is the crux of the matter. *What do you do?*

....

....

....

....

....

....

79 Sam Loyd Classics

1

The Puzzle of the Red Spade

During a recent visit to the Crescent City Whist and Chess Club, my attention was called to the curious feature of a red spade which appears in one of the windows of the main reception room. The design came from Dresden, and, after the manner of cathedral windows, is made of numerous small pieces of stained glass skilfully fitted together to make the desired pattern.

No reason was ever vouchsafed, nor even asked for, regarding the incongruousness of the colour. It was looked upon as a blunder which occasioned considerable comment at first, but came to be looked upon afterwards with favour, not only on account of the novelty of such a thing as a red spade, but also because a black spade would have made the room too dark.

Hearing, however, that a blunder had actually been committed by the manufacturer, in that the ace of hearts was to have been the insignia of the club, I was led to examine the window carefully. The space was composed of three pieces and I speedily discovered that by rearranging the pieces they would fit together to form the ace of hearts, as originally desired.

The members have become so accustomed, not to say endeared, to their unique emblem that they would not concent to having it changed. Nevertheless it makes a unique although simple puzzle.
Show how to change the spade into a heart by cutting it into three pieces.

2

The Canals of Mars

Here is a map of the newly discovered cities and waterways of our nearest neighbour planet, Mars. Start at the city marked **T**, at the south pole, and see if you can spell a complete English sentence by making a tour of all the cities, visiting each city only once, and returning to the starting point.

When this puzzle originally appeared in a magazine, more than fifty thousand readers reported, 'There is no possible way.'
Yet it is a very simple puzzle!

3

After Dinner Tricks

For readers interested in parlour tricks, here is an amusing puzzle which can be used advantageously to amuse the guests after a banquet or at an evening party. In the former case eight wine glasses – four empty and four partially filled – illustrate the trick to perfection.

In this, as in all exhibitions of a similar character, everything depends on the skill and clever acting of the performer. He must have his little book down to perfection, so as to be able to do the trick forwards or backwards without the slightest hesitation, while by the aid of a ceaseless flow of conversation he impresses upon his hearers the fact of its being the most simple trick that ever happened, which anyone can do unless he be a natural born muttonhead or hopelessly befuddled. It really looks so simple that

almost anyone will be lured into accepting an invitation to step up and test his sobriety by showing how readily he can perform the feat and then the fun begins – for it will rattle ninety-nine out of a hundred.

The problem is stated here. The glasses in the diagram are numbered to make it easy to describe the correct procedure.

Pick up two adjacent glasses at a time and in four moves change the positions so that each alternate glass will be empty.

4

Against the Wind

A bicycle rider rode a mile in three minutes with the wind, and returned in four minutes against the wind. Assuming that at all times he applies the same force to his pedals, *how long would it take him to ride a mile if there were no wind?*

....

5

Diminishing Power

Monsieur De Foie Gras, the noted French chauffeur, mentions that on a certain motoring trip his car went 135 miles during the first two hours and 104 miles during the next two hours. Assuming that the power steadily diminished during the next four hours so that each hourly run decreased in miles by the same amount, *how far did the car travel during each of the four hours?*

....

....

6

The Patrolman's Puzzle

Here is a problem that has been puzzling Clancy ever since he got on the force. He patrols the 49 houses shown on his map, beginning and ending his tour at the spot in the top left-hand corner. His orders are to pass an uneven number of houses along any street or avenue before he makes a turn, and he cannot walk twice along any portion of his route.

The dotted line shows the route he has been following. It takes him past the 28 houses that are shown white on the map.

Can you help Clancy find a route that will comply with his orders and take him past the greatest possible number of houses?

As before, the path must begin and end at the spot in the top left-hand corner.

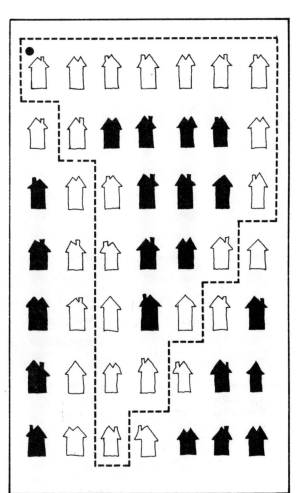

80 Questions of Science

1

An Elementary Quiz

In the world of chemistry, each of the various elements is usually represented by a symbol of one or two letters. For example, **B** is for boron, **C** is for carbon, **H** is for hydrogen, **Li** is for lithium, **Ni** is for nickel, and **Si** is for silicon.

But which elements are represented by these letters?

Ag ....   Mg ....

Au ....   Na ....

Cu ....   Pb ....

Fe ....   Ra ....

Hg ....,   Sn ....

K ....   W ....

2

ABC

The world of science abounds in all manner of strange and peculiar words. Given here are 26 such words and the 26 corresponding definitions. But they are not in the same sequence.

Which definitions go with which words?
Fill in the number of the correct definition.

The words

aduncate	iridotomy	royalette ....
biramous	julaceous	sherardizing......
cassideous......	knaur	tentilla...........
dystocia	lentic	ultor..............
eidograph	megaparsec	vittate ....
fluviatile........	navarho..........	warfarin..........
gutnik	obconic	xiphoid ....
hickie	petrail	YIG ....
	quilo..............	ziram ....

The definitions:
1. cone-shaped
2. a radio capsule which is to be swallowed
3. a swollen outgrowth from a tree trunk
4. surgical cutting of the iris
5. an anode
6. a heavy beam in a timber building
7. a rodenticide
8. a fungicide
9. sword-shaped
10. hooked
11. a radio-navigation system for aircraft
12. helmet-shaped
13. painful childbirth
14. occurring in streams
15. inhabiting ponds and swamps
16. branched
17. an instrument for reducing and enlarging plans
18. resembling a catkin
19. a blemish on a solid area of print
20. bearing longitudinal stripes
21. a type of crystal used in electrical engineering
22. a type of dress cloth
23. the branches of a tentacle
24. a unit of distance equal to approximately 3 million light years
25. a once-proposed name for a unit of mass equal to a kilogram
26. a process for coating steel or iron with a layer of zinc

3

Material Anagrams

There are numerous substances found in biology, chemistry, geology and medicine which can be anagrammed into other words or names. For example, the chemical element SILVER can be formed from the letters of LIVERS or SLIVER. Given here are 20 words and names, each of which can be anagrammed back into some substance.

What are the 20 substances?

groan	informal
....	....
carnies	Iceland
....	....
sanitate	Athlone
....	....
imbrue	argent
....	....
dale	bury
....	....
none	incase
....	....
renoting	oceanic
....	....
adorn	antinomy
....	....
inhumer	inhaled
....	....
imbrute	salient
....	....

4
Ologies

The suffix '-ology' derives from the Greek 'lego', to speak, or 'logos', a discourse. The earliest branch of science given this suffix was anthropology in 1593. Since the end of the 18th century, the application of the suffix has become widespread. Given here are 20 words ending in '-ology' and 20 areas of study that the ologies are associated with.
Which words go with which areas of study?

algology	reptiles
argyrothecology	clouds
balneology	weights and measures
cartology	beetles
coleopterology	putting to death
desmology	structure of wood
exobiology	seeds
herpetology	kidneys
ktenology	soils
metrology	fruit
nephology	ferns
nephrology	obstetrics
oology	ears
otology	seaweeds
pedology	moneyboxes
pomology	medicinal baths
pteridology	birds' eggs
spermology	maps
tocology	ligaments
xylology	life on other planets

5
Who invented It?

Given here are 20 articles and 20 inventors.
Which inventor is associated with which article?

adding machine	Benjamin Franklin
bakelite	Joseph Glidden
ballpoint pen	Sir Frank Whittle
barbed wire	Richard Gatling
carpet sweeper	Rudolf Diesel
Diesel engine	Charles Townes
elevator	Melville Bissell
fountain pen	Jacob Schick
gramophone	Elisha Otis
jet engine	William Hunt
laser	Blaise Pascal
lightning conductor	Samuel Colt
machine gun	King Gillette
electric razor	Leo Backeland
safety razor	John Loud
revolver	James Hargreaves
safety pin	Thomas Alva Edison
spinning jenny	Louis Waterman
tank	Whitcomb Judson
zip	Sir Ernest Swinton

81 Round in Circles

HERE ARE SIX CIRCULAR PUZZLES created by the great
H. E. Dudeney.

1
The Circles and Discs

During a recent visit to a fair we saw a man with a
table on the oilcloth covering of which was painted a
large red circle, and he invited the public to cover this
circle entirely with five tin discs which he provided,
and offered a substantial prize to anybody who was
successful. The circular discs were all of the same size,
and each, of course, smaller than the red circle. The
diagram, where three discs are shown placed, will
make everything clear.

He showed that it was 'quite easy when you know
how' by covering up the circle himself without any
apparent difficulty, but many tried over and over again

and failed every time. I should explain that it was a
condition that when once you had placed any disc you
were not allowed to shift it, otherwise, by sliding them
about after they had been placed, it might be tolerably
easy to do.

Let us assume that the red circle is six inches in
diameter.
*What is the smallest possible diameter (say, to the nearest
half-inch) for the five discs in order to make a solution
possible?*

....

156

2

The Three Fences

'*A man had a circular field*', said Colonel Crackham, '*and he wished to divide it into four equal parts by three fences, each of the same length. How might this be done?*'

'*Why did he want them the same length?*' asked Dora.

'*That is not recorded*' replied the Colonel, '*nor are we told why he wished to divide the field into four parts, nor whether the fence was of wood or iron, nor whether the field was pasture or arable. I cannot even tell you the man's name, or the colour of his hair. You will find that these points are not essential to the puzzle.*'

3

The Circling Car

The outside wheels of a car, running on a circular track, are going twice as fast as the inside ones.
What is the length of the circumference described by the outer wheels?
The wheels are five feet apart on the two axles.

....

4

Sharing a Grindstone

Three men bought a grindstone twenty inches in diameter.
How much must each grind off so as to share the stone equally, making an allowance of four inches off the diameter as waste for the aperture?
We are not concerned with the unequal value of the shares for practical use – only with the actual equal quantity of stone each receives.

....

5

Squaring the Circle

The problem of squaring the circle depends on finding the ratio of the diameter to the circumference. This cannot be found in numbers with exactitude, but we can get it near enough for all practical purposes.

It is equally impossible, by Euclidean geometry, to draw a straight line equal to the circumference of a given circle. You can roll a penny carefully on its edge along a straight line on a sheet of paper and get a pretty exact result, but such a thing as a circular garden bed cannot be so rolled.

The line when straightened out, is very nearly the exact length of the circumference of the accompanying circle. The horizontal part of the line is half the circumference.
Could you have found it by a simple method, using only pencil, compasses and ruler?

6

The Wheels of the Cart

'*You see, sir,*' said the farm-cart salesman, '*at present the front wheel of the cart I am selling you makes four revolutions more than the rear wheel in going 120 yards; but if you have the circumference of each wheel reduced by three feet, it would make as many as six revolutions more than the rear wheel in the same distance.*'

Why the buyer wished that the difference in the number of revolutions between the two wheels should not be increased does not concern us.
The puzzle is to discover the circumference of each wheel in the first case.
It is quite easy.

Front wheel ....

Rear wheel ....

82 Weigh Out

1

THIS IS A PUZZLE for those adept at weighing up the female form.

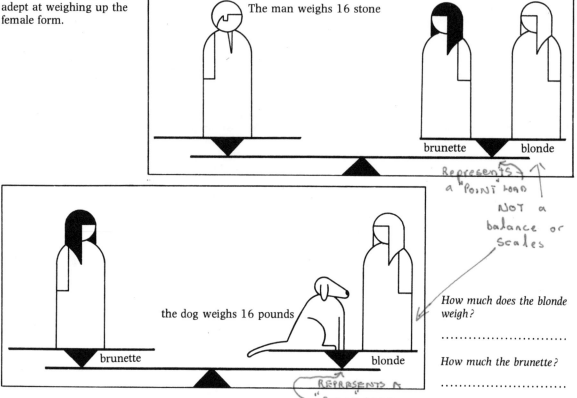

The man weighs 16 stone

brunette   blonde

Represents a "POINT LOAD NOT a balance or scales

the dog weighs 16 pounds

brunette   blonde

REPRESENTS A "POINT LOAD

How much does the blonde weigh?

....

How much the brunette?

....

2

FIVE MEN WEIGH altogether 60 stones. They are known as **A, B, C, D,** and **E,** and when arranged in a certain order, each man weighs a stone heavier than the one before him.

E is one stone heavier than A who is 2 stones lighter than B. D is a stone lighter than C, who is 3 stones heavier than E. *What are their respective weights?*

A ....

B ....

C ....

D ....

E ....

3

CONVERT the following maxims to metric:

a A miss is as good as

....

b ....

of prevention is worth

..................of cure.

c Build up your muscles men! Don't be a

..............weakling!

4

AT A FRUIT STALL on a market, 8 bananas, 7 apples and 3 grapefruit weigh as much as 3 apples, 6 bananas and 6 grapefruit. If a banana weighs $\frac{2}{3}$ as much as a grapefruit and a dozen apples weigh 3 kilograms, *how much does a grapefruit weigh?*

....

5

A MAN went to the same market to buy six bananas, six apples, and four grapefruit. When he arrived he found that there were no bananas left.
How many different combinations of apples and grapefruit does he need to buy in addition so that he goes home with the same weight of fruit as he had originally intended?

....
....
....
....
....
....

6

A GROCER wanted to put 20 lbs. of tea into 2 lb. packets, but most of his weights had been lost and all he could find were the 5 lb. and 9 lb. weights. *What was the quickest way for him to weigh out the tea?*

....
....
....
....
....

7

A CAKE, when put into one side of a pair of scales, appeared to weigh four ounces more than nine elevenths of its true weight, but when put into the other pan it appeared to weigh three pounds more than in the first pan. *What was its true weight?*

....

8

THREE MEN Tom, Tam, and Timmy went digging for gold and found these nuggets each marked with its weight in ounces:

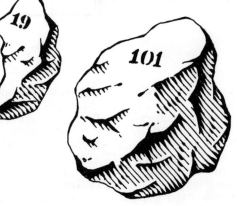

They found three nuggets each. Tom's nuggets were exactly double Tam's. *Which three nuggets were found by Timmy?*

1 ....

2 ....

3 ....

Crossland's Crosswords

David Crossland is one of the great crossword creators of the 1980s. Here are four of his cryptic classics.

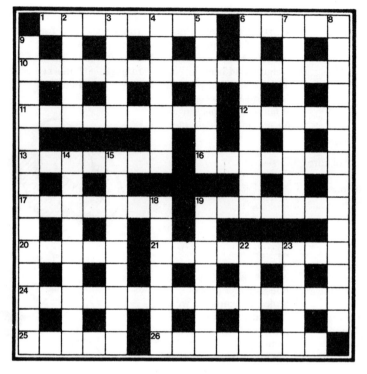

1

A Crossland Opener

ACROSS

1 Outlaw Southern thug pinching a pound (8)
6 Kind of film that has nothing in it abroad, nothing (5)
10 Make a terrible gaffe: as to the purpose of one's glove, for instance? (3, 4, 4, 2, 2)
11 This month, standing in front of gate, I get established (9)
12 Children's newspaper (5)
13 Noah's showing excitement at end of rain with a cry of joy (7)
16 Military man traded one with hesitation (7)
17 Roman who rationed sandwiches (7)
19 Grasshoppers also cut in pieces (7)
20 Lady's cartoon friend: she is one, according to Sinatra (5)
21 Concerned with choosing lo! treacle pudding (9)
24 If you think you've got this right, you've got the wrong idea (15)
25 Revolutionary Communist is a biased person (5)
26 The sound of nosey people (8)

DOWN

2 Friends graduate upset (5)
3 Clever people give information I repeated (5)
4 Where you might have seen a Callas turn (2, 5)
5 Rebels shaking up Tories on the right (7)
6 Like unkind criticism of one group of musicians learning in Old Theatre (9)
7 Extremely dangerously, horrible people form governments (9)
8 Working in sliced-loaf factory means having little money (2, 3, 9)

9 It's fashionable, getting out of bed clutching morning paper (2, 4, 3, 5)
14 Teacher, we hear, got through exams: was better than the others (9)
15 Composer's writing material? (9)
18 Go on and on getting little score after six balls (7)
19 Doctors finding bottomless chest beneath shelter (7)
22 Sounding somewhat out on a limb (5)
23 French king and holy man get together for revel (5)

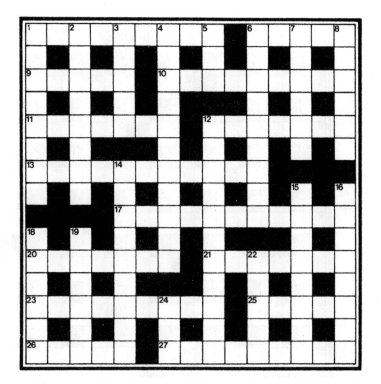

2

A Crossland Standard

ACROSS

1, 6 Topical greetings in verse: lad can become confused about end of couplet (9, 5)

9 Boy half gaga on French wine (5)

10 Cause of revolution on the railways (9)

11 Hold up: chief of bandits has gun-'older (7)

12 Fruit, South African, the reverse of something indispensible (7)

13 Steal social-security money over a long period for the juke-box (11)

17 Cockney character's elated sound about caper before long (11)

20 Low characters embraced by best of 6: damn! (7)

21 Sounds like I panic: this should keep things from view (3-4)

23 He gets a lot of money for suit, always (9)

25 Some saucy nickname for follower of Antisthenes (5)

26 Twin of 1, or offspring (5)

27 Girl I'm putting on side, mostly, making comeback – this comes with 6 (9)

DOWN

1 See Dave rise endlessly, about to chatter on, wandering (8)

2 Libertine, and what he offered to the novice and the expert? (8)

3 Part song, but no catch (5)

4 Introduce what happened at the World Police Dinner (11)

5 One part of loan sought by Antony (3)

6 Schizophrenic pet needs a kind of medicine (9)

7 Erase rugby fight (3, 3)

8 Month when female vampire makes appearance (6)

12 Attractive suit in 6, for recipients of 1, 6 (11)

14 Insure cox, perhaps, for day-out (9)

15 Overheads caused by marine fish, say (8)

16 From the Equator, you'll get stewed apricot, a pound (8)

18 Poet finds father turning up in curiosity shop (6)

19 You'll get good hauls from business operation in ship (6)

22 Revolution in Chile! Ambassador needed (5)

24 Final bits of clue in crossword, and this is it (3)

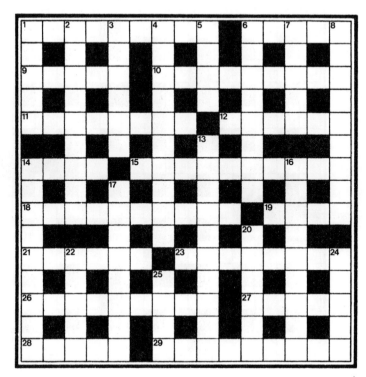

3

Give and Take
Half the clues across, and
half the clues down, have
one letter too many in
the definition part; the
remainder of the
definitions contain one
letter too few. Answers
are to be inserted
normally.

ACROSS
1 Inventor makes
European, we hear,
lean (5-4)
6 Make almost fertile
Greek stye (5)
9 I'm a friend in pan:
I'm upset during a
turn (5)
10 Nobble with info about
mental disorder (9)
11 Beast's caught,
swallowed by animal
via the mouth (8)

12 In Staffs town, king
cares (6)
14 Heard antic gets
curtailed (4)
15 Some graspers are
showing afterthought,
if little is tossed about
first (6-4)
18 Look: feline is
surrounded by a
different one, pacing
(10)
19 Movie shows knight
about start of
tournament (4)
21 They'll reveal each
drunkard reeling
about (6)
23 Fitters are usually
b-badly treated (8)
26 Past king of motor-
way junction (9)
27 Provider of tables is
ominous-sounding (5)
28 Bold lawyer Heath (5)

29 Old British chef
serving swan with
kinky dressing on (9)

DOWN
1 Applause about start
of show gives you
gripe (5)
2 Seed's making Pepsi-
Cola fizzy (9)
3 Gold off-spring next
to gold king, growing
(6)
4 I sprinkled gratin,
then tucked in to
find flavour (10)
5 Sack gets you some-
what entangled (4)
6 A cover-up by
Conservative is low (8)
7 Capital – nothing
over (5)
8 Pries for once, per-
haps, round ship (9)

13 Getting ale? It's
turned up, love –
there's happy feeling
all round (10)
14 Given hiding, has to
sit up during
December with
swelling (9)
16 Blocking up trendy
revolution, say (9)
17 Won points round
church, arched (8)
20 Factor in postage
refunds . . .(6)
22 . . . and factor that
shows the scheme to
a T (5)
24 See doctor in study
limp (5)
25 Bang caused by work
on street (4)

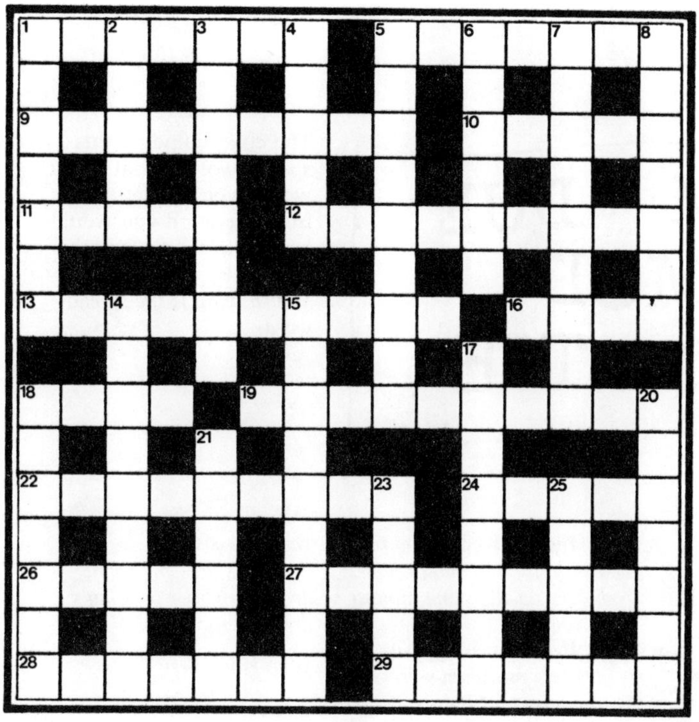

4

Printing Errors
There is a misprint of one letter in the definition part of each clue – answers are to be inserted correctly.

ACROSS

1 Yokes damage tailless cattle (7)
5 Sweeping tram out about noon, after party (7)
9 A race riot (not half!) on tube turned out properly (9)
10 In Spain, basic drama has one (5)
11 Internal fracture (5)
12 Shuffles, cuts with speed, when doubled (9)
13 I am, in French, an all-round whizz-kid, best (10)
16 Gals: one of Clotho, Lachesis or Atropos, we hear (4)
18 Area where you'll see young lad start growing (4)
19 You need guile to get sports cup craftily without energy (10)
22 Mock motor on motorway, pursued by the best (9)
24 Steak, and what it could be fried in, with top slice removed (5)
26 Golf-clubs event (5)
27 Sneak could be rotten, etc (9)
28 Getting porn rise after noon (7)
29 Being bid, insert 10 in remoulded clay (7)

DOWN

1 Lush walk by the railways (7)
2 Clown started tumbling in mud (5)
3 Sounds like those who pinch for parties (8)
4 Nimes? In France, we'll be seen round front of it (5)
5 More than one type of vinaigrette for these platters (9)
6 Hack who tore around London? (6)
7 It's fitting to get R.A. members in a flap (9)
8 Not t'way Donald will walk (7)
14 Waiting will make writer get angry, losing head (9)
15 I'm gripped by masculine mermaids at start of tiring jog (9)
17 Cowering with something to chew (English) in tent (8)
18 Past notices revised (7)
20 Making smells with apologies round church (7)
21 Name of Scottish mobster head, that is (6)
23 Left former crowd in the air (5)
25 Bunthorne's clutching a kind of whistle (5)

85 Mental Gymnastics

1

ONE OF THE WORDS listed below is a very special word:

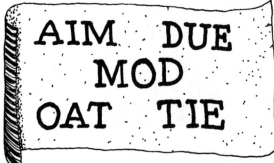

AIM DUE
MOD
OAT TIE

The clue to finding this special word is that if you were given one letter from the word you would be able to tell the number of vowels.
Which word is the special word?

....

2

VERA, AN ACTRESS in a play, was murdered in her dressing room. The following facts refer to the dressing-rooms shown here. Each of the five performers in the play – **Vera**, **Adam**, **Babe**, **Clay**, and **Dawn** – had his or her own dressing room.

a *The killer's dressing room and Vera's dressing room border on the same number of rooms.*
b *Vera's dressing room borders on Adam's dressing room and on Babe's dressing room.*
c *Clay's dressing room and Dawn's dressing room are* *the same size.*
d *Babe's dressing room does not border on Clay's dressing room.*

Who killed Vera?

....

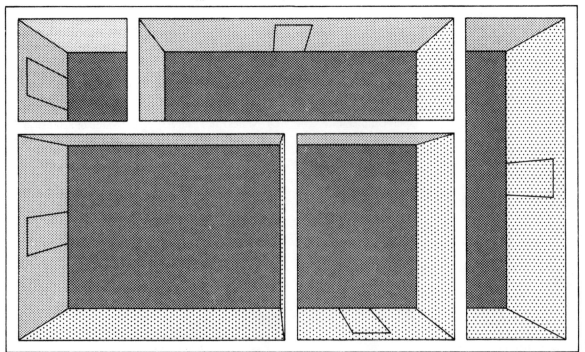

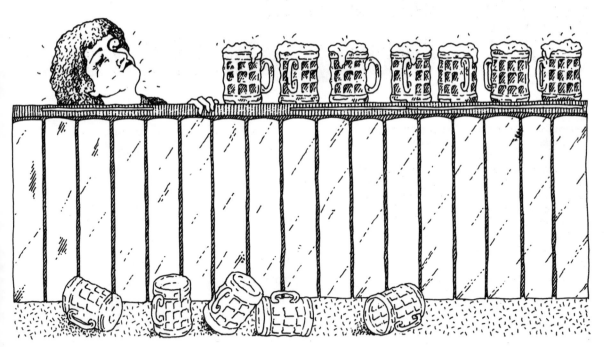

3

A MAN CAN DRINK a barrel of beer in 20 days, but if his wife also drinks, they can finish the barrel in 14 days.

How long would it take the wife to drink the beer alone?

....

4

A FATHER'S AGE is 40 years. His son is 13.

How many years ago was the father four times as old as the son?

....

5

How would you make four equilateral triangles with six matches?

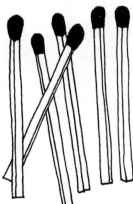

6

CONNECT the following square of nine points with the fewest possible connected straight lines.

7

CAN YOU COMPLETE this multiplication puzzle?

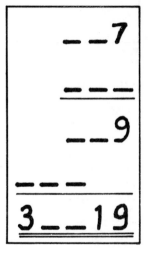

8

If A = 9 and G = 5 what is the sum of ATOM and BOMB, or in other words, what number does BINGO represent?

9

A CERTAIN YEAR in the future may be found from the following information: If that year is divided by 2, and the result turned upside down and divided by 3, and left right side up and divided by 2, and the digits in the result are turned upside down, the answer is 191.

What is that year?

....

10

THREE MEN registered in a hotel and asked for three separate rooms at ten dollars each, so the clerk received thirty dollars from the three men. The next day the clerk found that these three rooms should have been let for twenty-five dollars instead of thirty dollars, so he called the page boy and gave him the rebate to give back to the three men. The boy, however, was not very honest and gave the men one dollar each and kept two dollars for himself. This means that each man, instead of paying ten dollars, actually paid nine dollars. This makes twenty-seven dollars for the three men since the page boy kept two dollars. But 27 + 2 = 29, so *where did the other dollar go?*

....

....

11

How many trees twenty feet apart cover an acre?

....

1

Geographical Anagrams

It is a matter of common observation that many place-names can be anagrammed to form other words or names. For example, CHINA can be changed into CHAIN. Given here are the names of fifty places — countries, cities and towns. But each has already been anagrammed into some other word or name. *How quickly can you transform these 50 items back to their original geographical forms?*

amine....................	nerved	uranism.....................
enemy	planes....................	ywroken ....
erect	serial	angriest....................
laity.....................	sorted	diagnose ....
louse	sprucy	Havanans.................
pains	dottier....................	illision....................
pairs	ethanol	salvages...................
penal	granite	stashing...................
reign	Juanita	ancestral ....
rumba	launder....................	dominates ....
sexes	leaches	Englander.................
taxes	Maorian	nominates ....
unsad	oration	rechewing ....
analog	reddens	relanding ....
	retches	resoaping ....
	romance	Romanians ....
	rumbaed	tangerine ....
	testier	nowanights.................

2

Word Squares

A word square is an arrangement of words reading vertically and horizontally, like a cross-word puzzle but without any blacked-out squares. *Here is an example*

A P P L E
P O L E S
P L E A T
L E A S E
E S T E R

This type of square, where the vertical and horizontal words are the same, is known as a regular word square.

If the vertical and horizontal words are different, then the square is called a double word square. Double word squares are more difficult to construct than regular ones. *Here is an example*

S L I N K
W O M A N
O V A T E
R E G A L
D R O L L

Given here are three sets of clues for three double word squares. *How quickly can you complete them?*

1

Across clues
a padded sofa
unit of weight
potassium nitrate
sorrow
shabby

Down clues
ballads
one-twentieth of a ream
unbind
landed
stolid

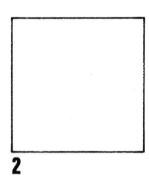

2

Across clues
bog
angry
bar on a fulcrum
to work on dough
pulls

Down clues
cloudy
sphere of action
bird
meat
flocks

3

Across clues
sin
set of wives
love
scale
machine for extracting moistu

Down clues
edible part of artichoke
electronic location system
hard
blend
high Turkish official

3

What's Special?

Given here are two groups of words, ranging in length from ten to 14 letters. The first group is composed of twenty words, and the second group is composed of just four words. Against each of the words is a thumbnail definition. These words are very, very special – items particularly dear to word-lovers. So rare are such words that they have been culled from a number of unabridged dictionaries and extensive gazetteers. These are not just any old words!

Can you determine what makes these words so special? How is the second list different from the first list? Are you able to add any words, longer than ten letters, to either of the lists?

The words and definitions (list 1)

arraigning	*calling to account*
cancellanses	*sheets of amendments in books*
Cicadellidae	*a large family of leafhoppers*
concisions	*mutilations*
Gradgrindian	*pertaining to an uninspired seeker of facts*
happenchance	*a circumstance regarded as due to chance*
insciences	*ignorances*
interinserts	*inserts between*
ma'amselles	*mademoiselles*
notionists	*holders of ungrounded opinions*
reproposes	*proposes again*
rereigning	*reigning again*
retardated	*an obsolete form of 'retarded'*
Riverville	*a town in Virginia, USA*
scintillescent	*twinkling faintly*
Succasunna	*a town in New Jersey, USA*
Tessellata	*certain prehistoric sea-lilies*
Transnistria	*a Romanian administrative division in the occupied Ukraine, between 1941 and 1943*
tromometer	*a device for measuring slight earthquake shocks*
unsufficiences	*insufficiencies*

....

....

....

The words and definitions (list 2)

horseshoer	*one who makes or affixes horseshoes*
intestines	*parts of the digestive system*
Taeniodontidae	*a family of prehistoric toothless creatures*
trisectrices	*certain types of curves in mathematics*

....

....

4

Words within Words

Consider the words FALSITIES and CALUMNIES. Delete the first, second, fourth, fifth and sixth letters of each. You should end up with LIES in each case, a word that means the same as both FALSITIES and CALUMNIES. Similarly, if the third, fifth, sixth and seventh letters of CURTAIL are deleted, what remains is CUT. And CUT and CURTAIL mean the same thing. There are many similar examples of words within words which are synonymous in this way.

Giver here are twenty longer words – *can you spot the shorter synonyms lurking within each of them?*

catacomb	....	hurries	....
chariot	....	illuminated	....
chocolate	....	instructor	....
deliberate	....	latest	....
destruction	....	masculine	....
encourage	....	pasteurized	....
evacuate	....	perambulate	....
exhilaration	....	precipitation	....
facetiousness	....	regulate	....
fatigue	....	satisfied	....

87 Cerebral Serebriakoff

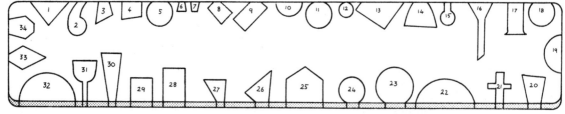

Victor Serebriakoff is the International Chairman of Mensa, the club whose members have remarkably high IQs.

Here are the kinds of puzzles that Victor manages almost to set – and solve – in his sleep.

1

Unorthodox Neighbours
This is a piece of plywood marked out for the jigsaw. All the shapes are different – but there is a pattern to their arrangement, except for one neighbouring pair of shapes which break the rule – which are they? *Encircle the numbers.*

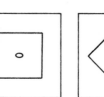

Logically, which of the lettered patterns fits here?

2

Cube of Cubes
What is the mark on the hidden cube?
Tick the correct sign.

A   B   C   D   E   F

3

Missing Pattern

A   B

C   D   E

4

All Bounce

This story is a good illustration of changes in standards

It concerns an indignant mother who approached her solicitor to sue the local council because they had deliberately taken action which resulted in her son having his nose broken by a flying brick.

The boy was in the habit of throwing a brick through the pane of a certain lamp-post whenever it was replaced and the council, apparently with malice aforethought, and in a very underhanded way, replaced the panes of glass with stiff plastic so that the brick bounced back and injured the poor child. The local social workers were appalled that instead of correcting the faults in the social system which caused the boy's behaviour they resorted to this mean and callous action.

This is not the only problem caused by bouncing.
A train of infinite mass is proceeding along a track at 60 mph and in front of it there is a perfectly elastic metal plate.

Another boy, equally the victim of 'faults in the social system', decides that it would be a good idea to throw a metal ball, which again is perfectly elastic, at the train from a bridge under which it is to pass. He does so, and the ball flies towards the train at 60 mph. The ball bounces back off the plate and fortunately misses the boy, thus saving the railway company a large sum in damages.

But the problem is, if it had hit the boy, at what speed would it have been travelling?

We can ignore friction with the air.

......................mph

5

Irresistible, Immovable

An indignant buyer returned to the horse dealer.

'I want my money back, that horse you sold me is stone blind.'

'What makes you think that?'

'He keeps walking into walls.'

'He ain't blind, he just don't give a damn.'

Here the wall was a relatively 'immovable object', and this brings us to the supposedly impossible question. What happens when an irresistible force meets an immovable object? I insist that there is an answer which is sensible in terms of the question. Think. *What happens?*

....

....

....

6

As Easy As Pie

Have you ever thought about series? If you haven't, don't. It's very muddling. What is a series? It is made of elements which must be arranged or be arrangeable in a linear fashion, they must be invariant in some way and the elements must all be one type of thing, numbers, letters, symbols. But in another way they must exhibit variance, the main point being that the varient aspect of each element must depend in some way on those that go before (and therefore, of course, with those that come after). A line of integers where there is *no* relationship between successive numbers is called a *random series*. But the muddling thing is that for any given series it is possible, if you look hard enough, to *find* a rule which justifies it and worst, if you like, an infinite number of rules of increasing complexity. No wonder puzzle setters love them.

Take this series

_ 3 1 4 1 5 _

Easy? Wait! You are invited to give the *second* most obvious answer. Give the integers which go at either end of this series.

7

Egging Them On by Calling Them 'Chicken'

A vast crowd assembled to see the skyscraper climber do his stuff. The respectful crowd parted to let him through. His pack on his back, he confidently took his first step on a crevice on the face of the twenty-storey building. The crowd was tense and silent as he climbed but, as he carefully considered each grip, he noticed a strange note in the noises from the crowd. Could it be tittering? Yes, they were laughing. Clinging precariously, he glanced down and noticed that he was being followed by a drunk. He climbed on, ignored by the crowd, who laughed, cheered and shouted in alarm according to their nature at the antics of the drunken man.

Miraculously, he reached the top soon after the official climber. But the latter thought that now it was his turn, for the pack on his back was a parachute. He stepped to the brink, smiled, spread his arms with a dramatic gesture, leaped off, pulled the cord, and was soon sailing towards the earth with arms folded and a smile of triumph on his face.

Half-way down the drunk hurtled passed him, saying as he did so 'Chicken'. Fortunately, the story stops at that point, the point at which it brings me to the next puzzle, that of the chicken and the egg.

I have never been able to understand why this is given as an example of an insoluble question. The answer ought to be absolutely obvious to any thinking person, so I pose it again. Think about it.
Which came first, the chicken or the egg?

88 Countdown/Countup

THE FOLLOWING GROUP of games are traditionally described as 'subtractive' games, for obvious reasons. They vary in degree of difficulty from simple to complex. In general, these games consist of several piles of objects such as coins or matches, denoted 'counters', and play involves the alternate removal of counters by two players. The variety of such games results both from the removal restrictions and the ultimate objective.

It is remarkable how many different games can be based on only a single pile of counters. To illustrate this point, the one-pile or countdown games, comprising the simplest of the subtractive family, will all employ a pile of thirteen counters. This number is just about right to allow the reader to perform his analysis with the help of some experimentation. A smaller number of counters might make such analysis

trivial; larger numbers would tend to raise the 'work factor' to unmanageable size.

In keeping with this choice of thirteen counters for the games here, they have all been designated by the appropriate family name TRISKIDEKAPHILIA.

Probably the most ancient (and simplest) subtractive game involves a single 'pile' of counters. The two players alternately remove one, two, up to N counters, and the winner is the player who removes the last one. This game and the more simple one-pile games will all be based on a pile of thirteen counters. General strategies for piles of arbitrary size will not be difficult to deduce.

In the present game, the 'limit' is three; that is, each player on his turn has the option of removing one, two or three counters. You have first play. *Your move.*

1

Second Player Option
Starting again with a pile of thirteen objects, your opponent has first play. To compensate for this disadvantage, you have the option of declaring the limit number N. On each move, a player may remove one, two, up to N counters.

Unless you choose the right value of N, your opponent will beat you with optimal play. *What N do you declare?*

2

Triskidekaphilia Misere
Once again there are thirteen counters. The limiting number is four, and you have first move. The objective, however, in this misere version is to force your opponent to take the last counter. You can remove one, two, three or four. *How many will it be?*

. . . .

. . . .

3

Nim
In the ancient game of Nim, the objective is to remove the last object, each play consisting of the removal from any one pile of as many objects as desired, from one to the entire pile.

You have first move at a stage in the game in which there is one triangular counter, a pile of five circular counters, and a pile of ten square counters. You have

sixteen choices: remove the triangular counter, remove 1, 2, . . . up to all five circular counters; or remove 1, 2, . . . up to all ten square counters. However, only one choice guarantees victory. *What is it?*

. . . .

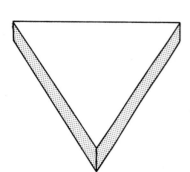

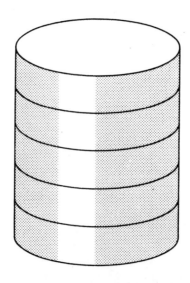

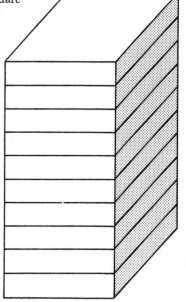

4

Tsyanshidzi

This is an ancient Chinese game, reinvented by W. A. Wythoff around the time of World War 1. Two players start with two piles of chips. Alternately, each player removes chips with the option of removing:

1 any number of chips from one pile or
2 the **same** number of chips from each pile.

As White, you have first play on piles of nine and twelve counters respectively. The advantage is yours if you make the one correct play. Otherwise, Black, who is experienced at the game, will beat you.

The objective is to remove the last chip or chips.

5

The Last Prime

A Five-Finger Exercise

Two players alternately hold up any number of fingers from one to five. The cumulative total is kept and the object is to keep the total prime. The first player who is unable to raise the total to a higher prime is the loser. You draw the first move. *How many fingers do you hold up?*

....

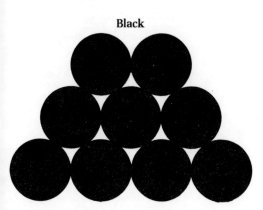

Black

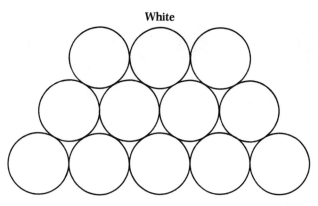

White

Criss-Cross

WITH THESE PUZZLES the words you are looking for may appear written forwards or backwards, upwards or downwards, or even diagonally.

2
The American Presidents
The surnames of all the Presidents of the United States of America are hidden in this diagram.
Can you find them?

J	E	F	F	E	R	S	O	N	I	X	O	N	T	O	B	E
O	E	E	C	R	E	I	P	L	I	N	C	O	L	N	A	G
H	O	O	V	E	R	O	B	S	T	H	A	Y	E	S	I	Z
N	R	T	S	W	A	U	L	N	N	A	V	A	V	G	N	T
S	N	F	O	O	C	I	A	K	O	N	Y	D	E	N	E	I
O	O	A	P	H	V	R	W	L	S	E	E	L	S	I	S	F
N	M	T	A	N	G	S	N	O	L	R	L	E	O	D	N	N
K	E	N	N	E	D	Y	M	P	I	U	N	I	O	R	A	A
J	A	C	K	S	O	N	O	A	W	B	I	F	R	A	G	M
N	E	G	D	I	L	O	O	C	D	N	K	R	S	H	A	U
D	N	A	L	E	V	E	L	C	R	A	C	A	R	T	E	R
P	A	N	O	S	I	R	R	A	H	V	M	G	T	U	R	T
W	A	S	H	I	N	G	T	O	N	N	O	S	I	D	A	M

1
Four-letter Words
This arrangement of letters contains four-letter words beginning with every letter of the alphabet. Some letters are represented more than once.
How many of these four-letter words can you find?

A	B	E	V	E	N	C	B	A	X	Q	I
T	A	N	G	F	M	E	T	I	R	M	P
D	I	A	L	E	L	D	G	H	A	U	J
C	K	C	A	B	F	E	K	O	Y	N	O
D	E	F	A	H	O	P	A	L	V	T	K
G	E	D	A	J	T	I	U	Q	E	S	R
J	L	L	H	I	N	L	A	M	Y	L	Z
P	F	O	K	L	M	L	O	M	A	W	J
Z	E	A	L	V	E	S	O	N	K	R	I
Q	R	L	X	A	N	L	U	B	I	X	H
U	I	S	D	N	E	R	M	C	L	E	G
W	U	T	W	Y	Z	O	N	D	E	F	V

3
Drinks

The names of fifty drinks, alcoholic and non-alcoholic, are hidden in this diagram. Some of the drinks are proper names, some are everyday words. *Can you find all fifty drinks?*

```
P R E S S A W H C S R I K C O H A
I O B A E T M A L A G A L O C B O
L E I T S A I O R A N G E A D E T
F D T O D D Y N N N I G N Y O E E
G E T I R R O Y G T R N O O P R I
G R E N A D I N E E I A A C L C V
E E R I C O C O A S R L S P O O R
N R A T H C N U P A L E L L N U O
I C N R A G T T B I A G I A K R S
T A O A T R U S R M G A V P D V A
C M R M O O I A A U E R O E R O R
I P B P T N P R B R R Y V R A I C
D A I S T A C I D E R E I I T S O
E R V H S S E N N I U G T T A I P
N I E R S T E I N E R Q Z I F E P
E B A R L E Y W A T E R S F I R I
B S I A L O J U A E B S Q U A S H
```

4
Towns and Cities

This diagram contains the names of twenty towns and cities from all over the world. *How quickly can you locate them?*

```
M A C N A L B A S A C A
W P G R E P E K I N G S.
O A R S T M A D R I D I
C N S E L E G N A S O L
S N E H T A L A P V T O
O I L P R S I I A I O P
M L I M A T E F S T L A
A R W V O H V H O B S E
E E O K T A A K C S O N
S B Y R O M E L N N V N
O O H E A T N A L T A I
T O R O N T O C I X E M
```

 **For the Numerate**

Digital Delights

1

ARRANGE ALL THE DIGITS 1, 2, 3, 4, 5, 6, 7, 8, 9, 0, so that they add up to 100. Fractions can be used if you wish.

....

2

FIND A NUMBER made up of 4 different digits.
The last digit is twice the first digit.
The second digit is three less than the third.
   If you add the first digit to the last digit the answer you get will be twice the third digit.
What is your number?

....

3

ARRANGE THESE FIGURES into two groups of four so that each group shall add up to the same sum.

1   2   3   4   5   6   7   8   9

....

4

TO DIVIDE the number **8,101,265,822,786** by 8, all we need to do is transfer the 8 from the beginning to the end!
Can you find a number beginning with 7 that can be divided by 7 in the same simple manner?

....

5

HERE ARE SIX NUMBERS:

4,784,887
2,494,651
8,595,087
1,385,287
9,042,451
9,406,087.

Three of these numbers added together will form a square.
Which are they?

....

....

....

....

....

....

6

ARRANGE the ten digits 0–9 in three arithmetical sums, employing three of the four operations of addition, subtraction, multiplication, and division, and using no signs except the ordinary ones implying those operations.
Here is an example to make it quite clear:

$3 + 4 = 7$
$9 - 8 = 1$
$30 \div 6 = 5$

But this is not correct because 2 is omitted and 3 is repeated.
What's your solution?

....

7

WHAT NUMBER composed of nine figures, if multiplied by
1, 2, 3, 4, 5, 6, 7, 8, 9,
will give a product with
9, 8, 7, 6, 5, 4, 3, 2, 1
(in that order), in the last nine places to the right?

....

8

FIND the smallest number that, when divided successively by 45, 454, 4545, and 45454 leaves the remainders 4, 45, 454, and 4545 respectively.

....

9

TAKE NINE COUNTERS numbered 1 to 9, and place them in a row as shown. It is required in as few exchanges of pairs as possible to convert this into a square number.

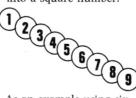

As an example using six exchanges we give the following:
Exchange 7 with 8,
8 with 4, 4 with 6,
6 with 9, 9 with 3 and
3 with 2, giving the number 139,854,276 which is the square of 11,826. But it can be done in many fewer moves.

....

....

....

10

THE NINE DIGITS may be arranged in a square in many ways, so that the numbers formed in the first row and second row will sum to the third row. Here are three examples, and it will be found that the difference between the first total, 657, and the second, 819, is the same as the difference between the second, 819, and the third, 981 – that is, 162.

Can you form eight such squares, every one containing the nine digits, so that the common difference between the eight totals is throughout the same?

2	1	8
4	3	9
6	5	7

2	7	3
5	4	6
8	1	9

3	2	7
6	5	4
9	8	1

11

IF YOU MULTIPLY British Thermal Units by 1054 you will get the equivalent in joules. If you multiply yards by 36 you will get the equivalent in inches.
Now you know the method, see if you can answer the questions.

Multiply this	By this	To obtain
1 bushels	3523.8	....
2 °C+17.78	1.8	....
3 centimeters	0.3937	....
4 cm-grams	980.1	....
5 chains	66	....
6 circumference	6.2832	....
7 cubic centimeters	0.0610	....
8 cu. feet	1728	....
9 cu. ft/min	62.43	....
10 cu.ft/sec	448.831	....
11 cu. inches	16.387	....
12 cu. meters	264.2	....
13 cu. yards	27	....
14 days	86,400	....
15 degrees/sec	0.1667	....
16 °F−32	0.5556	....
17 faradays/sec	96.500	....
18 feet	30.48	....
19 ft. of water	62.43	....
20 ft./min	0.5080	....
21 ft./sec	0.6818	....
22 fluid ounces	29.573	....
23 furlongs	660	....
24 gallons	231	....
25 gals/min	8.0208	....
26 grains	0.0648	....
27 grams	980.1	....
28 hectares	107.64	....
29 hectoliters	2,838	....
30 horsepower	33,000	....

Multiply this	By this	To obtain
31 inches	25.4	....
32 ins. of water	0.03613	....
33 kilograms	980,100	....
34 kg. calories	3086	....
35 kg. cal/min	51.43	....
36 kilometers	3280.8	....
37 km./hr	0.621	....
38 kilowatts	737.6	....
39 kilowatt-hrs	2,655,000	....
40 knots	6080	....
41 liters	61.02	....
42 meters	39.37	....
43 statute miles	5280	....
44 miles/hour	1,467	....
45 milligrams/liter	1	....
46 milliliters	0.0338	....
47 millimeters	0.03937	....
48 ounces avoidrupois	28.349	....
49 pecks	8.8096	....
50 pints liquid	473.2	....
51 pounds avoirdupois	444.600	....
52 lbs. (avdp)/sq.in.	70.22	....
53 quarts liquid	57.75	....
54 quires	25	....
55 radians	3437.7	....
56 reams	500	....
57 revolutions/min	6	....
58 rods	16.5	....
59 slugs	32.17	....
60 square centimeters	0.155	....
61 square feet	0.093	....
62 square inches	6,451	....
63 square kilometers	247.1	....
64 square meters	10.76	....

91 Alphametics and Cryptarithms

The word 'cryptarithmetic' was first introduced by Monsieur Vatriquant writing under the pseudonym Minos. In the May 1931 issue of *Sphinx*, a Belgian magazine of recreational mathematics, he proposed this problem with these remarks:

'Cryptographers, to hide the meaning of messages, put figures in place of letters. By way of reprisal, we will replace each digit of the following problem with a distinct letter.

```
    A B C
  × D E
  ───────
    F E C
  D E C
  ───────
  H G B C
```

What do each of the letters A through to H stand for?

A = ...   E = ...

B = ...   F = ...

C = ...   G = ...

D = ...   H = ...

Other Problems
Although the term 'cryptarithmetic' was new, the type of puzzle was older. An earlier one is from the *Strand Magazine* for July 1924.

1

What do each of the letters stand for?

T = ... H = ...

W = ... R = ...

O = ... E = ...

2 Here is a multiplication involving two three-digit numbers:

```
      A B C
    × B A C
    ─────────
    * * * *
      * * A
  * * * B
  ───────────
  * * * * * *
```

What are the two numbers ABC and BAC?

ABC = ...

BAC = ...

3 The Great Depression of the 1930s was no joke, but this puzzle came out of the Depression:

USA+FDR
=NRA

USA+NRA
=TAX

What are the numbers involved here?

....

Prime Problems

Here are four cryptarithmetic problems which all involve prime numbers (that is, numbers divisible only by themselves and 1).

First of all:
$$ALGER = R^2 \times NIG$$

$$DELTA = R \times ((AADR \times 0) + R)$$

And **R** is a prime number

Secondly: ADDD, AACA, BCDB and BDAC are four prime numbers. *What are they?*

ADDD ...... AACA ...... BCDB ...... BDAC ......

Thirdly: there are 24 possible combinations of the four digits **ABCD** and these combinations include:

4 prime numbers ....

7 products of two odd primes ....

1 square of a prime...

8 numbers divisible by 2, but not by 4, 8 or 16 ....

2 numbers divisible by 4, but not by 8 or 16............

1 number divisible by 8, but not by 16.................

1 number divisible by 16 ....
What are they?

Fourthly: ABC is a prime number and *AC*BC is its square.
What is ABC?

The Sphinx Problem

We mentioned above a Belgian magazine devoted to recreational mathematics, *Sphinx*.
Can you work out what the letters represent in this lengthy multiplication?

Printer's Devilry

In setting up the product of two powers:

$$a^b \times c^a$$

the printer accidentally composed a number of four digits:

abca

It just so happened that the two expressions have the same value.
What are the values of **a, b** *and* **c**?

....

....

....

Two More Problems

1 If you multiply **REDACTIONS** by **C**, the result is **TTTTTTTTSTS**.
What do the various letters stand for?

2 Thus far all the problems have been expressed in base-10, the system of counting which goes from 1 to 9, then 10 to 19, and so on. But different base systems can be invoked for cryptarithmetic problems. This one uses **base-5**, **base-7** and **base-8** systems. In a **base-5** system, numbers go from 1 to 4, then 10 to 14, and so on; in a **base-7** system, numbers go from 1 to 6, then 10 to 16, and so on; and in a **base-8** system, numbers go from 1 to 7, then 10 to 17, and so on. *Anyway, what is the value of* **ANNE** *given that:*

$$(ANNE)_{base\text{-}8} - (ANNE)_{base\text{-}5} = (ANNE)_{base\text{-}7}$$

....

 **Poet's Corner**

1

WHO WROTE each of these
verses?

a *Even such is Time, that takes in trust*
Our youth. our joys, our all we have,
And pays us but with earth and dust.

....

b *But if ye saw that which no eyes can see,*
The inward beauty of her lively spright,
Garnish with heavenly gifts of high degree,
Much more than would ye wonder at that sight.

....

c *Shall I compare thee to a Summer's day?*
Thou art more lovely and more temperate:
Rough winds do shake the darling buds of May,
And Summer's lease hath all too short a date.

....

d *Mortality, behold and fear!*
What a change of flesh is here!
Think how many royal bones
Sleep within this heap of stones.

....

e *Fly envious Time, till thou run out thy race,*
Call on the lazy leaden-stepping hours,
Whose speed is but the heavy Plummets pace;
And glut thyself with what thy womb devours.

....

f *And did those feet in ancient time,*
Walk upon England's mountain green?
And was the holy lamb of God
On England's pleasant pastures seen?

....

g *Till a' the seas gang dry, my dear,*
And the rocks melt wi' the sun;
I will luve thee still, my dear,
While the sands o' life shall run.

....

h *She walks in beauty, like the night*
Of cloudless climes and starry skies;
And all that's best of dark and bright
Meet in her aspect and her eyes.

....

i *Thou still unravish'd bride of quietness,*
Thou foster-child of Silence and slow Time,
Sylvan historian, who can'st thus express
A flowry tale more sweetly than our rhyme.

....

j *The splendour falls on castle walls*
And snowy summits old in story:
The long light shakes across the lakes
And the wild cataract leaps in glory.

....

2

ALL THE NAMES here have
something in common –
excepting two.
Which two?
And why?

T. S. Eliot
Stephen Spender
Louis MacNeice
Dylan Thomas
Thom Gunn

Ted Hughes
Peter Porter
Allen Ginsberg
Charles Olson
Robert Lowell
Bernie Schwarz
John Berryman

....

....

3

USE THE LETTERS here to
form the names of ten
poets:

A C U R E C H F R O T S
D E N U A S O N I N D I
C K S T E A K L I V E R
L E G D R E A M L E A
N O T R E C H E S T O P
E T E A S Y

....

....

....

....

....

....

....

....

4

HERE IS A POEM with 28 authors.
Who are they?

1 *Why all this toil for triumphs of an hour?*
2 *Life's a short summer, man a flower*

.........................and.........................

3 *By turns we catch the vital breath and die —*
4 *The cradle and the tomb, alas! so nigh.*

.........................and.........................

5 *To be is better far than not to be,*
6 *Though all man's life may seem a tragedy.*

.........................and.........................

7 *But light cares speak when mighty griefs are dumb;*
8 *The bottom is but shallow whence they come.*

.........................and.........................

9 *Your fate is but the common fate of all,*
10 *Unmingled joys, here, to no man befall.*

.........................and.........................

11 *Nature to each allots his proper sphere,*
12 *Fortune makes folly her peculiar care.*

.........................and.........................

13 *Custom does not often reason overrule*
14 *And throw a cruel sunshine on a fool.*

.........................and.........................

15 *Live well, how long or short permit, to heaven;*
16 *They who forgive most, shall be most forgiven.*

.........................and.........................

17 *Sin may be clasped so close we cannot see its face —*
18 *Vile intercourse where virtue has not place.*

.........................and.........................

19 *Then keep each passion down, however dear,*
20 *Thou pendulum, betwixt a smile and tear;*

.........................and.........................

21 *Her sensual snares let faithless pleasure lay,*
22 *With craft and skill to ruin and betray.*

.........................and.........................

23 *Soar not too high to fall, but stop to rise;*
24 *We masters grow of all that we despise.*

.........................and.........................

25 *Oh then renounce that impious self-esteem;*
26 *Riches have wings and grandeur is a dream.*

.........................and.........................

27 *Think not ambition wise, because 'tis brave,*
28 *The paths of glory lead but to the grave.*

.........................and.........................

5

FIND the missing first word for each line and you will find three acrostics giving you the names of four poets.

a .... *through many a year, 'mongst Cumbria's hills,*

.... *her wild fells, sweet vales, and sunny lakes,*

.... *stores of thought thy musing mind distils,*

.... *of poesy thy soul awakes:—*

.... *was thy life — a poet's life I ween;*

.... *though of Nature! every scene*

.... *beauty stirred thy fancy's deeper mood,*

.... *calmed the current of thy blood:*

.... *in the wide 'excursion' of thy mind,*

.... *thoughts in words of worth we still may find.*

b .... *wizard of the North,*

.... *with spells of potent worth!*

.... *to that greatest Bard of ours*

.... *mighty magic of thy powers:*

.... *thy bright fancy's offspring find*

.... *to his myriad mind.*

.... *the creations that we see —*

.... *Scotia's deeds, a proud display,*

.... *glories of a bygone day;*

.... *genius foremost stands in all her long array.*

c .... *like thine have many a charm;*

.... *thy themes the heart must warm.*

.... *o'er Slavery's guilt and woes,*

.... *and shame's deep hues it throws;*

.... *up Alpine heights is heard*

.... *now the stirring word;*

.... *Psalm, now, onward is inviting,*

.... *for nobler deeds exciting;*

.... *Britain now resounds thy name,*

.... *States unborn shall sell thy fame.*

179

93 Never Say Die!

Introduction

THE PICTURE HERE shows a die and its 'unfolded' pattern. The spots are arranged so that the sum of the points on all pairs of opposite faces is 7.

Why is a cube the best shape for a die? First, a die should be a regular solid so that when it is rolled each face has an equal chance to end on top. Of the five regular solids, the cube is the most suitable. It is easy to manufacture and, when you throw it, it rolls easily but not *too* easily. The tetrahedron and octahedron are hard to roll; the dodecahedron and icosahedron are so 'round' that they roll almost like balls. The principle of 7, the sum of opposite faces, is the key to many tricks with dice.

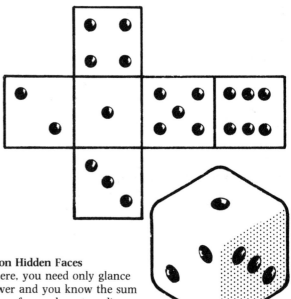

1

Guessing the Sum of Spots on Hidden Faces

In the tower of three dice here, you need only glance at the face on top of the tower and you know the sum of five faces: those on the four faces where two dice touch one another and the face on the bottom of the tower. In the diagram, the sum is 17.
Explain.

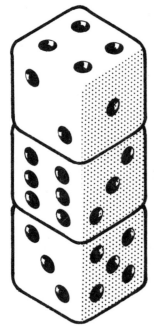

2

The Three Dice

Mason and Jackson were playing with three dice. The player won whenever the numbers thrown added up to one of two numbers he selected at the beginning of the game. As a matter of fact, Mason selected 7 and 13, and one of his winning throws is shown in the illustration.

What were his chances of winning a throw? And what two other numbers should Jackson have selected for his own throws to make his chances of winning exactly equal?

3

A Trick with Three Dice
The magician turns his back while someone throws 3 dice. He asks a volunteer to add up the spots on the top faces of the dice, then lift up any one of the three and add to the previous sum the number on the die's bottom face. He asks the volunteer to roll this same die again, and add to the last total the number of spots on its top face. He turns to the table, reminds the audience he does not know which die was thrown twice, picks up the three dice, shakes them in his hand, and, to the amazement of the audience, guesses the final sum.
The method: before picking up the dice, add 7 to the spots showing on the top faces of the dice.
Explain.

4

Turning the Die
This is played with a single die. The first player calls any number he chooses, from 1 to 6, and the second player throws the die at hazard. Then they take it in turns to roll over the die in any direction they choose, but never giving it more than a quarter turn. The score increases as they proceed, and the player wins who manages to score 25 or force his opponent to score beyond 25. Here is an example game. A calls 6, and B happens to throw a 3 *as shown in the illustration,* making the score 9. Now A decides to turn up 1, scoring 10; B turns up 3, scoring 13; A turns up 6, scoring 19; B turns up 3, scoring 22; A turns up 1, scoring 23; and B turns up 2, scoring 25 and winning.
What call should A make in order to have the best chance of winning?

5

In What Order are the Dice Arranged?
Give a friend three dice, a piece of paper, and a pencil. Turn your back and ask him to roll the dice and then arrange them in a row so that their top faces make a three-digit number. For example, the number on the dice shown is 254. Ask him to append the three-digit number given by the bottom faces of the dice. The result is a six-digit number (in our example 254,523). He is to divide this number by 111 and tell you the result. In turn, you tell him what is on the top faces of the three dice.
The method: subtract 7 from the number he tells you, then divide by 9.
In our example,
254,523 divided by 111 = 2,293
2,293 − 7 = 2,286
2,286 divided by 9 = 254.
Explain.

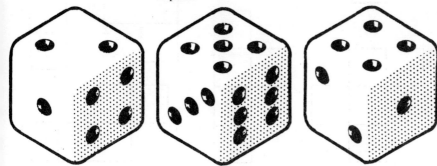

Polyominoes

Polyominoes are shapes made by connecting certain numbers of equal-sized squares, each joined together with at least one other square along an edge.

The simpler polyominoes — all possible shapes composed of fewer than five connected squares — are shown in the first diagram. These simpler polyominoes are called monominoes, dominoes, trominoes and tetrominoes.

The shapes that cover five connected squares are called pentominoes. There are twelve different pentominoes, and these are shown in the second diagram below.

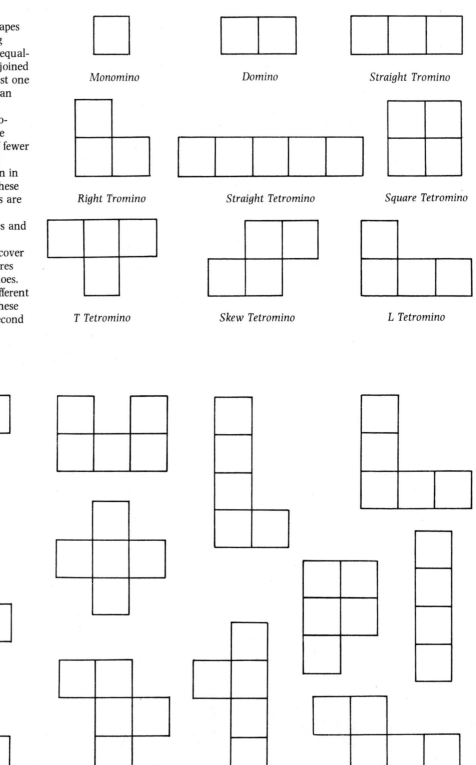

Monomino

Domino

Straight Tromino

Right Tromino

Straight Tetromino

Square Tetromino

T Tetromino

Skew Tetromino

L Tetromino

1

A Domino Problem
A domino is made of two connected squares and has only one shape, a rectangle. Given a chess-board measuring eight squares by eight squares, with a pair of diagonally opposite corner squares deleted, *is it possible to cover the board completely with dominoes* (allowing no vacant squares and no overlaps)?
The illustration shows the mutilated chess-board which is to be covered.

2

A Tetromino Problem
A tetromino is made of four connected squares, and has five different shapes, as you can see in the first diagram. They are
the straight tetromino
the square tetromino
the T tetromino
the skew tetromino
and the L tetromino.
It is possible to cover an eight-by-eight chess-board with any tetrominoes except the skew ones. Show how the four other types of tetromino can be used to cover an eight-by-eight chess-board.

3
Pentomino Problems

The figures shown here are all to be covered with the 12 pentominoes. Since each piece is five unit squares, each figure contains 60 squares.

The first five puzzles are eight-by-eight chessboards with holes of four single-unit squares in them. Following these are the four rectangles that can be constructed from 60 squares, with unit dimensions of 3×20, 4×15, 5×12, and 6×10. The first of these is the most difficult, and there are only two distinct solutions. There is a variety of different solutions for the other rectangles.

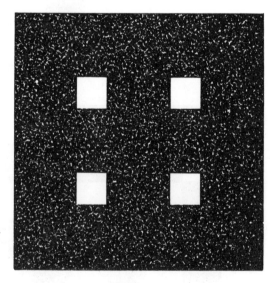

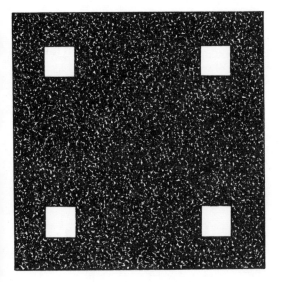

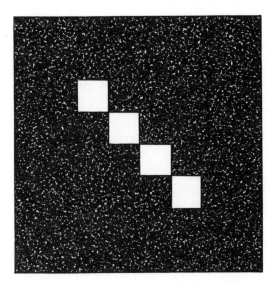

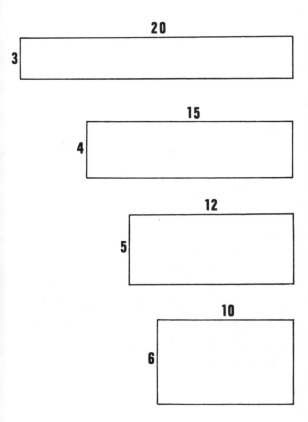

4

Bigger Polyominoes

Polyominoes built up from six constituent squares are called *hexominoes* seven squares *heptominoes* eight squares *octominoes* nine squares *nonominoes* and ten squares *dekominoes*

There is just one monomino; there is just one domino; there are two trominoes; there are five tetrominoes; and there are 12 pentominoes. *But how many hexominoes are there?* (A clue: there are between 30 and 50.) Likewise, *how many heptominoes are there?* (Another clue: between 100 and 120.) *And what about the numbers of octominoes, nonominoes, and dekominoes?* (Respective clues for these: between 350 and 400, between 1000 and 1300, and between 4000 and 4500.)

5

Polyominoes with Holes

None of the smaller polyominoes (up to and including hexominoes) contains any holes. But once larger polyominoes are encountered, a small number of them begin to have internal holes. For example, just one of the heptominoes has an internal hole, and looks like this:

And just six of the 350– 400 octominoes have internal holes. *How many of these 'hole-y' octominoes can you identify?*

95 A. Ross Eckler's Cryptology

THE OBJECT OF CRYPTOLOGY is to hide messages from those not authorised to receive them by means of various transformations on the letters known only to the sender and the receiver. Many of these are the same transformations used by logologists (or word puzzlers): transposals of letters within a word, substitutions of one letter for another, insertion or deletion of letters. It is hardly surprising, therefore, to uncover an area of wordplay that is neither pure logology nor pure cryptology. Here is a collection of puzzles with a cryptographic flavour.

Puzzle Number Two
The letters of the alphabet are converted into their International Morse Code equivalents, with a space between each pair of letters and two spaces between each pair of words. Each pair of elements (for example, dot-space, dash-dash, and so on) is then assigned a number from 1 to 9 (for example, 5 may correspond to dash-dot, and 3 to space-dash). A message written in this system becomes:
5 1 2 5 3 7 4 2 9 3 2 2 8 2 3 1 4 6 3 7 3 7 3 2 5 7 4 2 3 4 6 4 2 8 1 4 7.
What pair of elements corresponds to each number, and what does the message say?

....
....
....

For convenience, the International Morse Code is given below:

A . _	O _ _ _
B _ . . .	P . _ _ .
C _ . _ .	Q _ _ . _
D _ . .	R . _ .
E .	S . . .
F . . _ .	T _
G _ _ .	U . . _
H	V . . . _
I . .	W . _ _
J . _ _ _	X _ . . _
K _ . _	Y _ . _ _
L . _ . .	Z _ _ . .
M _ _	
N _ .	

Puzzle Number One
An automatic card shuffler always rearranges the cards in the same way if the setting is the same. A set of twelve cards bearing the letters

G O L D E N B I N A R Y

is put through the machine, and the cards, in the order in which they emerge, are put through the machine a second time. They come out

A N I N O Y G R E D B L

What message did the cards convey after the first operation, assuming the setting is left unchanged for the second operation?

....

Puzzle Number Three

Sixteen letters are written in a four-by-four square with rows and columns labelled 1 through 4. Thus, a letter in the second row and the third column can be converted into the pair of numbers 2 and 3. The word LUMBERJACK is converted into a series of numbers using these co-ordinates, and the number 1 is added at the beginning of the series and the number 4 at the end of this series. This new series of 22 numbers is broken up into pairs, and reconverted into letters using the same four-by-four square: the result is BESOLKHCUAI. Another word is similarly treated, using the same square, but with a 4 added at the beginning and a 1 at the end. This comes out TMOCHRBNSSE. *What is the original word?*

....

Puzzle Number Four

The words of a saying are written one below the other, lined up on the left. The initial letters are then taken off, followed by the second letters, etc., blanks being skipped. For example,

```
R O S E S
A R E
R E D
```

V I O L E T S
A R E
B L U E

becomes by this process
RARVA BOREI RLSED OEUEL ESETS.
Read the following:
TINFL ABTBU WAHSO SOWEI KOARA RGEKR LYEAD TSE.

Puzzle Number Five

A certain quotation containing 26 letters is written below a normal alphabet and used for the cipher equivalents of a simple substitution system. (Note that a cipher letter may stand for more than one plain letter with this scheme.) These equivalents are then used to encipher the quotation. For example, 'Give me liberty or give me death' becomes:

```
A B C D E F G H I J K L M
G I V E M E L I B E R T Y
L B D M Y M T B I M V M T
```

```
N O P Q R S T U V W X Y Z
O R G I V E M E D E A T H
R V L B D M Y M E M G M I
```

What message is given by:

YIYVNEAS
LRO
EEEE
UAIYV
A
UAUAL ?

Puzzle Number Six

For haggling purposes, a curio dealer enciphered the cost prices on his tags, replacing each digit by a letter. To improve his bargaining position, a shrewd customer noted the letters on the tags of three items, and at various times casually asked the price of each. The tags read NL.MI and CR.IK and AP.EI, and the prices asked were respectively $39.69, $53.46 and $87.75. The customer correctly assumed that these all represented the same percentage mark-up. *What did these items cost?*

....

....

....

Puzzle Number Seven

The word ALUMINUM (note the American spelling!) has the pattern 12345634 since the third letter is the same as the seventh letter, and the fourth is the same as the last, the others being all different. The word MOLECULE has the same pattern. Put them together and you get an ALUMINUM MOLECULE. Try to solve the pattern pairs below, aided by the clues.

1 12234536 Wrong-doer taken into custody.

....

2 12314536 Lady flier who cannot tell a lie.

....

3 12321456 Monster threatening evil.

....

4 12324256 Something denied to the military.

....

5 12324563 Tourists in native costumes.

....

6 12334536 Fighters easily taken in.

....

7 12343516 Unexpected pardon.

....

8 12345126 Shoulder bone that has been repaired.

....

9 12345316 Minor battle along the shore.

....

10 12345346 Portrait in oils done with skill and taste.

....

....

Noughts and Crosses?

Crosses and Noughts

The ancient and popular game of Noughts and Crosses is well known to end in a tie (cat's game) with best play. Against a corner opening, the correct response is to take the centre square, and any corner will frustrate a centre opening. Against any other responses, first player can force a win.

Against a side opening, the second player has a choice of responses that he can convert to a tie. However, few Noughts and Crosses devotees have taken the trouble to analyse the interesting branches that result from a side opening. There are traps lurking for both players.

In the game of Noughts and Crosses (or Crosses and Noughts Misere), the *loser* of the game, if any, is the player who first establishes three of his markers in a row. Play the game a few times with a friend, and you will find that the player with the first move can usually be forced into a loss, most often on the ninth play. You are under the disadvantage of having to move first.

Can you devise a strategy that will insure a tie?

....

....

3 x 3 x 3 Noughts and Crosses

In the 3 x 3 x 3 version of Noughts and Crosses, the first player's advantage is insurmountable if he is allowed to take the centre square **B5**. Therefore the restricted version permits the first player to take any square except **B5**. The three matrices are to be thought of as tiers of a 3 x 3 x 3 cube. Any three markers in the same line create a win. For example, **A4, A5** and **A6**; or **A4, B4** and **C4**; or **A4, B5** and **C6**.
Given the choice, would you prefer to play first or second? What would your strategy be?

....

....

....

Quick-Tac-Toe

Quick-Tac-Toe is an American version of noughts and crosses which is played in an unusual way. At each turn a player marks as many squares as he wishes, provided they are in the same vertical or horizontal row (they need not be adjacent). The winner is the one who marks the last square.

You are given the dubious advantage of playing second. Your opponent starts by marking the top squares of the first and third columns.

Your move.

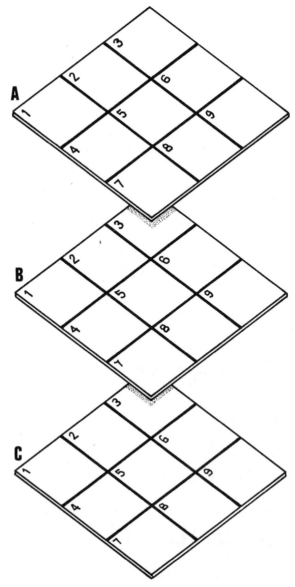

Connecto

In the game of Connecto, two players alternate in joining adjacent points, horizontally or vertically, on an infinite rectangular lattice, one using solid lines for his connections, the other using dotted lines. The winner is the first to enclose a region of any shape by a boundary composed of his line only. The dotted player has won in the diagram here.

You have undertaken to play Connecto against an experienced player. The flip of a coin gives your opponent the first move — obviously an advantage.
Can you, nevertheless, devise a simple strategy that will prevent him from winning?

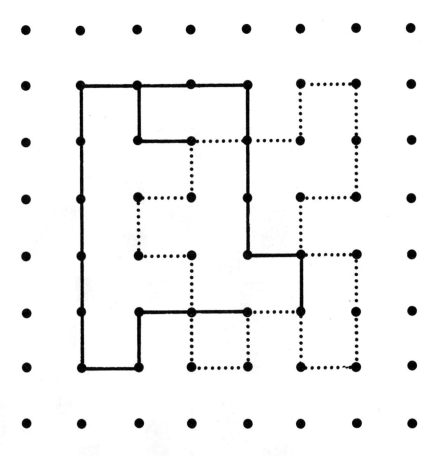

....

....

....

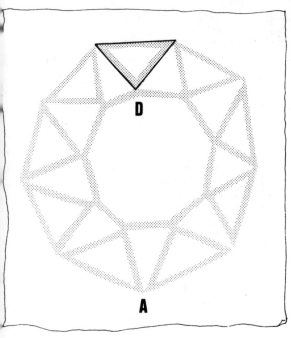

Fortress

Two opponents alternately move from an intersection to an adjacent intersection. The defender, originally situated at **D**, is confined to the three intersections of the heavily outlined 'fortress'. The attacker, starting at point **A**, has first move and operates only under the constraint that once having made a particular move, the path between those two intersections is barred in future.

The objective of the attacker is to enter the fortress on the same vertex that the defender is occupying, thus 'capturing' him. If the attacker succeeds, he wins. If he enters an unoccupied vertex of the fortress, he loses, since the defender can then capture him. The attacker loses also if he is negligent enough to stymie himself by moving into a cul-de-sac. Apparently this is a difficult game to analyse.
Whose role would you prefer, and what would be your strategy?

....

....

....

Classic Crosswords

HERE ARE FOUR classic puzzles created by four of the masters of the art (and craft) of crossword creation.

Elizabeth Kingsley's Double-Crostic

From 1934 to 1953, the year of her death, Elizabeth Kingsley contributed almost a thousand of her unique brand of puzzles to *The Saturday Review. Here is the very first:*

1	2	3		4	5	6		7	8		9	10	11	
12	13	14		15	16	17		18	19	20	21		22	23
24	25	26	27	28	29		30	31	32	33	34		35	36
	37	38	39		40	41	42	43		44	45	46	47	48
	49	50	51	52	53		54	55	56		57	58	59	60
61	62		63	64	65	66		67	68	69	70	71		72
73		74	75	76		77	78		79	80	81		82	83
84		85	86	87	88	89		90	91	92	93	94	95	
96	97		98	99	100	101	102	103		104	105	106	107	118
109		110	111	112	113		114	115	116	117		118	119	
120	121	122	123		124	125	126		127	128	129	130		131
132	133		134	135	136	137	138	139		140	141		142	143
144	145		146	147		148	149	150	151	152	153		154	155
	156	157	158	159		160	161		162	163	164	165		166
167	168		169	170	171		172	173		174	175	176	177	178

To solve this puzzle you must guess twenty-five words, the definitions of which are given in the column headed DEFINITIONS. The letters in each word to be guessed are numbered (these numbers appear at the beginning of each definition) and you are thereby able to tell how many letters are in the required word. When you have guessed a word each letter is to be written in the correspondingly numbered square on the puzzle diagram. When the squares are filled in you will find (by reading from left to right) a quotation from a famous author. Reading up and down, the letters mean nothing. The black squares indicate ends of words: therefore words do not necessarily end at the right side of the diagram.

Either before (preferably) or after placing the letters in their squares you should write the words you have guessed on the blank lines which appear to the right in the column headed WORDS. The initial letters of this list of words spell the name of the author and the title of the piece from which the quotation has been taken.

DEFINITIONS

I 1-14-23-50-95. A perfume of roses.

II 145-6-28-90-137. Child's game played with cards and numbers.

III 97-8-79-146-98-61-75-77-76-32-27-19-133. Light as a feather.

IV 80-85-60-113-51-58-48. Held in high esteem; worshipped.

V 81-172-31-84-24-176-65-89. Insubstantial.

VI 112-45-114-164-149-173-142-36. The business section of a city.

WORDS

I.....................

II.....................

III.....................

IV.....................

V.....................

VI.....................

Torquemada's Torture

Taking his pseudonym Torquemada from the Grand Inquisitor of Spain, Edward Powys Mathers (1892–1939) began producing his series of brilliantly original puzzles for the *Observer* in 1926. Here is a vintage sample, *By the Waters of Shannon:*

VII 144-102-2-63. Material for bandages.

VIII 37-4-66-82-110-116-62. Upholstered backless seat.

IX 100-106-33-5-122-41-138-69-83-13-162-127. A Russian pianist.

X 40-59-52-25. A drupe with a single seed.

XI 135-175-3-73. Movement of the ocean.

XII 130-43-129-107-111-55-139-47. To alienate.

XIII 15-121-92-136-101-39. A mighty hunter.

XIV 167-9-140-46-105. Artless; simple.

XV 119-54-104-17-153-34. Hebrew God.

XVI 134-63-128-168-16-30. Flat, dark image.

XVII 155-125-78-148-143-165-158-56. Prejudiced (compound).

XVIII 12-96-120-11-7-170-150-21-68-174. Significant, unusual.

XIX 87-141-171-161-67-20-10-126. Not propitious.

XX 177-99-152-163-108-115. Member of the tribe of Levi.

XXI 42-88-26-159-49-91. Doodle dandy.

XXII 22-71-151-118-131-147-38-94-160-29. Watchword (Bibl.).

XXIII 109-86-132-124-72-117-123-178. Uttered a harsh sound.

XXIV 157-44-93-53-166-18-35-103. Forceful.

XXV 156-154-74-169-70-57. To stop the flow.

VII.....................
VIII.....................
IX.....................
X.....................
XI.....................
XII.....................
XIII.....................
XIV.....................
XV.....................
XVI.....................
XVII.....................
XVIII.....................
XIX.....................
XX.....................
XXI.....................
XXII.....................
XXIII.....................
XXIV.....................
XXV.....................

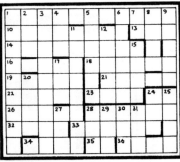

Clues consist of one word or consecutive words in each line.

ACROSS

1 Issue this warning to them

10 Who praise the uproarious Brem:

13 Ere you visit the lair

14 Of a newly wed pair

16 Have notches cut out of your hem.

18 Should it ever befall that the Grung

19 Simply must disinherit its young,

12 & 24 It will first climb a tree

22 And glean sprats for their tea

23 By a weird rise and fall of its tongue.

26 If a Michaelmas daisy should please

28 The green-crested Pot-stick or Kreze,

32 'Tis a custom of old

33 That the bird should be told

34 rev. That the thing is a deadly disease.

35 Little Edward once pelted a Plo

36 With fragments of glacial snow

DOWN

1 Till it fell from the swing:

2 I regret that its wing

3 Now extends nearly down to its toe.

4 When the Snats move away in the Spring

5 They're remarkably swift on the wing

6 And I think that they coin

8 (As they tear to the Boyne)

9 rev. That they coin little lyrics to sing.

11 & 7 A snail is a fool to a Woft;

12 I have seen a Woft seat itself oft

15 At my aunt's little Zoo

17 rev. On a slip of bamboo

20 Since a slip of bamboo is so soft.

24 With enough beer and bromide and borax

25 & 30 To fill a crustacean's thorax

27 Any may sheep can be

28 & 31 In a threefold degree

29 Concealed from the fangs of the Lorax.

Afrit's Afright

Prebendary Alistair Ferguson Ritchie (1887–1957) derived his pseudonym from his own name which led him to an evil demon of Arabian mythology called Afrit. His most taxing puzzles appeared in the *Listener*, his easier ones in the *Sphere*. This one would have appealed to readers of both papers:

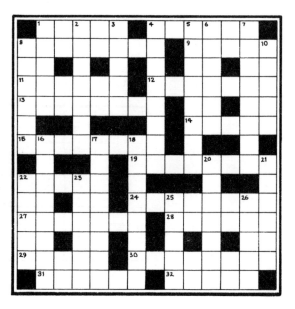

ACROSS

1 He may be a'richt in the heid, but he's aye wandering (5)
4 Curious fellow: he usually has to pay sixpence (6)
8 The fragrance of an old amour. It seems to have gone off a bit! (8)
9 Pat says he made all the running, and of course things have to be run smoothly (5)
11 The sum I do here has chemical results (6)
12 They have ends, but they're really beginnings – twelve a year (7)
13 Summary way of making a cab start (8)
14 Stop! – or proceed slowly if the road is (5)
15 To make these you begin with leaves, and end with roots – even if they end in smoke (8)
19 Is it his unnatural need and baffled rage which makes him so false, the rat? (8)
22 Men go like this, little man (5)
24 Truly rural, he is, though not till he's had his beer (8)
27 It takes two on 'em to do it properly (7)
28 Not experienced, so if you haven't got the right 'un try the left 'un (6)
29 It's dear and old when you sing about it, but it sings for the camper when it's new and cheap (5)
30 Hides away, but shows that the island lies between the South and South-east (8)
31 You may safely do so to the baby; otherwise you might get landed! (6)
32 Lots and lots, though they may be reduced to a shred (5)

DOWN

1 You can't say he hasn't got a shilling to his name (5)
2 He'll keep you in order, and the motor, too. There's something in that (7)
3 A laying down of the law. Still, it doesn't tell you to follow Father (5)
4 Do as the doctor does, and the praise will be equally divided (8)
5 There's a hindrance en route, and that makes the game merely one of chance (8)
6 It really is a moving spectacle to see Mother after the cows! (6)
7 'Tear asunder a broken reed' is one account of it, but it's another kind of account which usually is (8)
8 A design which is revealed in the name of the Law (6)
10 An untidy study is naturally bound to be (5)
16 She doesn't sound as if she were mass-produced, so she should render good service (8)
17 Considerably abashed, as Vera would be by a proposal like this! (8)
18 To get across, let art go one way and poetry the other (8)
20 You can't approve his way of getting money, especially as he's got enough under his head to keep a roof over his head (7)
21 Foxes had them long before the wireless was thought of (6)
22 This is desire in an immoderate degree, so the degree should be modified and diminished (5)
23 Spoil a good drink? Why, it's the outside edge! (6)
25 Pitch and Toss. If you're right in this you won't be left in this (5)
26 They make an end of themselves, being mere creatures of fancy (5)

Ximenes

Just as Cardinal Ximenes de Cisneros succeeded Torquemada in the Spanish Inquisition, so Derrick Macnutt (1902–1971) adopted the name Ximenes when he succeeded Torquemada as the *Observer's* crossword compiler. Here is one of his famous Misprint puzzles.

Half of the Across and half the Down clues contain a misprint of one letter only in each, occurring always in the definition part of the clue: their answers are to appear in the diagram correctly spelt. The other eighteen clues are correctly printed: their answers are to appear in the diagram with a misprint of one letter only in each. No unchecked letter in the diagram is to be misprinted: each twice used letter is to appear as required by the correct form of at least one of the words to which it belongs. All indications such as anagrams etc. in clues lead to correct forms of words required, not to misprinted forms.

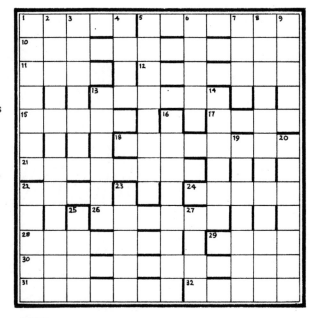

ACROSS

1 Essential Latin school – dark blue (5)
5 Windmill pieces, with it – the admiral's type (7)
10 Crash of gate stops you with a colossal jump (12)
11 Get farmer to show what's wrong (4)
12 Vulgarian boldly interrupts girl without respect (7)
13 Deliberate collision in London street – I'm fired (6)
15 He would evade work but proverbially never lies (5)
17 Nasty hook – reverse of what a fisherman uses (4)
18 I may be called lather-proof, therefore most fit (8)
21 Sheep in having got lost calls for finesse (8)
22 To steal the dog's dinner is very hard (4)
24 Pocket picker to be seen in funds (5)
26 Soft clots: get the doctor – a very short distance (6)
28 Fish like carp among catch in rough water (7)
29 Very nifty round hat (4)
30 Trying to cure Ma, hugging her, deary? No! (12)
31 Is this slayer more infernal? (7)
32 Marriage no longer violated by Sepoy (5)

DOWN

1 This is old hat, darling, like you and me (7)
2 Once simple mixed emotions, typical of a wish (12)
3 This old royal fish is always fed (7)
4 The Painted Perch can be upset by oats (4)
5 Arch-binder will give you an evening in Paris (8)
6 The sea's sounding very rough, my boy (5)
7 I used to be sweet: now I'm a slut (4)
8 Jobs for operators become suddenly slack afloat (12)
9 I'm moping in a place of confinement (5)
13 A household makes husbands get senile (6)
14 Trip off? That was well known in Scotland (6)
16 Formerly peaty ground, light for tall plant (8)
19 A livery upset? Try old-fashioned French thyme (7)
20 Stuff the French play casually (7)
21 Female don, by no means a lovable woman (5)
23 Lesson's no use to me: I sound opposed to it! (5)
24 Turn upside down a brat with a flat bottom (4)
27 A notion that is somewhat less than perfect (4)

The Philadelphia Maze

The Philadelphia Maze
This maze is unique.
There are 320 different
ways of travelling from
the outside of the maze
to the centre.
If you don't believe it, try.

Saint Bertin's Maze
This maze was once on
the floor of the old abbey
at St Bertin in St Omer,
in northern France.
*You must start on the
outside and work your way
to the centre.*

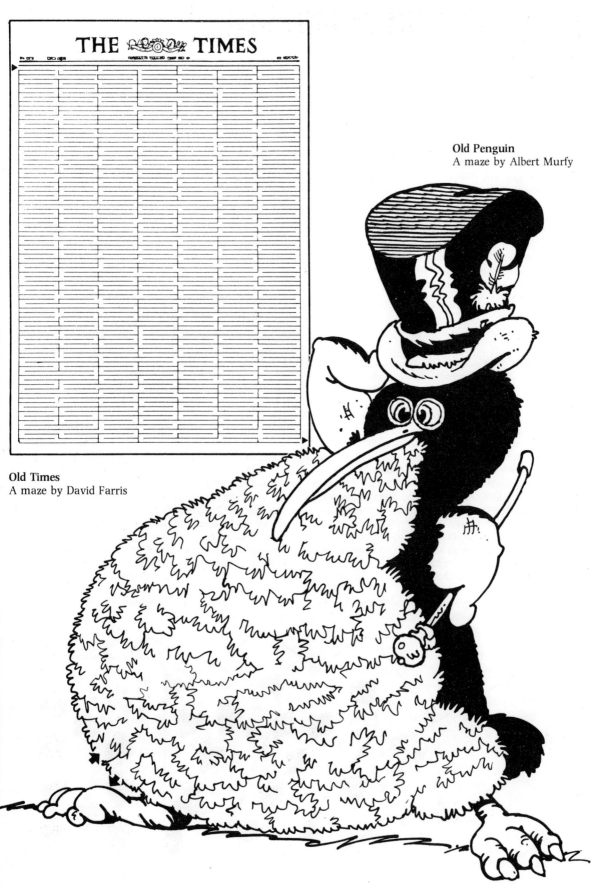

THE TIMES

Old Times
A maze by David Farris

Old Penguin
A maze by Albert Murfy

99 No Solution

HAVING STARTED ON OUR ASCENT of the Puzzle Mountain with a selection of elementary puzzles without solutions, as we near the summit here are more puzzles for you to consider without benefit of the Answers pages. The difference between these and the ones at the beginning of the book is that they did have definite solutions, while these do not. Play the games here in your head or against a brilliant opponent – like David Silverman, one of the grand panjandrums of puzzledom, who actually devised them – and you will find that you are still puzzling over them years from now when the pages of *The Puzzle Mountain* have turned yellow and the grand prize has long been won – and spent.

1

Minipoker

Each player is dealt one card from a pack of 52, following an initial stake of one chip. Hands rank in value from deuce up to ace with suits irrelevant as in standard poker. If a show is called and the players hold cards of the same denomination, a tie results. The first player's options are either to fold (the second player thus wins the first stakes) or to bet one chip. In the latter case, the second player may either call at the cost of one chip, in which case the hands are compared to determine the winner of the pool; or fold, in which case the first player wins the preliminary stakes.

Assuming that this game is played repeatedly, only two facts are clear: players should always bet or call with an ace, and the probability with which they bet or call on a lesser hand should be an increasing function of the value of the hand.

With what probabilities should one bet or call, holding the various card denominations?

If both players employ optimal mixed strategies, what is the first player's probability of winning?

What is his expectation?

2

Semi-Blind Poker

After an initial stake of one chip each, Red and Black are dealt one card from a shuffled deck containing only a King, a Queen, and a Jack. Red looks at his card and may either fold, yielding the stakes to Black, or bet four chips. If he bets, Black, who is unable to look at his own card, has four options:

1. he may fold, yielding the stakes
2. he may call at the reduced price of three chips
3. he may pay one chip to the pool for the privilege of looking at the third, undealt card or
4. he may pay two chips for the privilege of looking at his own card.

If Black elects option 3 or 4, after paying and looking, he may either fold or call for four chips. *What are the optimal mixed strategies, and what is Red's expectation?*

3

Buy or Fold

The thirteen spades are shuffled, and after a first bet of one chip, each player is dealt one card face up. The player with the lower ranking card may either fold and yield the pool to his opponent, or he may, for the price of one chip, purchase a new card from the pack. He may continue to buy replacements until he receives one higher than his opponent's card. Discards are all left face up and are not subsequently drawn from. If and when a player buys a card higher than his opponent's current card, the buy-or-fold option shifts to his opponent. Whenever a player folds, he loses the entire pool, including all chips paid for replacements.

Under what conditions is it advisable for the low man to fold?

4

Grid

This game is played on an infinite square lattice, though for practical purposes a sheet of graph paper with quarter-inch grids is sufficient. The players alternately 'appropriate' intersection points, the first player labelling them with circles, the second with crosses, or any other convenient distinguishing mark such as circles of a different colour.

The winner is the first player, if any, to appropriate the four vertices of a square, which may be of any size, but must be oriented in the direction of the lattice. For example, the mid-points of the sides of a two-by-two square form the vertices of an unacceptable square.

What is the first player's best strategy?

5

The Dating Game

Two players alternately tear out sheets from a loose-leaf desk calendar with the restriction that, after the first move, each play must involve a date that agrees with the preceding date with respect either to number or month. The last player able to make a legal move wins. Experimentation on small 'calendars'

indicates that the first player has the advantage if and only if the total number of dates is odd, implying that the second player should win only if a leap-year calendar is used.

Verify or disprove this conjecture.

This game lends itself to numerous generalisations and variations.

6

Regulus

Two players alternately connect pairs of vertices of a regular polygon with straight-line segments. No vertex may be used more than once, and no previously drawn segment may be crossed. The last player able to make a legal move wins. In the case of a polygon with an even number of vertices, the first player wins easily

by connecting opposite vertices, effectively dividing the remaining vertices into two identical groups. Now he simply replies symmetrically to each of his opponent's plays.

For polygons with an odd number of vertices, which player has the winning advantage, and what is his optimal strategy?

It is better never to begin a good work than, having begun it, to stop.   *Venerable Bede*

100 The Summit

Welcome to the summit of the Puzzle Mountain — and the challenge that could win you the Grand Prize.

The puzzle comes in four stages and speaks for itself. Study the rules on page 202 and when you have arrived at the solution, simply fill in the entry form and mail it to reach the address given before September 30th, 1982.

STAGE 1

Some box numbers hide
Their letters inside
　In the cities, we grant,
And two others beside.

Computing their placing
And squarely embracing,
　Just a bird is disordered
With its eye closely facing.

On your third word bestow
A value below
　Continuously added
To the numbers that show.

To check if you've done it
　Efficiently, your
Should come to five one
　Six four five six six four.

STAGE 2

In London meantime
Without any rhyme,
The lady is waiting
For rapturous fêting.

2657

543457353855

46485442365543

65555345583544

753264

783465

58332464

732465

6225576435

STAGE 3

Her figure in mind,
You now need to find
An additional figure
From this lexical rigour.

Post all your letters
(But without our old fetters).
What remains from the right
Puts the answer in sight.

ACROSS

1 A trembling class caused my hopes to falter (13)
8 Sport's award for pool (7)
9 First to run in game around the deck (5)
10 Cook without a prop before the fire (5)
11 A time before ignorant use of that kind – except on the Sabbath (7)
12 'CCCHHHHHH' sounds like a parrot the wrong way round – tough stuff this (13)
15 In American race one in ten backing outsiders (7)
17 Load up around an intoxicant (5)
19 'The tide rolls in, the sound of the sea,' proclaims King (5)
20 Complaint causing first one in the lead to drop out (7)
21 What could make noisy chap snore endlessly? (13)

DOWN

1 A producer of some tissues – I left Poet's Corner very untidy (13)
2 Last of money going on each way double could make you sweat (5)
3 Horrific height (7)
4 Married friend taking in a smart forward one bigamously? (13)
5 Soak beginning to rise all right (5)
6 Big splash made by a couple of sportsmen on the box (7)
7 Prime Minister standing up in my seat – House in uproar about serious inflation (13)
13 Stronger drink almost rank (7)
14 Why we hear the Beatles' walrus following a safe-breaker? (7)
16 Anthem? Jazzmen start with 'take it away'! (5)
18 Approaches a nasty trap (5)

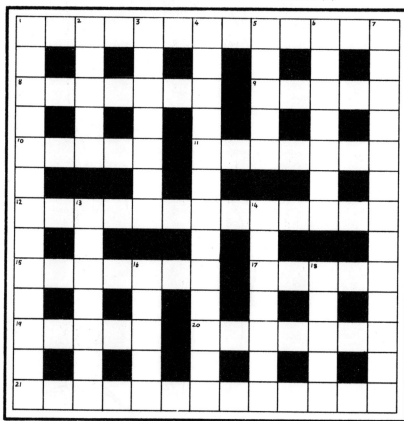

Taking one from the other
Will give you no bother;
But more problems bedevil
You at the next level.

CAB
CAB
CAB
CAB
DAF
DAF
DAF
HAC
HAC
HAC
LAG
LAJ
LEJ
LEJ
LEJ
LEK
LEK
LEK
LEM
MEN
MEN
MEN
MEN
NEP
NIP
RIP
RIP
RIP
RIP
RIP
RIP
ROQ
ROQ
ROQ
TOS
TOS
TOS
TOS
TOS
TOV
TOW
TOW
YOW
YOW
YUX
YUX
SUZ
SUZ

200

STAGE 4

A valuable sherpa
Now comes to usurp a
Usage of the word
Once used as a key word.

Adding this to the last,
A new figure is cast.
Adding up to the sum
To the summit you come.

Up there there's a goat
With no beard o'er his throat.
The height has deranged him,
And a mark's prearranged him.

But now that you've made his
Identity certain,
Research for a question
To ring down the curtain.

Have you looked, have you found
(Despite detours extended
Around the high mountain
You've nearly ascended)?

Three hundred and four days
(Not fewer, not more days)
From the day you ascended
Your journey's nigh ended.

It is dark, we must hear:
'Align first', and you're here —
And to show how you've come
Rightly set out the sum.

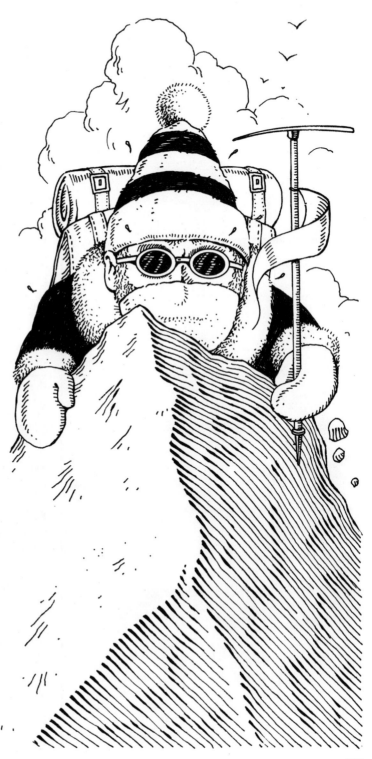

The Puzzle Mountain

THE SUMMIT

To: Shuckburgh Reynolds Ltd,
8 Northumberland Place,
London W2 5BS,
England.
Below is my solution to the Summit of the Puzzle Mountain. I agree to abide by the rules and to accept the published result as final and legally binding.

NAME ....

ADDRESS ....

....

....

daytime telephone no ....

MY SOLUTION : ....

....

....

....

....

....

....

signed :............................... dated :................

THE RULES

1
All entries must be sent to Shuckburgh Reynolds Ltd, 8 Northumberland Place, London W2 5BS, England.

2
The closing date for the competition is September 30, 1982, and no entry received after this date will be accepted.

3
The first correct entry drawn from all those received by the closing date will be declared the winner.

4
The winner will be notified by mail at the address indicated on the entry form.

5
The competition is open to residents of any country in the world but is void where prohibited by law.

6
Those persons employed by the publishers of this book (or any subsidiary or associated company), or any others involved in any way in the production of the book, their families or agents, are not eligible to enter.

7
All entries received become the property of Shuckburgh Reynolds Ltd, and no correspondence can be entered into regarding them.

8
In all cases, the decision of the Board of Directors of Shuckburgh Reynolds Ltd is final and binding.

9
All entries are free and shall be on the entry form provided or a facsimile thereof but are limited to one entry per person. No purchase is necessary to enter.

10
No liability shall be accepted for entries that may be lost, damaged, or delayed in the mail.

11
Entry in the competition constitutes agreement to abide by these rules.

12
The correct solution has been lodged at Lloyd's Bank Ltd, London, England, and in the event that no entry received by the closing date corresponds with this, no prize shall be awarded.

◀ Entries will only be accepted on this official entry for

202

Answers

SEEING IS BELIEVING
page 8

1 Both are the same length. It is the positioning of the lines that makes the lower one look longer
2 AB looks longer, but in fact both lines are the same length
3 A Mexican cycle race
4 They are both the same size
5 Both bricks are the same size
6 Both circles are the same size

OUT FOR THE COUNT
page 10

1 The husband is 52
  The wife is 39
2 4368
3 The film is nearly three hours long – but the bridge is 1200 feet!
4 None, of course!
5 $26\frac{2}{3}$ mph
6 $2\frac{2}{3}$
7 2519
8 Paris was $27\frac{1}{2}$ and Helen was $16\frac{1}{2}$
9 1 and 7
10 7.00 pm
11 With those dimensions you couldn't actually form a triangle!
12 17 beasts and 26 birds
13 668578
14 3, 5, 7, 9, 11, 13, 15, 17
15 24 eggs. At this ratio the chicken will lay $\frac{1}{3}$ of an egg in a day: 6 chickens would lay four eggs in a day, and 24 in 6 days
16 The sons are aged 24, 20, 17, 16, 12
18 3 lbs
19 15+36+47+2=100

WORDS, WORDS, WORDS
page 11

1 AT-TEN-U-ATE
2 FIG, HIP, DATE, APPLE, PEACH, NECTARINE, MELON, PEAR, ORANGE, OLIVE, GOURD, LEMON, RAISIN
3 EIGHT, BIGHT, LIGHT, NIGHT, WIGHT, MIGHT, RIGHT, SIGHT, TIGHT, FIGHT
4 SOVEREIGNTY, CONGRATULATE, DIAPPOINTMENT, MATRIMONY, SWEETHEART
5 ABSTEMIOUSLY
6 CAT, EWE, CUR, RAM
7 SKILL—KILL—ILL
8 'The quality of mercy is not strained' CATCHPHRASE

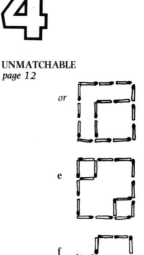

UNMATCHABLE
page 12

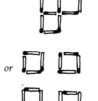

3

4 a

5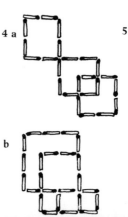

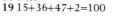

204

5

AMAZING
page 14

SILVER SCREEN
page 16

1 **Who have we here?**
   1 Clark Gable
   2 Vivien Leigh
   3 Jayne Russell
   4 John Travolta
   5 Snoopy
   6 Rudolph Valentino
   7 Liza Minnelli
   8 Rin Tin Tin
2 Faye Dunaway and
   Warren Beatty
3 Marie Schneider
4 Al Jolson, 1927
5 *Funny Girl*
6 *Blithe Spirit*
7 Liza Minelli
8 1928
9 Michael Caine
10 Jane Asher
11 Robert Donat
12 The Who
13 George Lazenby
14 He is better known as
   Ringo Starr of The Beatles.
   His first film was called
   A Hard Day's Night
15 Julie Andrews
16 Glenda Jackson
17 They were both married
   to Clark Gable
18 Theda Bara, which is an
   anagram of Arab Death
19 Bud Abbott and Lou
   Costello
20 Humphrey Bogart

WORLD WORD WAYS
page 18

1 a You can't fool me
   b Get a move on
   c Everything is all right
   d Not half!
   e Someone who can't
     hold their drink
   f At the back of beyond
   g Anything goes

2 a French
   b French
   c Latin
   d Latin
   e Spanish
   f French
   g Italian

3 a Rhythms
   b Pushchair
   c STRENGTHLESSNESS
   d Floccinaucinihilipilification

4 1 Flat
   2 Reversing lights
   3 Elastoplast
   4 Dressing gown
   5 Bank note
   6 Draughts
   7 Cupboard
   8 Semolina
   9 Lift
   10 Tap
   11 Torch
   12 Mince
   13 Broad bean
   14 Black treacle
   15 Truncheon
   16 Mileometer
   17 Tights
   18 Public school
   19 Sultana
   20 Pavement

5 1 Duckling
   2 Artichokes
   3 Clear soup
   4 Pastry
   5 Spinach
   6 Tiny peas
   7 Snails
   8 Cold chicken and
     potato-based soup
   9 Mixed vegetables or
     fruits
   10 Assorted sea foods
   11 Seafood preparation in
     scallop shells
   12 Calves' sweetbreads
   13 Peach
   14 Creamy stew
   15 Sauerkraut
   16 Sea-food soup
   17 Small thick beefsteaks
   18 Chicken livers
   19 Lettuce
   20 Topped with crumbs or
     cheese
   21 Cauliflower
   22 'Irish' potatoes (chips!)
   23 Kidneys
   24 Veal chops or cutlets
   25 Raspberries
   26 Pepper
   27 In jelly
   28 Lamb
   29 Strawberries
   20 A corruption of
     'beefsteak'

6 a Digger/Anzac
   b Swag
   c Safe thing
   d The bush
   e Pass in one's cheek
   f Pommy
   g Sheila
   h Fair dinkum
   i Bottle shop
   j Bowser
   k Billabong
   l Good on you
   m Pink Pages

VICTORIANA
page 20

1 A rolling stone gathers no
  moss

2
C a l F
R i a l t O
O t t O
W h e a T

3 1 China as(s)ter
     = China Aster
   2 Gold (h)en rod
     = Golden Rod
   3 La vend er(r)
     = Lavender
   4 Hol(e) (f)ly hock
     = Hollyhock

4
```
        C
B U D
T A P E R
F I G
        D
```

MONEY MATTERS
page 22

1 £49
2 £10
3 A: $12; B: $20; C: $30
4 1st: $240, 2nd: $200,
  3rd: $80, 4th: $280
5 From A: £88, from B: £44
6 Wife: £4,650
  Son: £6,200
  Elder daughter: £3,100
  Younger
  daughter: £1,550
                   _____
                   £15,500
7 5 dollars 13 cents
8 27 pounds of meat
9 $100
10 $50, $100, $120
11 12 days
12 $10,737,418.24
13 10 tons of chicken feed
   2 tons of pigs' swill
   88 tons of cattle fodder
14 $160

OUR ISLAND STORY
page 24

1 Celebes
2 Tierra del fuego
3 Skye
4 Philippine Islands
5 Isle of Wight
6 Spitzbergen
7 South Island, New Zealand
8 Newfoundland
9 Jamaica
10 Bermuda
11 Corsica
12 Shetland Islands
13 Cape Breton Islands,
   Nova Scotia
14 Vancouver Island
15 Cyprus
16 Japan
17 Iceland
18 Madagascar

DUDENEY'S GEMS
page 26

1 The number is 987,654,321, which when multiplied by 18 gives 1,777,777,778 with 1 and 8 at the beginning and end. And so on.

2 Twice 4 added to 20 is 28. Four of these (a seventh part) were killed, so they were the ones that remained. The others flew away of course

3 24 birds and 12 beasts

4 54 years

5 Each had three when married – six were born afterwards.

6 The difficulty is to know where to start, and one method may be suggested here. In reading the clues across, the most promising seems to be 18 across. The three similar figures may be 111, 222, 333, and so on. 26 down is the square of 18 across, and therefore 18 across must be either 111 or 222, as the squares of 333, 444, etc. have all more than five figures.

From 34 across we learn that the middle figure of 26 down is 3, and this gives us 26 down as the square of 111, i.e. 12321.
We now have 18 across, and this gives us 14 down and 14 across. Next we find 7 down. It is a four-figure cube number ending in 61, and this is sufficient to determine it. Next consider 31 across. It is a triangular number – that is, a number obtained by summing 1, 2, 3, 4, 5, etc. 210 is the only triangular number that has one as its middle figure. This settles 31 across, 18 down, 21 down, and 23 across. We can now get 29 across, and this gives us 30 down. From 29 down we can obtain the first two figures of 15 across, and can complete 15 across and 29 down. The remainder can now be worked out.

7 Change the 8 and 9 around – turn the 9 upside down to make a six. Both columns add up to 18.

6

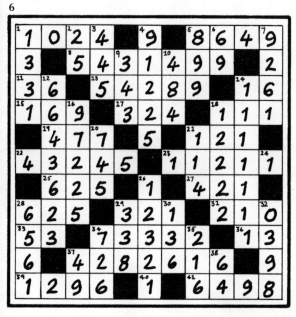

PAPER POSERS
page 28

1 Folding an Octagon
By folding the edge CD over AB we can crease the middle points E and G. In a similar way we can find the points F and H, and then crease the square EHGF. Now fold CH on EH and EC on EH, and the point where the creases cross will be I. Proceed in the same way at the other three corners, and the regular octagon, as shown, will be marked out by the creases and may be at once cut out

2 Square and Triangle
Fold the square in half and make the crease FE. Fold the side AB so that the point B lies on FE, and you will get the points G and H from which you can fold HGJ. While B is on G, fold AB back on AH, and you will have the line AK. You can now fold the triangle AJK, which is the largest possible equilateral triangle obtainable

3 Strip to Pentagon
By folding A over, find C, so that BC equals AB. Then fold as in Fig. 1 across the point A, and this will give you the point D. Now fold as in Fig. 2, making the edge of the ribbon lie along AB, and you will have the point E. Continue the fold as in Fig. 3 and so on, until all the ribbon lies on the pentagon. This, as we have said, is simple, but it is interesting and instructive

4 A Crease Problem
Bisect AB in C and draw the line CG, parallel to BH. Then bisect AC in D and draw the semicircle DB, cutting the line CG in E. Now the line DEF gives the direction of the shortest possible crease under the conditions

5 Key Ring Puzzle
First cut out the keys and ring in one piece, as shown. Cut half through the paper along the little dark lines and similarly turn the paper over and cut half through the little dotted lines. Insert a pen-knife and split the card below the four little squares formed by these lines, and the three pieces will come apart with the keys loose on the ring and no join

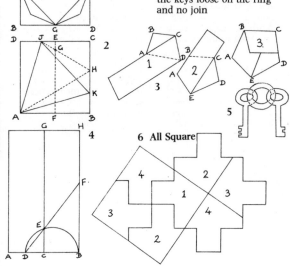

6 All Square

AGE OLD PROBLEMS
page 30
1 Jane will have been married 25 years in 5 years time, so she will have been married 20 years on her anniversary next week. Since she will then have been married half her lifetime she will be 40 next week. Jane is is now 39
2 99 years old. There was no year 0
3 Tom is 7; Mary is 13
4 Mrs. Dickens 39, Edgar 21, James 18, John 18, Ethel 12, Daisy 9. James and John are twins
5 They were 64 and 20
6 60
7 30 and 12
8 The boy is 10; his sister is 4
9 The ages are 2, 5, 8, 11, 14, 17, 20, 23, 26. The father is 48
10 There were 129 years between the birth of Cleopatra and the death of Boadicea; but as their combined ages amounted to 100 years only, there must have been 29 years when neither existed – that is between the death of Cleopatra and the birth of Boadicea. Therefore Boadicea must have been born 29 years after the death of Cleopatra in 30 BC which would be in the year 1 BC
11 Robinson's age must be 32; his brother's 34, his sister's 38, and his mother's 52
12 The father and mother were both of the same age, 36 years old, and their three children were triplets of 6 years of age, thus the sum of all their ages is 90 years
13 I am 40, he is 10
14 I am 73. She is 37
15 Punch is 52, Judy is 39

THE BRILLIANCE OF BORGMANN
page 32
Homonymic Humdingers
The ten mutually homonymous words:

1 ere	2 air
3 Ear	4 e'er
5 eyre	6 are
7 Ayer	8 Ayr
9 Ayre	10 heir

Our sixth word, ARE, requires explanation. To begin with, it is not a form of the verb 'to be' but a surface measure in the metric system equal to one hundred square metres, or to 0.0247 acre. The word is also spelled AR. The symbol or abbreviation for 'are' is 'a', always written as a lower-case letter, with or without a period (full stop) following it. Definitions are customarily started with a capital letter; but to conceal the symbolic nature of 'a' without mis-writing it, we did not capitalise the definitions in this problem. Definitions usually end with a period; we used that period as the abbreviation period for 'a'.

A Jug of Wine, a Loaf of Bread – and Thou
Our question is also our answer. **WHAT** is the essence, substance or distinctive quality of the passage quoted. The verse is an accidental acrostic. The initial letters of the four lines constituting the rubai (tetrastich), read in succession, spell the word **WHAT**. That word, used as a noun, means 'the essence, substance or distinctive quality of something'.

Sight and Sound
Here are our efforts, to match against your own:
1 Pneumatic Dnepropetrovsk gnomes knew mnemonic names.
2 Pshaw! – psychotic Peiping philosophizes Pnom-Penh's phthalein ptomaine poisoning.
In the second sentence, the successive initial sounds are those of SH, S, B, F, N, TH, T

and P. Dnepropetrovsk is a city in Russia; Peiping is another name for Peking; Pnom-Penh is the capital of Cambodia.

Un-French French
The correct translations into French:
1 *Soutien-gorge*. The French word *brassière* is used only for a child's bodice or vest.
2 *Double entente, or 'expression à double entente'.*
3 *Bis!*
4 *Vêtements de dessous*, or *Sous-vêtements*.
5 *La carte*: the customary term used in a restaurant when asking the waiter for a menu.
6 *Moral*, or *Etat d'esprit*, or *Force d'âme*.
7 *Nom de guerre*, or *Pseudonyme littéraire*.

An Odd Problem
Numbers, the supposed key to cosmic secrets, are certainly the key to this problem. Replace each letter in the words ODD and EVEN with its numerical position in the alphabet:

O D D
14 4 4

E V E N
5 22 5 14

Next, add the numerical equivalents of ODD – their sum is **23** – and add the numerical equivalents of EVEN – their sum is **46**. You will observe that **23** is an ODD number; multiply it by **2**, and the product is **46**, an EVEN number.

THERE WAS A YOUNG LADY FROM CREWE
page 34
1 And the second was worse than the first 'un
2 But the other won several prizes
3 When I wear it I'm only called vermin
4 As to who should be frightened of whom
5 I have bitten myself underneath
6 But once in the garden, oh Lord!
7 When she saw some budgie manure
8 I'll tread on your teeth and I'll squash 'em!'
9 I am trying to get in Who's Zoo
10 He ought to have known better – now didney?

ARTISTIC ENDEAVOUR
page 35
1 a Frans Hals
  b Reynolds
  c Leonardo da Vinci
  d Bruegel
  e Van Gogh
  f Millais
  g Hogarth
  h Landseer
  i Rembrandt
  j Gainsborough
  k J. L. David
  l Tintoretto
  m Millet
  n Botticelli
  o Veronese
  p Rembrandt
  q Holbein

2 a American
  b Flemish
  c French
  d French
  e French
  f Dutch
  g Spanish
  h German
  i French
  j British
  k Spanish
  l Italian
  m Dutch
  n Flemish
  o Italian
  p Flemish
  q Spanish
  r French

3 Vincent Van Gogh
4 Sir Peter Paul Rubens and
  Sir Anthony Van Dyck
5 Bernini, Michelangelo,
  Raphael

DRAW, O COWARD!
page 36
1 a Deed
  b Noon
  c Nun
  d Sexes
  e Solos
  f Level
  g Sagas
  h Peep
  i Shahs
  j Repaper
  k Ma'am
  l Redder
  m Rotator
  n Reviver
  o Pull-up

2 a on evil
  b test on Erasmus
  c Roy went on
  d again
  e Roman way
  f Roses, Simon
  g a cat I saw?
  h is, Eva can I stab live
  i Noel and Ellen sinned
  j nine memos
  k a myriad of fits
  l sees trade's opposition
  m are negro jam-pots won?
  n a bad log for a bastion!
  o no lost one rise distressed
  p at Toronto, son

3 The missing words in order
  are: noon, eve, Bob,
  Hannah, peep, ewe,
  Dad, tit, Aha, sees, eye,
  pup, keek, bib, pap, tot,
  deified, pip, nun, redder,
  tut, madam, deed, refer,
  level, eke, poop, gig, oho,
  reviver, mum, gag, toot,
  civic, sexes, tenet

DOMINO DELIGHTS
page 38

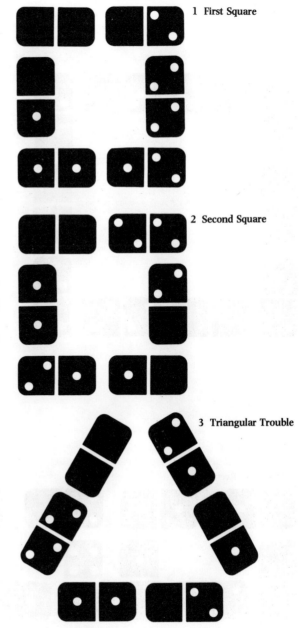

1 First Square

2 Second Square

3 Triangular Trouble

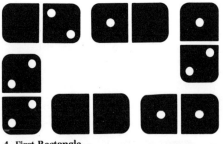

4 First Rectangle

7 The Five Lines

8 The Seven Lines

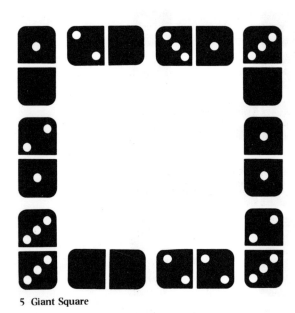

5 Giant Square

6 The Three Rectangles

9 Three More Rectangles

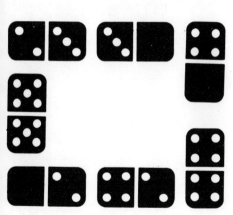

10 The Seven Squares

19

CLOCKING IN
page 40

1 15 hours
2 300 times
3 The hour indicated would be $23\frac{1}{3}$ minutes after four o'clock, but because the hand moves in the opposite direction you must deduct this number of minutes from 60 to get the real time, which is 36 12/13 minutes after four
4 It began at 59 minutes past ten. It is now 54 minutes past eleven
5 41 minutes past three o'clock
6 5 minutes past two
7 0. The figures are part of a sequence representing the figures on a digital clock showing hour, minutes and seconds, as one pm approaches: 125957, 125958, 125959, 130000
8 5 5/143 minutes past twelve. It could be 60/143 past one o'clock
9 8.23 am and 4.41 pm
10 3 minutes
11 $1\frac{2}{3}$ minutes
12 4 seconds

20

WORD SEARCH
page 42
1 Needle in a haystack

```
E L D E N E E D E L N E E N E D L
L E E N E D L E N E E D E L N E E
D E E L E N D L E E D E N E E D L
E D N E L E E N E L E E L E E N E
N E E L D E E D N L E D E N D E N
E N L E E D E L E D E E N E L E L
E E D E N N E E L E D L E N D E E
D E D E L E E D N E E L D E L L D
N L E N E L D L E N E E L D N E E
E D E D L N E E E D L E N E E D L
L E L D E L N E L E N E D E D N E
N E E D N E D E D E E D E N L E L
N E L D E E E E L N E E L E D E E
N E D E L D E N E E D L N E E L D
E N D E E L E N E N E E L D E E E
E L E N N E E E D L E N E E L N N
E E D L E N E L E N E L E N E N D
```

2

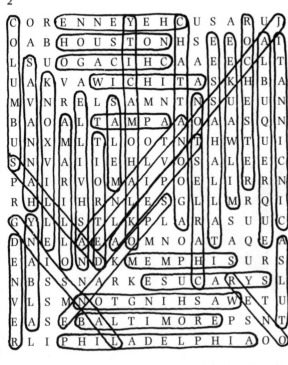

3

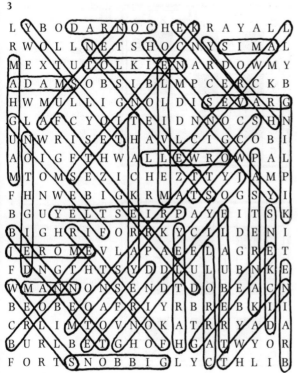

PATIENCE IS A VIRTUE
page 44

1 The most obvious solution is to place the four main cards in order of value in row No. 1 as shown here, then reverse a set of A, K, Q, J, cards in row No. 2. Completing the other two rows without breaking a rule is then fairly easy

Here are two further solutions:

Many more are possible

2 Nine moves in all
This is just one solution:
Col 1, card 2 to bottom
Row 4, card 2 to left
Col 4, card 4 to top
Row 3, card 3 to right
Col 2, card 3 to bottom
Row 3, card 2 to left
Col 4, card 4 to top
Row 2, card 3 to right
Col 4, card 3 to bottom
3 Bill had the Joker and 2 Kings
4 The King of Hearts has a J in one corner; the bottom club is the wrong way up; the third card is correct

5

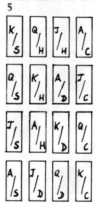

6

WORD CROSS/CROSS WORD
page 46

Crosswords Ancient

1

2

Crosswords Modern

Miniature Crossword 1
ACROSS:
1 Dogstar *dogs tar*
5 Reading 2 *meanings*
6 Implore *imp lore*
7 Eyelids *anagram*
DOWN:
1 Dormice *dorm ice*
2 Grapple *G. R. apple*
3 Tripoli *trip and anagram*
4 Regrets *r. egrets*

Miniature Crossword 2
ACROSS:
1 Incense 2 *meanings*
5 Maigret *anagram*
6 Replace *rep lace*
7 Earnest *ear nest*
DOWN:
1 Immerse *hidden*
2 Clipper 2 *meanings*
3 Narrate *rev. of 'ran'
and rate*

READING BETWEEN THE LINES
page 48

1 Vowel play
a PERSEVERE YE PERFECT MEN EVER KEEP THESE PRECEPTS TEN
b ORTHODOX OXFORD DONS DON'T KNOW OLD PORT FROM LOGWOOD

2 Fine phrases
a Much Ado About Nothing
b In-between times
c Reversal of fortune
d He is under arrest
e I before E except after C
f Sing a song of sixpence
g Music hath charms

3 Numbers up
a PUZZLE MOUNTAIN IS THE BEST PUZZLE BOOK EVER
b CODES ARE EASY WHEN YOU KNOW HOW

4 Pig Latin
a THE AVERAGE LENGTH OF WORDS IN THE ENGLISH LANGUAGE IS ABOUT FOUR AND A HALF LETTERS
b IN ALL THE COMMON LANGUAGES OF WESTERN EUROPE AND AMERICA E IS THE LETTER THAT IS USED THE MOST OFTEN

5 Morse the merrier
a Knowledge is power
b Death is evil, it cuts off hope
c Actions speak loudly

6 Natural break
ALL OUR LIVES WE ARE CRUSHED BY THE WEIGHT OF WORDS

7 False start
ALL THE FIRST AND ALL THE LAST LETTERS ARE FALSE

WORDS AT PLAY
page 50

1 Dual Duel
1 Wholly/holy
2 Right/rite
3 Choose/chews
4 Desert/dessert
5 Links/lynx
6 Slow/sloe
7 Suede/swayed
8 Furze/firs
9 Ball/bawl
10 Strait/straight
11 Pact/packed
12 Assent/ascent
13 Maid/made
14 Foul/fowl
15 Maize/maze
16 Banned/band
17 Lax/lacks
18 Course/coarse
19 Hew/hue
20 Laud/lord

'Ologies'
1 i 2 j 3 p 4 n 5 g 6 t
7 m 8 s 9 a 10 q 11 h
12 e 13 b 14 c 15 r 16 o
17 l 18 f 19 d 20 k

Hidden Countries
1 Iran, Vietnam
2 Malta, India
3 Sweden, Lebanon
4 Panama, Spain
5 Tonga, Togo
6 Lesotho, Ghana
7 Dahomey, Nepal
8 Peru, Uganda
9 Chad, Andorra
10 Gabon, Mali

4 Alphabetic Extractions
1 Evergreen
2 Rhythm
3 Minimum
4 Quinquireme
5 Anagram
6 Nineteen
7 Gargling
8 Wigwam
9 Cyclic
10 Puppies
11 Kinky
12 Gypsy
13 Success
14 Xerxes
15 Thirty
16 Fanfare
17 Evasive
18 Suburb
19 Horror
20 Liable
21 Jazzy
22 Damned
23 Ululate
24 Jejune
25 Voodoo
26 Ironic

TIME FOR TANGRAMS
page 52

page 54

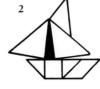

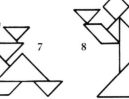

THE FOOD OF LOVE
page 55

1 **a** German
  b American
  c French
  d German
  e Polish
  f Bavarian
  g German
  h British
  i Russian
  j Hungarian
  k German
  l Austrian
  m British
  n French
  o Austrian
  p American
  q Russian
  r German
2 **a** Rossini
  b Elgar
  c Leoncavallo
  d Weber
  e Wagner
  f Rimsky-Korsakov
  g Purcell
  h Beethoven
  j Offenbach
  k Glinka
  l Walton
3 **a** Mendelssohn
  b Robert Schumann
  c Chopin
  d Greig
  e Schubert
4 **a** Debussy
  b Rachmaninov
  c Chopin
  d Mussorgsky
  e Mendelssohn
  f Chopin

FAIR AND SQUARE
page 56

1 S A G E S
  A D A G E
  G A U G E
  E G G E D
  S E E D Y

2 O P A L S
  P E T A L
  A T O N E
  L A N C E
  S L E E T

3 7 and 12 must be interchanged

4

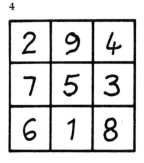

6 There are 23 in all:
apple, banana, citrange,
cob, coconut, cranberry,
fig, gooseberry, lemon,
lichee, lime, mango, melon,
nut, orange, peach, pear,
pineapple, plum,
pomegranate, quince,
redcurrant, strawberry.

And this is where they are:

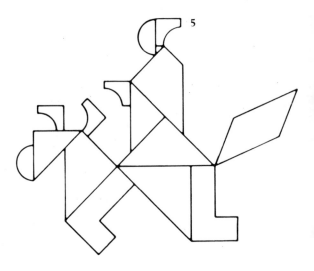

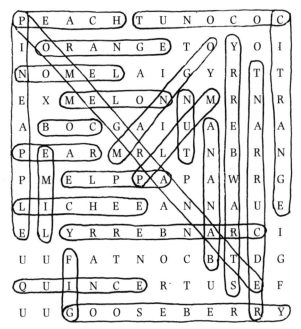

28

VERSE AND WORSE
page 58

1 The four men were musicians and played their instruments for payment.

2 *When I was young and in my prime, I could eat a muffin any time. But now I'm old and going grey, It takes me nearly half a day.*

3 Crust, Ace, e'e, eh?
= *Crustacea*

4 G u f f a W

   L a s s   O

   O r d e R

   W i g w a M

5 BANK WET = BANQUET

29

IN FOR A SPELL
page 59

1 The following were spelt incorrectly:
rhythm
sacrilegious
perseverance
staccato
iridescent
occurrence
supersede
parallelogram
ecstasy
accommodate
harassment
rarefy
apocryphal
gauge
manageable
besiege
disappointment
battalion
weird
definitely
irresistible
diphtheria

2 a Anaesthesia
  b Cacophony
  c Chronology
  d Dubious
  e Ellipse
  f Forfeit
  g Frequency

h Furore
i Idiosyncrasy
j Neurohypnology
k Adjournment
l Vicious

3 1 Daughters-in-law
  2 Attorneys general
  3 Brigadier generals
  4 Judge advocates
  5 Chargés d'affaires
  6 Potatoes
  7 Notaries public
  8 Laws merchant
  9 Opera
  10 Pelves
  11 Sergeants major
  12 Teaspoonfuls
  13 Piccolos
  14 Tables d'hôte
  15 Courts-martial
  16 Paymasters general
  17 Messrs.
  18 Mesdames
  19 Crises
  20 Men-of-war
  21 Lieutenant colonels
  22 Banditti or bandits
  23 Cannon
  24 Phenomena
  25 Aviatrixes
  26 Menservants
  27 Oboes
  28 Oxen
  29 Valets de chambre
  30 Data

30

MIXED BAG
page 60

1 $0 = 4 + 4 - 4 - 4$
$1 = 44/44$
$2 = (4/4) + (4/4)$
$3 = (4 + 4 + 4)/4$
$4 = 4 + (4 \times (4 - 4))$
$5 = \dfrac{(4 \times 4) + 4}{4}$
$6 = \dfrac{4 + 4}{4} + 4$
$7 = (44/4) - 4$
$8 = 4 + 4 + 4 - 4$
$9 = 4 + 4 + (4/4)$
$10 = (44 - 4)/4$

5 (word search grid with F I V E)

2 Wellington

3 50 pence and 5 pence piece. One of the coins isn't a 50 pence piece, but the other is.

4 1 ton
250 centimetres
3 raised to the 5th power
Zero degrees Centigrade
Inches in a kilometre
−40 degrees Centigrade and −40 degrees Fahrenheit are equally cold.

6 There are several ways. Here are three:
  a Orientals, latrines, nastier, satire, irate, tear, rat, at, a.
  b Orientals, relations, elation, entail, alien, nail, nil, in, I.
  c Orientals, entrails, salient, saline, leans, seal, sea, as, a.

7 'Chess is a foolish expedient for making idle people believe they are doing something very clever, when they are only wasting their time.'

8 $17531908 + 7088062 = 24619970$

9 Cater, certain, crate, crater, erect, erection, inter, nicer, niece, reactions, recant, recite, resin, sinter, siren, trace, trice. These are all shown in the diagram.

217

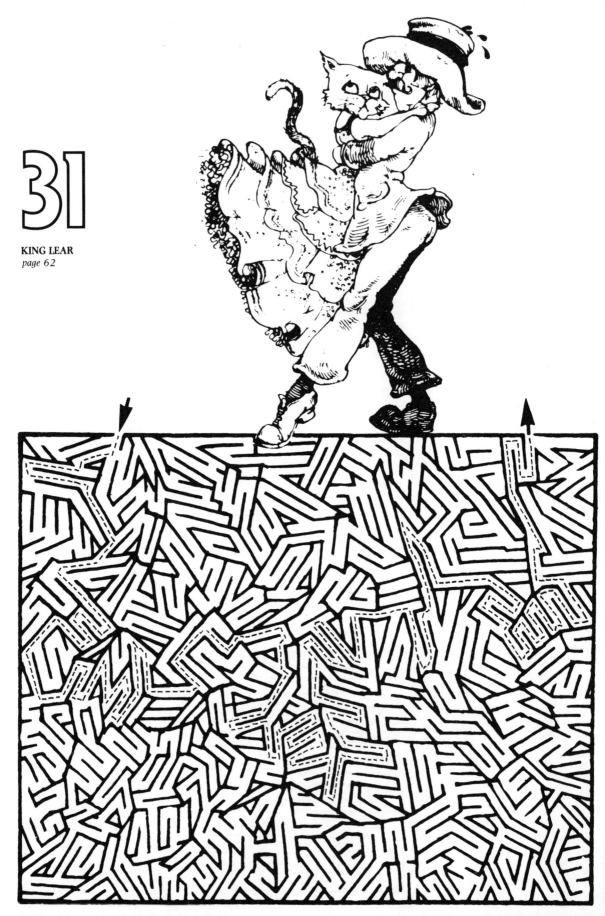

31

KING LEAR
page 62

OUT OF SHAPE
page 64
1

2

3

4

5 14 triangles
6 Yes, the tiles would fit
  together if placed in vertical
  rows with every other row
  inverted

MENSA GYMNASTICS
page 66

1 The answer is C. These are Binary numbers
◻ =1   ● =0
inside=least significant digit. Binary 1000=8=C

2 The groups give the number of curved lines and of straight lines in the capital letters A to G. Answer A

3 Answer C. Count the number of terminations – 0, 1, 2, 3, etc. C has 7

4 Answer D, the letter A. The letters order is of the descending squares, i.e. y=25th letter (5) Q=16th letter (4) and so on

5 Answer F. It is the only "stable" figure – not "falling over". The series is – "1 stable, 2 unstable" figures repeated

6 Answer D
Letters outside= plus letters inside= minus
+2−3=−1
−3+4=+1
−1+1=0

7 Answer 16–17. The line followed the pattern turn right – turn left – turn left, repeated except at 16/17 there are two right turns together

FLY THE FLAG
page 68

1 Jamaica
2 Brazil
3 Taiwan (Republic of China)
4 Maldive Is.
5 Bahrain
6 Panama
7 Cuba
8 Thailand
9 Mauritius
10 Lebanon
11 Canada
12 Greece
13 India
14 Cyprus
15 Burma
16 Argentina
17 Honduras
18 St. Lucia
19 South Yemen
20 Pakistan
21 Japan
22 Barbados
23 (Kingdom of) Yemen
24 Central African Republic

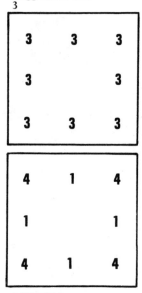

NUMBER CLASSICS
page 70

1 12 square miles
2 Give the last person an egg on the dish.
3

3	3	3
3		3
3	3	3

4	1	4
1		1
4	1	4

4 275625 leaves
5 £1 each. There were 3 people: a grandfather, father and son.
6 3 animals
7 126
8 72 persons
9   39
      12
      —
      78
      39
      —
      468
      —
10 2513.28 square yards
11 A 13 times; B 8 times
12

13 Represent the whale's length by 1. The body is $\frac{1}{2}$ of the length. The tail is 6ft+($\frac{1}{2}$+$\frac{1}{2}$). The length of the head is 6ft.
$1-\frac{1}{2}=\frac{1}{2}$, the rest of the length, consisting of (6ft+6ft)+($\frac{1}{2}$+$\frac{1}{2}$). If 12ft=$\frac{1}{4}$, the rest of the length, then invert $\frac{1}{4}$ to 4/1 and multiply by 12, giving you the whale's length at 48 feet.

14 15

15 A camel lives 75 years, a carp 150, a cat 15, a dog 17, an elephant 300, a chicken 18, a horse 30, an ox 21, a guinea pig 15, a stork 100, and a whale 400 years.
The toal amounts to 1,141 years.

16 In 2$\frac{1}{2}$ hours

17 Originally B had 24, and finally 72. Which was the original number of geese owned by A.

18 You can see 12 dozen or 144 apples and couldn't see 36 dozen or 432 apples, therefore, there is a total of 576 apples that you have or 48 dozen.

19 A will get 2,500 pennies, B 1,500 and C 700 pennies.

20 5×7, or 35 ways in which to choose.

21 The upper piece is 31 feet, the middle 47 feet and the lower 22 feet long.

22 Assuming the tail weighs 9 pounds and $\frac{1}{3}$ of the body's weight, then 3 times 9 would represent the body's weight of 27 pounds. The weight of the head would be the difference of 27 pounds and 9 pounds, giving you 18 pounds as the weight of its head, so the whole fish weighs 45 pounds.

23 15
24 36 feet
25 80 miles 1587 yards.

TRUE OR FALSE
page 72
83 of the statements are true.
Seventeen of them are false:
 1 Cat gut comes from sheep.
 8 The gestation period of a
   rhinoceros is 560 days.
23 There are at least
   100,000 million stars in
   the Milky Way.
24 It was in 1804.
36 There is no Heaven in
   Norway, but there is a
   place there called Hell!
42 It's totally untrue!
58 No, it weighs 10 lb.
64 Not at four months, but
   certainly at four years.
71 In 1848 Karl Marx was
   working in London, but as
   a journalist not a circus
   clown.
75 At least 845 different
   dialects are spoken in
   India.
80 There is no evidence to
   support this slander!
84 No, it weighs more like
   $1\frac{3}{4}$ lb.
85 Not so: the duck-billed
   platypus has.
90 It's totally untrue.
96 No he didn't.
98 It's totally untrue.
100 It's totally untrue.

WATCH THE BIRDIE
page 76
 1 Great Northern Diver
 2 Grey-lag Goose
 3 Shelduck
 4 Gannet
 5 Tufted Duck
 6 Water Rail
 7 Avocet
 8 Little Gull
 9 Common Sandpiper
10 Whimbrel
11 Raven
12 Ring-Ouzel
13 Nightjar
14 Tree Sparrow
15 Starling

HIDE AND SEEK
page 78

2 Zoo Quest

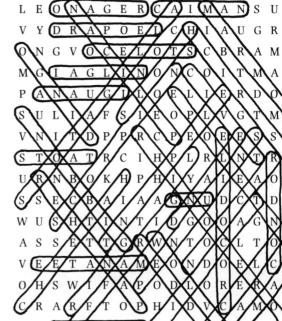

1

```
    O W O T O T O T O T
  T T O O W O W O O W O O
  W O W O T O W O T O T T W
  W O O T           T O W O
                    W O T W
                    W W O O
                    T W T W
                  W O W W O
                T O O O W
              T O T W W
            T O W O W
          T T T O W
        O W O T T
      T W T W T
    W T O T O
  W O W W W
  W O T O T T O W O W O W W
  T O W O W O O T T W T W T
  W O T W W O O O W O W O O
```

```
        T R E E T H
        T H R R E E R T
      R H E E T H R T R E
      H T E E H E R T H E E R
      T H E R T H E E R T H E
                        E R T E
                        T R E E

        R E H T E R E H T
      T R E E E H R E H T
      T H R T E R H E R
      E T H E R E E H T
        T H T E E R E T H
                    T E T
                    H R E E
      T E E T H R E H T H R E
      R T E T H R E T R T T H
      R H E T T R E E T H
        T H E R T E T E
          T E T H R E
```

222

HEADS OR TAILS?
page 80

1 Move 4 to touch 5 and 6
Move 5 to touch 1 and 2
Move 1 to touch 5 and 4

2

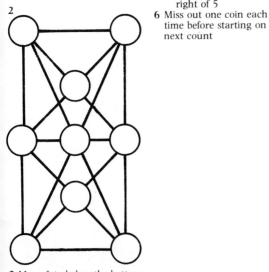

3 Move 1 to below the bottom row and place it between and under 8 and 9
Move 7 up two rows and place it to the left of 2
Move 10 up two rows and place it to the right of 3

4

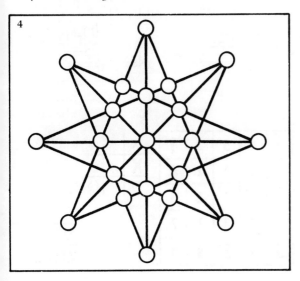

5 Move coins 1 and 2 to the right of 6
Move coins 6 and 1 to the right of 2
Move coins 3 and 4 to the right of 5

6 Miss out one coin each time before starting on the next count

MISSING NUMBERS
page 82

1 19. Vertical pattern applies to each row. Add first and second numbers and subtract six to get bottom numbers $(7+9-6=10)$

2 28. Vertical pattern applies to consecutive pairs only. Divide first number by seven to get second number $(14 \div 7 = 2)$

3 32. Horizontal pattern applies to consecutive pairs only. Reverse digits of first number and add five to get second number $(12 + 5 = 17)$

4 102. Horizontal pattern applies to each row. First number is added to itself to get second number. It is added again to get third number $(19 + 19 = 38 + 19 = 57)$

5 24. Starting at the right, double top number and subtract one to get the bottom number $(5 \times 2 = 10 - 1 = 9)$; then double next number and subtract 2 etc

6 2. Horizontal pattern applies to consecutive pairs only. Second digit of first number is divided by first digit of first number to obtain second number $(6 \div 1 = 6)$

7 9. Pattern applies to horizontal lines only. Sum of outside numbers is equal to the sum of inside numbers $(101 + 1 = 102; 47 + 55 = 102)$

8 43. Starting with smallest number, multiply each number by three and subtract five to get next number $(3 \times 3 = 9 - 5 = 4)$.

9 36. All numbers are multiplied by 9

10 360. Horizontal pattern applies to entire puzzle. First number multiplied by one to get second number. Second number multiplied by two to get third number etc $(3 \times 1; 3 \times 2 = 6)$

'... THAT IS THE QUESTION'
page 84

1 Antony & Cleopatra *IV.xiv.*18
2 King Lear *V.ii.*9
3 Richard III *IV.iii.*12
4 The Merchant of Venice *IV.i.*184
5 A Midsummer Night's Dream *II.i.*175
6 Much Ado About Nothing *II.i.*184
7 The Two Gentlemen of Verona *IV.ii.*40
8 The Winter's Tale *III.iii.*58
9 Romeo and Juliet *I.v.*142
10 The Taming of the Shrew *II.i.*38
11 The Tempest *V.i.*183
12 Titus Andronicus *IV.iv.*82
13 Troilus and Cressida *III.iii.*165
14 Othello *I.iii.*208
15 Othello *II.iii.*264
16 The Merry Wives of Windsor *III.ii.*19
17 The Merchant of Venice *IV.i.*223
18 Measure for Measure *II.ii.*117
19 Macbeth *V.v.*17
20 King John *V.vii.*112

A RIOT OF REBUSES
page 86

1 *A Tale of Two Cities*
2 In D, A=India
3 Partner-ship
  Lady-ship
4 a Europe *U rope*
  b Asia *Ace-see-A*
  c America *A merry K*
5 a Embed
  b Detail
  c Deface
6 Capitalists
7 *Under Milk Wood*
8 *An N in ME*=enemy
9 a Intend
  d I understand you
  c Never a cross word
  d Upsidedown
  e Insecure
  f Man overslept
10 a Sea Serpent
  b *U nigh corn* – unicorn
11 a Tench
  b Carp
  c Dace
12 a The Seven Seas
  b one in a million
  c Unfinished Symphony
  d not before time
  e Long Island
  f Lover come back to me
  g tin-opener
  h six-shooters

SUITABLY PUZZLING
page 88

1 Entrance **B** is the only one
  that leads to the centre

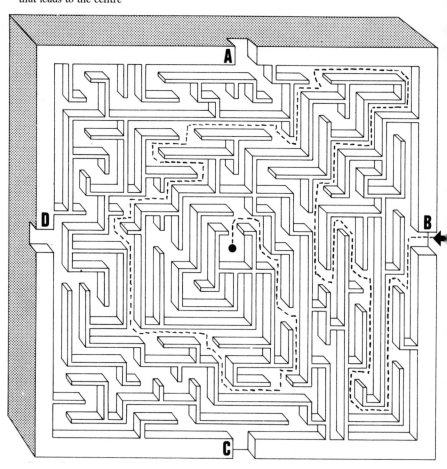

2 i C+D
  ii D+E+F
  iii B+D+E
3 There are 27 squares in
  the figure

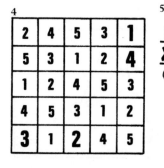

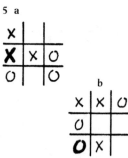

A MAN'S RAG
page 90

1. Administration
2. Calculate
3. Instigate
4. Panorama
5. Destination
6. Conglomerate
7. Kleptomania
8. Estimation
9. Ornithological
10. Malevolent
11. Catalogues
12. Punishment
13. Desperation
14. Remuneration
15. Steamer
16. Waitress
17. Upholsterers
18. Hustlers
19. Softheartedness
20. Hearthstones
21. Indomitableness
22. Misrepresentation
23. Therapeutics
24. Degradedness
25. Disconsolate
26. Families
27. Desegregation
28. Measured
29. Prosecutors
30. Supernaturalisms
31. Endearments
32. Incomprehensibles
33. Steaminess
34. Twinges
35. Villainousness
36. Militarism
37. Misfortune
38. Legislation
39. Infection
40. Filled
41. Anarchists
42. Violence
43. Funeral
44. Protectionism

METRIC MIXTURE
page 91

1. Let **x** equal the length of each necklace the jeweller made, and **y** equal the number of necklaces; the total length of the chain he bought equals the length of each necklace times the number of necklaces, **xy**. This total length remains the same, whether he makes a greater number of shorter necklaces: $(x-5)(y+2)$ or a smaller number of longer necklaces: $(x+10)(y-3)$. By setting each of these alternatives equal to the original xy and simplifying, we can solve for both the length of each necklace he made – 50 centimetres – and the number he made – 18 – which multiplies out to a 9 metre long piece of chain

2. The least number of pourings which will divide the milk into exactly equal 1-litre portions is 7. The chart shows the seven pourings and the amount left in each container after the pouring:

Pourings	Containers		
	ml.	ml.	ml.
	750	1250	2000
Start	0	0	2000
1	0	1250	750
2	750	500	750
3	0	500	1500
4	500	0	1500
5	500	1250	250
6	750	1000	250
7	0	1000	1000

3. The important part of this problem is to remember how we stand books on a shelf.
The first page of volume one is indicated by the left arrow, and the last page of volume 6 by the right arrow. Beginning and ending at these points the worm passes through 10 covers totalling 30 millimetres, and 4 texts totalling 12 centimetres, for a completed journey of 15 centimetres.

4. The tailor cut the 4×9 centimetre piece into two *L*-shaped sections as shown left, and stitched them together as shown right.

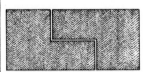

5. By dividing the distance the light must travel by the speed of light, we find that the second astronomer should come back in 1.28 seconds.

6. The magician folded the sheet of paper in half and made cuts reaching almost across the whole width of the paper alternating from side to side. When the paper is opened up it makes a very large loop, big enough to climb through.

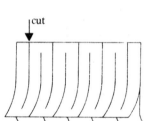

7. The two engines are moving towards each other at 230 kilometres per hour, the total of their individual speeds, so it will take $1\frac{1}{2}$ hours to cover the distance between them.

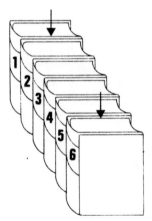

LETTER BY LETTER
page 92

1 uncomplimentary
  unnoticeably
  subcontinental
2 strengths
3 uncopyrightable
4 pti – placing an O before
  and after each of the
  others results in a valid
  word or name
5 rhythms
6 defencelessness
7 boldface
  feedback
8 indivisibilities
9 all the words in the list
  can be reduced by one
  letter at a time (from
  front or back) and form
  complete words all the
  way to a one letter word
  – for example, *brandy*,
  brand, *bran*, *ran*, *an*, *a*.
10 overnervousness
11 teepee
  voodoo
  assess
  muumuu
12 dreamt
13 horrendous
  stupendous
  hazardous
  tremendous
14 palladous
  vanadous
  iodous
  ˉnodous
15 eel, eerie
  llama, llano
  oodles, ooze
16 aitch
17 r
  ar
  the canine letter
  the dog's letter
  littera canina
18 w
19 ushers
  (*us, she, he, her, hers*)
20 smithery
  (*he, her, hers, him, his, I,
  it, its, me, my, she, their,
  theirs, them, they, thy, ye*).
21 valve – replacing the
  second v with a u leads
  to value
22 hijklmno
  milk and *John*
23 understudy
  superstuff
  overstuffs

24 the plurals of rhinoceros
  are:
  rhinoceroses
  rhinoceri
  rhinocerotes
  and *rhinoceros*
25 adventurers
  impersonate
  retaliations
  interpolates
  misinterpreted
26 *zenzizenzizenzic*
  meaning 'in mathematics,
  the square of a square of
  a square'
27 beginning with *cold*, shift
  each of the four letters
  three spaces along the
  alphabet; thus:
  c becomes f
  o becomes r
  l becomes o
  and d becomes g
  cold thus becomes *frog*
28 queueing
  cooeeing
29 *proprietory, proterotype* and
  rupturewort are eleven-
  letter specimens.
  prettypretty is a twelve-
  letter specimen found
  only in the *Century
  Dictionary*
30 *flagfalls* and *galagalas* are
  nine-letter specimens;
  Khalakhkha is a ten-letter
  specimen
31 *bzzzbzzz* is slang for gossip
  or idle talk
32 *higglehaggled* is a 13-letter
  specimen;
  Hamamelidaceae is a
  14-letter specimen, a
  family of shrubs and
  trees.
33 *echoic* – an anagram
  effected merely by moving
  the last letter of *choice* to
  the beginning.
34 *poppyworts, prosupport,
  puttyroots, synsporous,*
  and *zoosporous* are five
  ten-letter specimens
35 billowy
36 spoon-fed
37 each can take an s either
  at the beginning or end
  so as to form a new word
38 the odd letters spell the
  word *tinily* and the even
  letters spell the word *renal*
39 indicatory.

MOVIOLA
page 94
The Film of the Book
1 Hitchcock's *The Lady
  Vanishes* (1938)
2 *Village of the Damned*
3 *The Pride and the Passion*
4 *Behold a Pale Horse*
5 *Crossfire*
6 *The Old Dark House*
7 *The Mark of Zorro*
8 *Bullitt*
9 *The Best Years of Our Lives*
10 *Seven Brides for Seven
  Brothers*
11 *Topkapi*
12 *Stagecoach*
13 *The Professionals*
14 *The Pajama Game*
15 *It Happened One Night*
16 *The Inn of the Sixth
  Happiness*
17 *The Heiress*
18 *Foreign Correspondent*
19 *Sabotage* (US title: *A
  Woman Alone*). When he
  made this film in 1937,
  Hitchcock was unable to
  use the original title, as
  only the previous year he
  had made a quite different
  film called *Secret Agent*.
20 *Dr Strangelove*
21 Hitchcock's *Spellbound*
22 *White Cargo*
23 Hitchcock's *Young and
  Innocent (The Girl was
  Young)*
24 Hitchcock's *Stage Fright*
25 *Bad Day at Black Rock*
26 *The Fallen Idol*
The Animal Kingdom
1 *Dragon Seed*
2 *Cry Wolf*
3 *The Fallen Sparrow*
4 *A Gathering of Eagles*
5 *Flying Elephants* (with
  Laurel and Hardy) or
  Flying Tigers (with John
  Wayne)
6 *After the Fox*
7 *Poor Cow*
8 *Brother Rat*
9 *Horse Feathers*
10 *The Spider's Stratagem*
11 *The Rabbit Trap*
12 *Track of the Cat*
13 *The Flight of the Phoenix*
14 *The Sleeping Tiger*
15 *Dear Octopus*
16 *Straw Dogs*
17 *Madame Butterfly*

18 *Eagle Squadron* or
  Dragonfly Squadron
19 *The Voice of the Turtle*
Who Said That?
1 David Niven describing
  his profession in interview.
2 Director Michael Curtiz,
  whose command of
  English was somewhat
  haphazard, is alleged to
  have issued this
  instruction during the
  location filming of *The
  Charge of the Light Brigade*
  (1936).
3 An oft-repeated line (by
  Sig Roman and Jack
  Benny) in Lubitsch's *To
  Be or Not To Be* (1942).
4 Walter Abel as the
  harassed editor in Wilder's
  Arise My Love (1940).
  The line became some-
  thing of a catch-phrase in
  the forties.
5 Shirley Booth's intro-
  duction to *The Matchmaker*
  (1957).
6 Alfred Hitchcock,
  invariably, when asked
  what, if anything, scared
  him.
7 Ingrid Bergman to Paul
  Henried in *Casablanca*
  (1942).
8 Bernard Shaw, allegedly,
  to Samuel Goldwyn when
  they were trying to
  negotiate terms for the
  filming of Shaw's plays.
9 Tony Curtis in *The Black
  Shield of Falworth* (1954).
  His Brooklyn accent was
  derided: he was playing
  an English nobleman.
10 Walter Huston's advice
  to his son John.
12 Cary Grant to James
  Stewart (speaking about
  Henry Daniell) in *The
  Philadelphia Story* (1940).
13 Everett Sloane speaking of
  old age in *Citizen Kane*
  (1941).
14 From the suicide note of
  Jean Harlow's husband,
  Paul Bern. What he
  meant has never been
  ascertained.
15 An instruction from D.W.
  Griffith during the filming
  of *The Birth of a Nation*.

16 George Sanders as
Addison de Witt in *All
About Eve* (1950).
17 Howard Hughes' only
instructions to the staff of
RKO Studios which he
had just acquired.
18 The wireless message from
the other world in *Orphée*
(1949).
19 A comment by Richard
Rowland of Metro when
United Artists was taken
over by Chaplin, Pickford,
Fairbanks and Griffith.
20 Hunt Stromberg on taking
over the production of
Flaherty's *White Shadows
in the South Seas* (1928).
21 Gig Young as MC of the
marathon dance contest
in *They Shoot Horses,
Don't They?* (1970).
22 Hattie McDaniel as the
black mammy in *The
Great Lie* (1941).
23 Katharine Hepburn of
Spencer Tracy in *The State
of the Union*.
24 The slogan that won the
all-important competition
in *Christmas in July*.
25 Eddie 'Rochester'
Anderson on a 1970 TV
show, when asked once
again to play Jack Benny's
manservant.

Nicknames
1 Marie McDonald
2 Clara Bow
3 Ann Sheridan
4 Florence Lawrence
5 Veronica Lake (from her
hair-do which covered
one eye)
6 Buddy Rogers (in 1928)
7 Laurel and Hardy
8 Mary Pickford
9 Brigitte Bardot
10 Lizabeth Scott
11 John Barrymore
12 Jean Harlow
13 Luise Rainer
14 Joan Crawford
15 Jeanette Macdonald
16 Nelson Eddy
17 Tom Mix
18 Erich von Stroheim
19 D. W. Griffith, *or* (more in
the theatre) Noel Coward
20 Monty Woolley
21 Lon Chaney Senior

22 Pola Negri
23 Norma Shearer
24 Elissa Landi
25 John Wayne
26 John Barrymore
(especially for *Don Juan*,
1927)
27 Lon Chaney Junior
28 George Arliss
29 Clark Gable
30 Francis X. Bushman
31 Charles 'Buddy' Rogers
32 Marie Dressler
33 Jessie Matthews
34 Silvana Pampanini

THE PUZZLES OF SAM LOYD
page 96
1 The 14–15 Puzzle
The original problem is impossible to solve except by such
skullduggery as turning the 6 and 9 blocks upside down. One
of the puzzle's peculiarities is that any such interchange,
involving two blocks, immediately converts the puzzle to a
solvable one. In fact, any odd number of interchanges has the
same effect, whereas an even number leaves the puzzle
unsolvable as before.
The other three problems are solved as follows:
44 moves are required to get the vacant square in the top
left-hand corner: 14, 11, 12, 8, 7, 6, 10, 12, 8, 7, 4, 3, 6, 4,
7, 14, 11, 15, 13, 9, 12, 8, 4, 10, 8, 4, 14, 11, 15, 13, 9,
12, 4, 8, 5, 4, 8, 9, 13, 14, 10, 6, 2, 1.
39 moves are required to solve the third problem: 14, 15, 10,
6, 7, 11, 15, 10, 13, 9, 5, 1, 2, 3, 4, 8, 12, 15, 10, 13, 9, 5,
1, 2, 3, 4, 8, 12, 15, 14, 13, 9, 5, 1, 2; 3, 4, 8, 12.
The magic square can be produced in fifty moves: 12, 8, 4, 3,
2, 6, 10, 9, 13, 15, 14, 12, 8, 4, 7, 10, 9, 14, 12, 8, 4, 7, 10,
9, 6, 2, 3, 10, 9, 6, 5, 1, 2, 3, 6, 5, 3, 2, 1, 13, 14, 3, 2, 1,
13, 14, 3, 12, 15, 3.

2 A Horse of Another Colour
The black pieces of paper are nothing but a delusion and a
snare. The pieces are placed to make a little white horse in
the centre as shown. Hence, the name of the puzzle – *A Horse
of Another Colour!*

3 False Weights
If the broker weighed the goods with a pound weight one
ounce too heavy, he got 17 ounces for a pound. When he
sold them by weight one ounce light, he gave 15 ounces for
a pound, and had two ounces over. If these two ounces were
sold at the same price, so as to make 25 dollars by cheating,
it is plain that the two ounces represent 2/15 of what he paid
for the whole and charged for the 15 ounces. One-fifteenth
being worth 12.50 dollars, fifteen-fifteenths, or the whole,
would be 187.50 dollars, which, if there was no question of
commission, would be what he paid for the goods.
We find, however, that he received 2 per cent from the seller,
3.75 dollars, and 4.25 dollars from the purchaser, making 8
dollars brokerage in addition to 25 dollars, by cheating. Now,
if he had dealt honesty, he would have paid for 17 ounces,
which, to be exact, would have been 199.21875 dollars. His
brokerage for buying and selling would therefore only be
7.96875 dollars, so he has made an additional 3 and one-
eighth cents by cheating. As the story said that he made
exactly 25 dollars by cheating, we must reduce the 187.50
dollars price so that his two cheatings will amount to just
25 dollars.
Now, as 3 and one-eighth cents is exactly 1/801st part of
25.03125 dollars, we must reduce 187.50 dollars by its
1/801st part, which will bring it down to 187.27 dollars, so
that he will make just 25 dollars and the 0.0006 of a cent by
cheating. To such as wish to be very exact, I would suggest
that the seller be paid 187.2659176029973125 less the 2
per cent brokerage of 3.745 dollars plus.

4 The Mixed-up Hats
The probability that not one of the six men will get his own
hat is 265/720, or 0.36805556. This is arrived at as follows.
The number of ways that n hats can be taken at random
without a person getting his own hat is:
$$n! \, (1 - 1/1! + 1/2! - 1/3! + 1/4! \ldots + 1/n!)$$
This over factorial n (the total number of ways the hats can
be selected) gives the answer. As n increases, the answer
approaches closer and closer to $1/e$ as a limit, thus providing
a curious empirical technique for calculating the
transcendental number e.

DEFINITIVELY
page 98

1
N I M B L E
O R D E A L
V A L I S E
E R O T I C
M A R K E T
B A N Z A I
E M B R Y O
R O T T E N

2
C A L L O W
H Y A E N A
E N T E R S
R E L I S H
R A S H T I
Y E O M A N
T R Y I N G
R O C K E T
E S C U D O
E N S I G N

3
F L O R A
L I T E R
O P T I C
A B A S H
T U T T I
A B E A M
T A S T E
I L I A D
O L I V E
N E S T S

4
J U D G E D
E S T A T E
F A T H O M
F R E S C O
E X O T I C
R A N G E R
S A L I V A
O X Y L I C
N O B O D Y

LITERARY LAPSES
page 100

1 *Power* **tends** *to corrupt and absolute power corrupts absolutely.*
2 *. . . in want of a* **wife.**
3 *. . . the beginning of* **fairies.**
4 *One here will* **constant** *be . . .*
5 *How to* **Win** *Friends . . .*
6 *. . . beware the* **Jub jub** *bird . . .
. . . Come to my arms, my* **beamish** *boy!*
7 *And time* **future** *contained in time past.*
8 *. . . and Galileo, and* **Newton** *. . .*
9 *. . . you may use any* **language** *you choose . . .*
10 *. . . to move immediately* **upon your works.**
11 *The last time I saw* **Paris**
12 *The heathen* **Chinee** *is peculiar . . .*
13 *Here of a* **Sunday** *morning . . .*
14 *We hold these truths to be sacred and undeniable; that all men are created equal and* **independent,** *that from that equal creation they derive rights inherent and inalienable, among which are the* **preservation of life, and liberty, and the pursuit of happiness.**
15 *There's plenty of* **boys** *. . .*
16 *. . . that round the* **thatch-eaves** *run.*
17 *. . . Daughter of the Moon, Nokomis . . .*
18 *In this* **Kingdom** *by the sea . . .*
19 *. . . Flopsy, Mopsy,* **Cottontail,** *and Peter.*
20 **Weep** *and you* **weep** *alone . . .*

PERFECTLY PERPLEXING
page 102

1 a The saucer weighs four ounces
  b Jane spent twelve pence
  c The clock would show the right time at 7.06

2

3 16 routes
4 80 cents

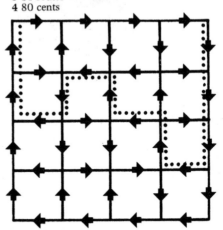

5 Nine fire stations

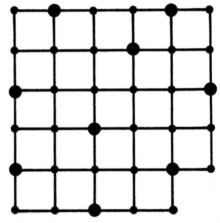

228

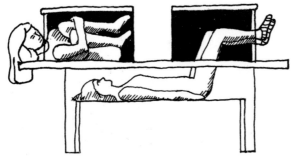

MIXED BLESSINGS
page 104

Just for the Birds!
The 20 birds:
Canary, chaffinch, cormorant, crow, cuckoo, duck, emu, gull, hen, kite, kiwi, kookaburra, merganser, nightingale, owl, pigeon, rook, swan, teal, tit.

This is where to find them:

Poor But Honest
1 So no one will ever find him out.
2 Because he's candid.
3 Chessmen.
4 Because he follows you only in sunshine.
5 Because it has no scruples.
5 Because the best of them are all meer-schaums.
7 Ad-vice.
8 Time out of mind.
9 Because the heads were on the wrong end.
10 Spending one's last penny on a purse.
11 Because he is equal to any post.
12 Because his head prevents him going too far.
13 Milestones, you never see two together.
14 The air.
15 A paying one.
16 Because nothing satisfies him.
17 None, because they were all copycats.
18 Sarcasm.
19 Through the customhouse.
20 Look on the bed for a comforter.
21 Give them chairs and let them sit down.
22 When she becomes a little bolder.
23 It is better not to get into a stew.

Find Fourteen Words
LEVER-REVEL
LEPER-REPEL
DEVIL-LIVED
DRAWS-SWARD
LIAR-RAIL
ROOD-DOOR
MOOD-DOOM

Dated Look
1 A walking dress of 1899
2 The *'New Look'* of 1947

Houdunnit
The great Houdini reveals all: *'The secret is that there are really two secrets. The innocent-looking table you are watching seems to have the usual narrow top but if you look closely at it you will see a thin line painted round it in a bright colour. Your eyes concentrated on that thin line and so did not notice the rest of the table's thickness which, in fact, is the thickness of a girl's body! Which brings me to the other secret. In the table itself is hidden a second girl who, once the box is constructed on the table, will lift her legs up through a panel in the bottom of the box and push her feet through the hole at one end of the box. When the two halves of the box are moved apart, her half will not be moved much, just slid about on the table top. And all the while she will thus be able to wiggle her feet.*

The other half of the sawn box contains the entire other girl, the one who you saw stepping into the box in the first place, and she has drawn up her legs to squeeze into the smallest area possible. So her half can be moved about anywhere, taken any distance away from the other half of the box.

You were mystified as to how her feet were able to wave to the separated top half of her body, weren't you? Now you know — because they weren't her feet!'

PLAY AT WORDS
page 106

1 Catchwords
1 Cataract
2 Ducat
3 Catsup
4 Locate
5 Catamaran
6 Vacate
7 Scatter
8 Catapult
9 Decathlon
10 Indicate
11 Secateurs
12 Advocate
13 Unscathed
14 Catastrophe
15 Implicate
16 Intricate

2 O What A Lovely Word
1 h 2 l 3 e 4 n 5 o 6 j
7 m 8 p 9 a 10 r 11 f
12 b 13 t 14 k 15 g 16 s
17 i 18 d 19 c 20 q

3 Girls Wanted
1 Bigamy
2 Kayaks
3 Armada
4 Saracen
5 Summary
6 Jejune
7 Almanac
8 Dilemma
9 Truthful
10 Patella
11 Bandanna
12 Veracity
13 Satirist
14 Plethora
15 Adorable
16 Pregnancy
17 Spherical
18 Harmonica
19 Vacillate
20 Paranormal
21 Cloistered
22 Universally
23 Declaration
24 Destination

4 Blank Verse
1 Glare, Regal, Large, Lager
2 Cretan, Nectar, Trance, Canter
3 Lemnos, Lemons, Solemn, Melons
4 Angered, Enraged, Grandee, Grenade

5 A Novel Anagram
A Farewell To Arms

6 Proverbial Anagram
A stitch in time saves nine

PUZZLES THROUGH THE LOOKING GLASS
page 108

1 One is\black, the other white
2 *a* 19 *b* The Easterly traveller 12,
the other 8
3 No. $1 = 5\frac{1}{2}$ lbs
No. $2 = 6\frac{1}{2}$ lbs
No. $3 = 7$ lbs
No. $4 = 4\frac{1}{2}$ lbs
No. $5 = 3\frac{1}{2}$ lbs
4 They went to the Bank of England:
one stood in front of it and the
other behind it!
5 The order is **M, L, Z**
6 $60 \times 60\frac{1}{2}$ yards
7 10 per cent
8 15 and 18
9 *In Shylock's bargain for the flesh was found*
No mention of the blood that flowed around:
So when the stick was sawed in pieces eight
The sawdust lost diminished from the weight.
10 60,000
11 Place 8 in the first, 10 in the second,
none in the third and 6 in the fourth.
10 is nearer ten than 8, nothing is
nearer ten than ten, 6 is nearer ten than
nothing, and 8 is nearer ten than 6.
12 Regardless of how the monkey climbs,
he and the weight will remain opposite.
13 One guest.
In this family tree males are denoted by
large letters and females by small ones.
The Governor is **E** and his guest is **C**.

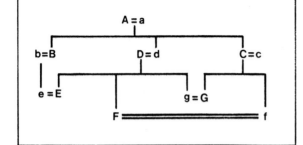

14 a The weight is sent down;
the empty basket comes up.
  b The son goes down,
the weight comes up.
  c The weight is taken out,
the daughter goes down,
the son up.
  d The son gets out,
the weight goes down,
the empty basket up.
  e The Queen goes down;
daughter and weight come up.
Daughter gets out.
  f The weight goes down,
empty basket up.
  g Son goes down,
weight comes up.
  h Daughter removes weight,
and goes down,
son comes up.
  i Son sends down weight,
empty basket comes up.
  j The son goes down,
weight comes up.
  k Son gets out.
the weight falls to the ground.

MATHEMATICAL MARVELS
page 110

1 The only way to score exactly
50 in three shots is to topple
first the 7 on the right, then
the 8 on the left hand pile
(which doubled gives you 16)
and finally the now exposed
9 on the right hand pile
(trebled gives you 27);
$23 + 27 = 50$
2

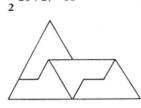

3 A rectangular piece of laminex
23in. × 9in. can be cut as
required with a wastage of
only 5in. The shaded area in
the diagram represents the
wastage.

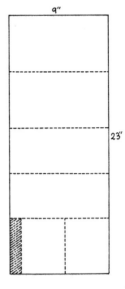

4 The Bath Towel and Face
Flannel should cost 25
coupons. If you were to take
the first and third offers the
total would be 50 coupons,
for which you would get one
of each article. According to
this the Hand and Guest
Towels, which she does not
want, come to 25 coupons.
Therefore the remaining two
must also come to 25 coupons.

ANTIQUARIAN EXCURSIONS
page 111

1 The rivers are: Dee, Tyne,
Wye, Tiber, Don, Seine.
They were reversed in the
sentences eg. '**see** de**scend**',
'**deny that**', etc.
2 a Are o's *Rose*
  b Pea ink *Pink*
  c Pan sigh *Pansy*
  d Lobe Elia *Lobelia*
  e Larks purr *Larkspur*
  f Bal sam *Balsam*
3 East or West, home is best
4 a (R)ash *ash*
  b Asp(h)en *aspen*
  c (Cr)oak *oak*
  d (H)elm *elm*
  e Pop(py), lar(k) *poplar*
  f (S)will, (sh)ow *willow*
  g P(ea), lane *plane*
  h Li(p), me(at) *lime*
  i Bee, ch(at) *beech*
  j Al(e), (fod)der *alder*
  k Map, le(g) *maple*
  l Pi(g), ne(t) *pine*
5 C A R T

  A L O E

  R O P E

  T E E S

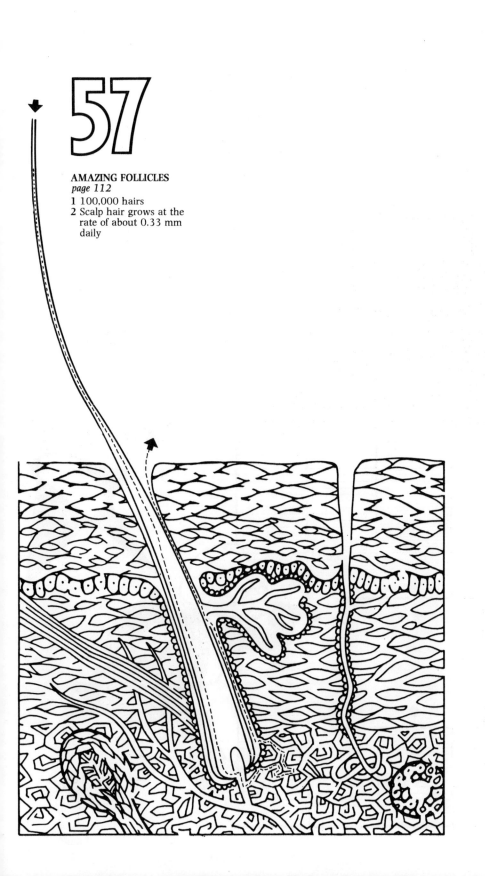

AMAZING FOLLICLES
page 112
1 100,000 hairs
2 Scalp hair grows at the
rate of about 0.33 mm
daily

FULL MARX
page 113
1 Remarks **a**, **c**, and **e** were
made by Karl Marx
(1818–83)
Remarks **b**, **d** and **f** were
made by Groucho Marx
(1890–1977)
2 You need the missing
vowels, because with them
you will have the titles of
six of the Marx Brothers
films: **Animal Crackers**,
Monkey Business, **Horse
Feathers**, **Duck Soup**,
A Night at the Opera and
A Day at the Races.

MOUNTAIN RETREAT
page 114
1 Pets of the Month
There remained five hamsters
worth £11 retail and two
parakeets worth £2.20 retail
– a combined value of
£13.20
2 Map Folding
Fold it in half, so that **4** is
under **1**, and **5** is under **2**.
Now fold this in half so that
1 and **8** are in front, and
2 and **3** are at the back.
Look 'inside' and bend **4** and **5**
round together to tuck them
between **6** and **3**. Finally
fold in half again
3 Seven Lines
The diagram shows how
seven lines can produce
eleven non-overlapping
triangles

60

4 Missing Persons

1 Vic	2 Ivan	3 Sam
4 Pat	5 Abe	6 Tom
7 Hal	8 Leo	9 Sid
10 Eric	11 Alan	12 Dan
13 Len	14 Carl	15 Emil
16 Ivor	17 Roy	18 Ian
19 Tim	20 Ray	

5 Animalgrams
1 Raccoon
2 Bearcat (also cat-bear)
3 Leopard
4 Terrier
5 Lioness
6 Samoyed
7 Echidna
8 Centaur
9 Spaniel
10 House rat
11 Carthorse
12 African lion

6 Magic and Antimagic
You will know whether you found a solution or not. This just proves it can be done

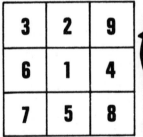

3	2	9
6	1	4
7	5	8

7 The Birds and the Trees
a fulmar, aspen
b yew, owl
c larch, robin
d cedar, heron
e elm, chough
f lime, hawk
g dove, pine
h grouse, ash

8 Quickies
1 The northernmost point of Eire
2 Sovereignty
3 Let a=2 and b=4
4 After eleven weeks
5 Episcopal
6 2 raised to the power of 333
7 The positive tenth root of 10. Raise each number to the 30th power to see clearly which is smaller

ANATOMICAL ATROCITIES
page 116

a Heart
b Two lungs
c Liver
d Spleen
e Kidneys
f Gall bladder
g Large intestine
h Small intestine
i Bladder

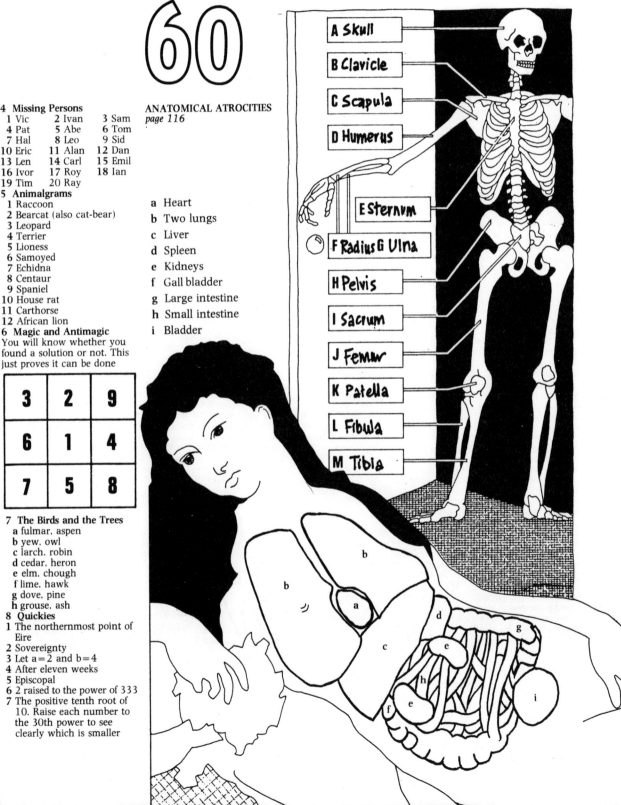

A Skull
B Clavicle
C Scapula
D Humerus
E Sternum
F Radius G Ulna
H Pelvis
I Sacrum
J Femur
K Patella
L Fibula
M Tibia

THAT'S LOGICAL
page 118

1

From **a** and **b**, if Adrian orders ham, Buford orders pork and Carter orders pork. This situation contradicts **c**. So Adrian orders only pork. Then from **b**, Carter orders only ham. So only Buford could have ordered ham yesterday, pork today.

2

From **i**, **iii** and **iv**, either Deb or Eve must be in the same age bracket as Ada and Cyd; so Ada and Cyd are under 30. From **vii**, Freeman will not marry Ada or Cyd. From **ii**, **v** and **vi**, either Cyd or Deb must have the same occupation as Bea and Eve; so Bea and Eve are secretaries. So from **vii** Freeman will not marry Bea or Eve. By elimination, Freeman will marry Deb, who must be over 30 and a teacher.

3

From **ii**, the doctor has an offspring among the five people; so the doctor can be anybody but the daughter's son. Also from **ii**, the patient has a parent among the five people; so the patient is either the daughter or the daughter's son. From **iiia**, if Mr Blank or his wife is the doctor, his daughter is not the patient; while if his daughter's husband or indeed daughter are the doctor, his daughter's son is not the patient. So one of the following must be the doctor-patient pair:

	DOCTOR		PATIENT
A	Mr Blank	....	his daughter's son
B	His wife	....	his daughter's son
C	His daughter	....	his daughter
D	His daughter's husband	....	his daughter

Pair C is eliminated from **i**. For pair A and pair B, the doctor's offspring is Mr Blank's daughter; but from **ii** the patient's older parent is also Mr Blank's daughter. This situation contradicts **iiib**; so pair A and pair B are eliminated. Pair D must be the correct pair and the doctor is the husband of Mr Blank's daughter. This conclusion is supported by the fact that the doctor's offspring and the patient's older parent can be different males, as required by **ii** and **iiib**.

4

The following chart shows the manner of Dana's death assuming each of statements **i** to **iii** is false.

Statement **i** – *If false: murder, but not by Bill*
Statement **ii** – *If false: murder by Bill*
Statement **iii** – *If false: accident*

The chart reveals that no two statements can be false. So either none or one is false. From **iv**, just one man could not have lied. So no man lied. Since no man lied, it was neither murder nor an accident.
So the manner of Dana's death was suicide.

5

From **ii** and **iii** one man must be kept on the first side of the lake until the last crossing; otherwise **ii** and **iii** cannot be satisfied for the last two crossings.
Then from **i** and **iv** the crossings were accomplished in the following manner:

W represents woman,   **Mc** represents Clinton,
M represents man,   **Md** represents Douglas,
Ma represents Abraham,   and **M?** represents the last rower.
Mb represents Barratt,

Crossing
no.

1	Mc W W W W		Ma Mb Md ⟶	
2	Mc W W W W	⟵ Mb		Ma Md
3	Mb W W		Mc W W ⟶	Ma Md
4	Mb W W	⟵ Md		Ma Mc W W
5	M ?		M ? W W ⟶	Mc Mc W W
6	M ?	⟵ M ?		M ? M ? W W W W
7			M ? M ? ⟶	M ? M ? W W W W

From **ii** Douglas could not have rowed during crossing **5** so Barrett did. Then, from **ii** whoever rowed during crossing **6** did not row during crossing **7**; so Douglas rowed last.
To complete the details: from **ii** neither Barrett nor Douglas could have rowed during crossing **6** so either Abraham or Clinton did.

6

At least one of the statements **ii** and **iv** is true.
If both **ii** and **iv** are true, then Curtis killed Dwight and, from **i** statements **v** and **vi** are both false. But if Curtis killed Dwight **v** and **vi** cannot both be false. So Curtis did not kill Dwight. Then only one of the statements **ii** and **iv** is true.
Then from **ii** it is impossible for just one of statements **i**, **iii** and **v** to be true, as required by **i**. So **i**, **iii** and **v** are all false and **vi** is the only true statement.
Since **vi** is true, a lawyer killed Dwight. Since Curtis did not kill Dwight from previous reasoning, Barney is not a lawyer because **iii** is false, and Albert is a lawyer because **i** is false. It follows that: **iv** is true; and **ii** is false; and Albert killed Dwight.

IT MUST BE A SIGN
page 119

1 The sun
2 Opposition
3 Cancer the Crab
4 Cube root
5 Less than
6 Is not greater than
7 Taurus the Bull
8 Biennial
9 At; to
10 Because
11 Therefore
12 Latitude
13 Equivalent
14 Is equal to
15 Difference
16 Sagittarius
17 Male
18 Female
19 First quarter of the moon
20 Gallon
21 Is greater than
22 Feet and inches
23 Leo
24 Woody-stem plant
25 Angles
26 Australian dollar
27 Is perpendicular to

AROUND THE WORLD IN 80 SECONDS
page 120

1

Alabama *Montgomery*	Montana *Helena*
Alaska *Juneau*	Nebraska *Lincoln*
Arizona *Phoenix*	Nevada *Carson City*
Arkansas *Little Rock*	New Hampshire *Concord*
California *Sacramento*	New Jersey *Trenton*
Colorado *Denver*	New Mexico *Santa Fe*
Connecticut *Hartford*	New York *Albany*
Delaware *Dover*	North Carolina *Raleigh*
Florida *Tallahassee*	North Dakota *Bismarck*
Georgia *Atlanta*	Ohio *Columbus*
Hawaii *Honolulu*	Oklahoma *Oklahoma City*
Idaho *Boise*	Oregon *Salem*
Illinois *Springfield*	Pennsylvania *Harrisburg*
Indiana *Indianapolis*	Rhode Island *Providence*
Iowa *Des Moines*	South Carolina *Columbia*
Kansas *Topeka*	South Dakota *Pierre*
Kentucky *Frankfort*	Tennessee *Nashville*
Louisiana *Baton Rouge*	Texas *Austin*
Maine *Augusta*	Utah *Salt Lake City*
Maryland *Annapolis*	Vermont *Montpelier*
Massachusetts *Boston*	Virginia *Richmond*
Michigan *Lansing*	Washington *Olympia*
Minnesota *St. Paul*	West Virginia *Charleston*
Mississippi *Jackson*	Wisconsin *Madison*
Missouri *Jefferson*	Wyoming *Cheyenne*

3

A India	H Kampuchea
B China	I Vietnam
C Nepal	J Laos
D Bangladesh	K Bhutan
E Burma	L North Korea
F Thailand	M Sri Lanka
G Malaysia	N South Korea

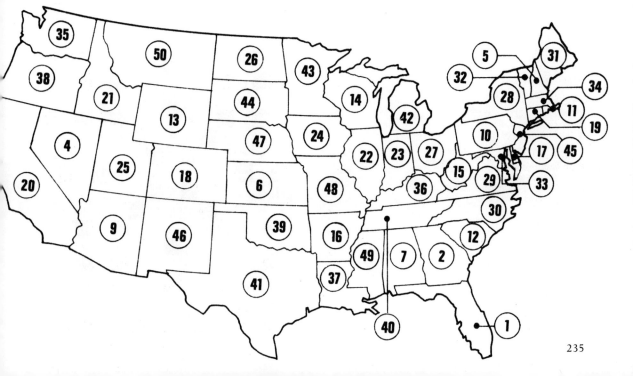

OF A LITERARY BENT
page 122

Cover to Cover
1 Evelyn Waugh
2 Denis Wheatley
3 Maurice Maeterlink
4 Dylan Thomas
5 Agatha Christie: *The Mirror Crack'd from Side to Side*
6 Gustave Flaubert
7 Thomas Hardy
8 Anne
9 Elizabeth Cleghorn Gaskell
10 Jane Austen: *Emma*
11 Irwin Shaw
12 E. M. Forster
13 *Edwin Drood*
14 The Duchess of Windsor
15 *Erewhon* – an anagram of Nowhere

Soul Searching
Her shoe!

Arabian Knight
* = Asterisk (ass to risk)
// = Parallel

Only Connect
Etienne de Silhouette (1709–1767) was the French Minister of Finance who gave his name to silhouette outline portraits – and the silhouettes here are of Jane Austen (1775–1817); her uncle James Leigh Perrot; Mrs. George Austen; and Jane Leigh Perrot, Jane's aunt.

Wilde About Oscar
1 *The Importance of Being Earnest*
2 *The Portrait of Dorian Gray*
3 *The Critic as an Artist*
4 *The Importance of Being Earnest*
5 *The Ballad of Reading Goal*
6 *An Ideal Husband*
7 *The Portrait of Dorian Gray*
8 *A Woman of No Importance*
9 *Lady Windermere's Fan*

Literary Riddles
1 Hamlet's uncle because he did 'Murder most foul'.
2 Because it is 'More in sorrow than in anger'.
3 Because we wish her to lay on.
4 Because they cannot help making 'Aphalia' of the heroine.
5 He was a tawny general of Venice.

6 Because he could a tail unfold.
7 The sackbut.
8 Because it was written by Harriet Beecher Stowe (Beecher's toe).
9 Bunyan.
10 The first thing he saw was a big swell pitching into a little cove.
11 Because it is before you (beef or ewe).
12 Because it can't be beet.
13 Because it is always drawn with the drag-on.
14 Because it is an Attic story.
15 Because you never see him without a lyre.

CROSSWORDS WITH A DIFFERENCE
page 124

1

2

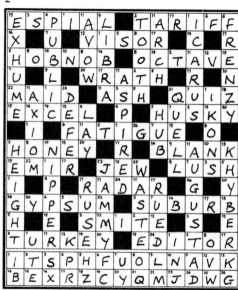

66

**PUSH BUTTON
BRAINTEASERS**
page 126
1 a SOS
  b LO LLI(POP)
  c BOGGLE
  d HI
  e HOHOHO
  f OBOE
  g HOG
  h HE IS BOSS
  i BELLE
  j EEL
2 The answers should be:
  3784
  3159
  1395
  1827
  2187
  1435
  In all the sums the digits in
  the answers are exactly the
  same as the digits in the
  two multipliers.
3 1963
  $\times 4$
  ——
  7852
  ——

  198
  $\times 27$
  ——
  5346
  ——

  1738
  $\times 4$
  ——
  6952
  ——

  159
  $\times 48$
  ——
  7632
  ——

  138
  $\times 42$
  ——
  5976
  ——

4 i $1066 \times 13 = 13858$
  ii $13858 \times 366 = 5072028$
  iii $5072028 - 28 = 5072000$
  iv $5072000 \div 1000 = 5072$
  v $5072 - 6 = 5066$
  vi $5066 - 1066 = 4000$
  vii $4000 \div 100 = 40$
  viii $40 - 39 = 1$

67

PROBLEMATIC
page 128
1 3 lines

2 2e middle of top row
3 D J L Y M N S A
4 If we letter the square as
  shown, then all the figures
  follow the formula:
  $$\frac{(D \times B) - C}{A} = E$$

A [ ] B   9 [ ] 6
  E   6
D [ ] C   11 [ ] 12

5 a 09.23
  b 8 minutes
  c 12.34
6 a Mr. Foyle
  b dark hair
  c Mr. Foyle is bald

68

VISUAL VARIATIONS
page 130
1 1 and 3
2 2
3 1
4 1 and 2
5 3
6 1 and 2

69

HIDDEN WORDS
page 132

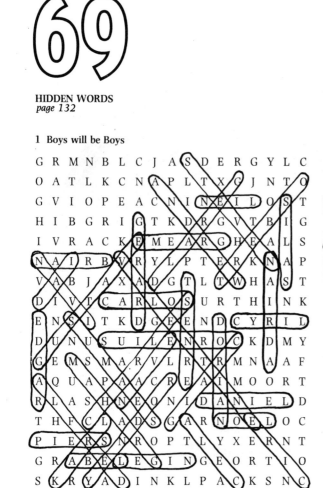

1 Boys will be Boys

```
G R M N B L C J A S D E R G Y L C
O A T L K C N A P L T X G J N T O
G V I O P E A C N I N E I L O S T
H I B G R I G T K D R G V T B I G
I V R A C K F M E A R G H E A L S
N A I R B V R Y L P T E R K N A P
V A B J A X A D G T L T W H A S T
D I V T C A R L O S U R T H I N K
E N S I T K D G E E N D C Y R I L
D U N U S U I L E N R O C K D M Y
G E M S M A R V L R T R M N A A F
A Q U A P A A C R E A I M O O R T
R L A S H N E O N I D A N I E L D
T H F C L A D S G A R N O E L O C
P I E R S N R O P T L Y X E R N T
G R A B E L E G I N G E O R T I O
S K R Y A D I N K L P A C K S N C
```

2 Cherchez la Femme

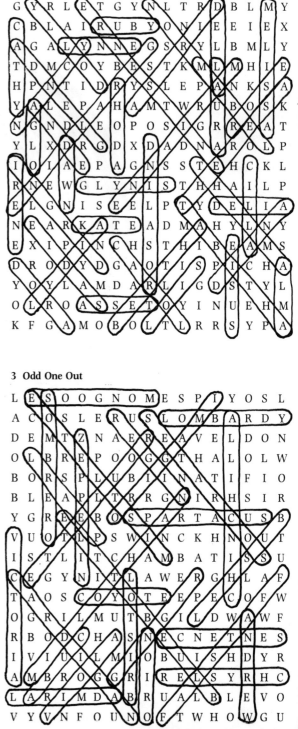

```
G Y R L E T G Y N L T R D B L M Y
C B L A I R U B Y O N I E E I E X
A G A L Y N N E G S R Y L B M L Y
T D M C O Y B E S T K M L M H I E
H P N T I D R Y S L E P A N K S A
Y A L E P A H A M T W R U B O S K
N G N D L E O P O S I G R R E A T
Y L X D R G D X D A D N A R O L P
I O I A E P A G N S S T E H C K L
R N E W G L Y N I S T H H A I L P
E L G N I S E E L P T Y D E L I A
N E A R K A T E A D M A H Y L N Y
E X I P I N C H S T H I B E A M S
D R O D Y D G A O T I S P I C H A
Y O Y L A M D A R L I G D S T Y L
O L R O A S S E T O Y I N U E H M
K F G A M O B O L T L R R S Y P A
```

3 Odd One Out

```
L E S O O G N O M E S P I Y O S L
A C O S L E R U S L O M B A R D Y
D E M T Z N A E R E A V E L D O N
O L B R E P O O G G T H A L O L W
B O R S P L U B I I N A T I F I O
B L E A P L T R R G N I R H S I R
Y G R E E B O S P A R T A C U S B
V U O T L P S W I N C K H N O U T
I S T L I T C H A M B A T I S S U
C E G Y N I T L A W E R G H L A F
T A O S C O Y O T E P E C O F W
O G R I L M U T B G I L D W A W F
R B O D C H A S N E C N E T N E S
I V I U I L M I O B U I S H D Y R
A M B R O G G R I R E L S Y R H C
L A R I M A B R U A L B L E V O
V Y V N F O U N O F T W H O W G U
```

BORIS KORDEMSKY'S PUZZLES
page 134

1
Three Moves
Seven matches from first pile to second; six matches from second to third; four from third to first

2
Count!
Thirty-five

3
A Duel in Arithmetic
There are two ways to get 1,111 by replacing 10 digits with zeros, five ways by using 9 zeros, six ways by using 8 zeros, three ways with 7 zeros, one way with 6 zeros, and one way with 5 zeros – a total of eighteen in all. The last variant is:

```
 111
 333
 500
 077
 090
-----
1,111
```

Try to find the other seventeen variants on your own!

4
Cat and Mice
Start from the cross in the diagram (position 13) and go clockwise through positions 1, 2, 3, ..., crossing out each thirteenth dot: 13, 1, 3, 6, 10, 5, 2, 4, 9, 11, 12, 7 and 8. Call position 8 the white mouse, and Purrer starts clockwise from the fifth mouse clockwise from the white mouse (i.e. position 13 relative to position 8). Or he starts counterclockwise from the fifth mouse counterclockwise from the white mouse

5
The Sliced Cube
6 cuts, 27 little cubes. There are no little cubes with 6 black faces; 8 cubes with 3 black faces (the corners of the cube); 12 with 2 black faces (edges of the cube); 6 with 1 black face (faces of the cube); 1 with no black faces from the centre of the cube

6
What is the Engine Driver's Name?
The passenger who lives nearest the guard is not Petrov (4–5). He does not live in Moscow or Leningrad, since at best these are only tied for nearest to the guard (2), so he is not Ivanov (1). By elimination, he is Sidorov. Since the passenger from Leningrad is not Ivanov (1), by elimination he is Petrov, and the guard's name is Petrov (3). Since Sidorov is not the fireman (6), by elimination he is the engine driver

7
The Idler and the Devil
Before the third crossing, the idler had 12 roubles. Adding the 24 roubles he gave the devil after the second crossing, he had 36 roubles, twice the 18 roubles he had before the second crossing. Adding 23 roubles again, he had 42 roubles, twice the 21 roubles he started with

8
Three Puzzles
1 There is an infinity of such numbers. The difference between divisor and remainder is always 2. Then 2 plus the desired number is a multiple of the divisors given. The lowest common multiple of 3, 4, 5 and 6 is 60, and $60-2=58$, the smallest answer
2 The lowest common multiple of 7, 8 and 9 is 504. This is the answer since no multiples of it have three digits
3 The left side of the equation is divisible by 9, so the right side is too. It follows that the sum of the digits on the right side is divisible by 9, so a is 8, which gives t a value of 4

EYE CATCHING
page 136
1 All five fields are exactly the same size. The different shapes make them appear to be different sizes
2 Both lines are the same length. The angle they are at makes them look different
3 All three are the same length. It is the angles that make the straight parts of the lines look different lengths
4 You could be looking at this optical illusion from above or below. There are no two ways about the line however: it is perfectly straight
5 All three are arcs from the same circle, but the more you see of each arc the greater the bend seems to be
6 The distance between A and B and B and C is identical
7 Both the angles are the same

INDOMITABLE
page 138

1 The Two Lines

2 The Two Columns

3 The Two Rectangles

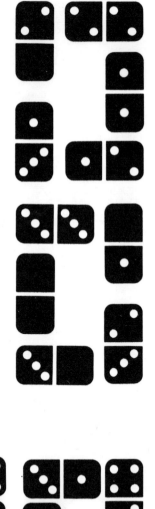

5 The Three Columns

4 Another Three Rectangles

6 The Giant Eight

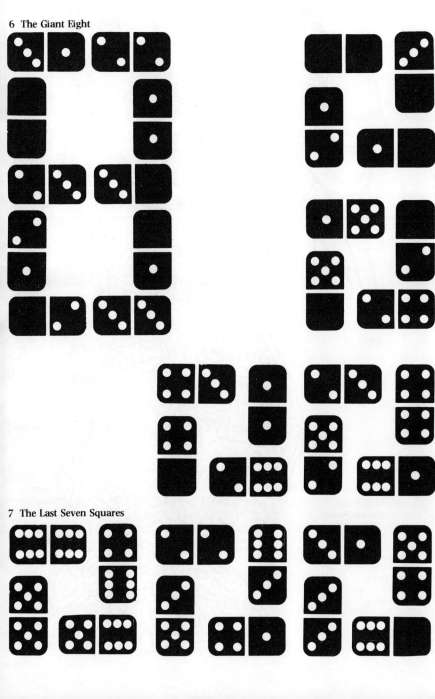

7 The Last Seven Squares

73

WHAT'S YOURS?
page 140
Spirited Words
1 Sir Walter Scott
2 Robert Burns
3 George Bernard Shaw
4 Richard Bentley
5 Rupert Brooke
6 John Masefield
7 Samuel Johnson
8 Ogden Nash
9 Richard Brinsley Sheridan
10 William Shakespeare
11 Ambrose Bierce

Alcoholic Anagrams
Ale, bingo, posset, vin rosé,
Guinness, tequila, rosé, Mosel,
vino santo, ruby, mead, lager,
claret, retsina, Cointreau,
geneva, Sauterne, spätlese,
Dao, Perlan, sack, stout,
porter, resinata, Pernod,
marc, Saint Amour, rotwein,
vintage port, Sudbahn

Where's It From?
Aguardiente *Dominican Republic*
Applejack *USA*
Bucelas *Portugal*
Cotnari *Romania*
Fendant *Switzerland*
Genever *Holland*
Kislav *Russia*
Mavrodaphne *Greece*
Nahe *Germany*
Orvieto *Italy*
Patrimonio *Corsica*
Poteen *Ireland*
Pulque *Mexico*
Rakia *Bulgaria*
Rioja *Spain*
Santenay *France*
Tokay Aszu *Hungary*
Trebern *Austria*
Verdelho *Madeira*
Viniak *Yugoslavia*

Pot Pourri
1 The best song
2 3.2 seconds
3 1885
4 plums
5 Red Biddy is a Glasgow
Irish name for cheap red
wine laced with methy-
lated spirits, a favourite
in the city's slums at one
time. The name and drink
spread elsewhere, and is
now applied to a variety
of similar nauseous
concoctions
6 Cuban rum, lime juice,

and sugar
7 A mixed drink of
champagne and stout
8 appellation contrôlée,
denominazione di origine
controllata, Pedro
Ximenez, vin délimité de
qualité supérieure, very
special old pale
9 Portugal, Spain,
Switzerland, West
Germany, Australia,
Israel
10 Champagne
11 Poinchy
12 Episcopal

74

INS AND OUTS
page 142

SOLITAIRE SENSATIONS
page 144

1 Centre to Centre
46-44, 65-45, 57-55, 54-56, 52-54,
73-53, 43-63, 75-73-53, 35-55, 15-35,
23-43-63-65-45-25, 37-57-55-53, 31-33,
34-32, 51-31-33, 13-15-35,
36-34-32-52-54-34, 24-44.

2 Latin Cross
43-23, 45-43, 53-33, 23-43, 42-44.

3 Greek Cross
45-47, 43-45, 64-44-46, 24-44,
47-45-43, 42-44.

4 The Five Crosses
64-66, 44-64, 74-54, 42-62-64-44-42,
41-43, 24-22-42-44-24, 14-34,
46-26-24-44-46, 47-45, 46-44.

5 The Lonely Cross
24-44, 32-34, 53-33, 23-43, 35-33,
55-35, 25-45, 52-32-34, 75-55, 63-65,
55-75, 57-55, 36-56, 55-57.

6 The Tilted Square
53-73, 33-53, 46-44, 65-45-43-63,
35-33-31-51-53-55-57-37-35-15-13-33,
73-53, 74-54-52-32-34, 24-44.

PARLEZ-VOUS?
page 146

1 Pseudo-French Rhymes
The sounds of the first verse
approximate to Old Mother
Hubbard; of the second,
Hickory Dickory Dock.

2 Spoken Like a Native
1 Burma
2 Ceylon
3 Taiwan
4 China
5 Tibet
6 Athens
7 Iceland
8 Iran
9 South Korea
10 Japan

3 Inter-Language Reversals
Retiled, déliter
reveler, relever
red-robed, déborder
retinges, segniter
mutative, evitatum
Catalan, nalatac
refiner, renifer

4 Trans-Lingual Anagrams
Monarchiste
Leptinotarse
algorithme
astreindre
Richtungen
ausrichten
Monarchien
Eintragungen
rinascimento
incolpatore
pronosticare
incantatore
lusingatore
tolerancia

5 Palindromic Sentences
The languages are,
respectively, Danish, Dutch,
Esperanto, Finnish, French,
German, Hungarian,
Icelandic, Italian, and Latin.

LOGICAL LOGOGRAMS
page 148

1 BEARD
bar, rad, are, read, bed.

2 LEAVES
ale, sea, vale, seal, lea,
eve, veal, ave, eel, lave, save,
vase, sale, else, elves, eaves,
ease, lease, slave.

3 ROMANCE
name, ream, earn, mace,
amor, arm, can, Rome, moa,
cone, race, mar, core, man,
more, near, Amen, care, ram.

4 SEAMS
Sam, sea, ma, same, mass,
Ems, mess, ass, as, me, ess, am.

5 EUROPEAN
ear, rope, pea, pear, peer,
neap, rape, nap, nape, rap,
pare, ape, pure, reap, rue,
near, pore, pan, preen, pour,
pen, roup, prune, proa,
Nore, upon, pun.

SILVERMANS GOLD
page 150
Yes or No?
Your strategy should be quite
different from that best
pursued in Twenty Questions.
One way to proceed is to
start with the question 'Is
your number bigger than 1?'
If you get a 'yes' response,
your next question will be 'Is
it bigger than 2?' and so on
up the line. In this manner,
the first 'no' answer you
receive will pinpoint your
opponent's number, which
you will promptly guess the
next time you assume the
role of questioner.

The only way your
opponent can win, therefore,
is to guess your number on
his first round of questions.
His chance of doing so is 1
out of 100, so your advantage in this game, as first
questioner, is 99 to 1. As the
size of the range of numbers

increases, the first player's
advantage increases
correspondingly.
Modified Russian Roulette
Let P be the probability of
winning for the first player
who spins. In one out of six
cases, he loses immediately.
In the other five, the other
player will have the same
probability P of winning.
Thus $P = 5/6 (1-P)$ and
$P = 5/11$. Now let N be the
number of chambers
remaining, assuming neither
player has yet exercised the
spin option. The chance of
winning is not better than
$(N-1)(1-P)/N$ if no spin is
made, and this chance is
always less than 5/11 except
when $N = 6$, in which case it
is equal to 5/11. (Obviously
spinning prior to the first shot
does not affect the first
player's odds, provided his
opponent plans to spin on his
turn.)

It follows that, after the
first shot, it is always
desirable to spin, and that
prior to the first shot it
apparently makes no
difference. Ah, but it does
make a difference! For if you
elect not to spin and get a
'click', your opponent, who
may not have worked out
the game, is liable not to
spin either, in which case
(provided he also gets a
'click') you will spin prior
to the third shot. By not
spinning, you offer him the
opportunity of foolishly
lowering his odds by 4 per
cent. Had you spun prior to
the first shot, he would have
had no opportunity of making
a mistake, and would be
compelled to adopt the best
strategy. So your best chance
is obtained by not spinning
prior to the first shot, and
spinning on all successive
shots.

In the *misère* version,
analysis is more difficult.
Working backward, on the
fifth shot, spinning gives
odds of 6/11 against $\frac{1}{2}$
without spinning. So spinning

is superior at shot five. At shot four, spinning gives odds of 6/11 against $\frac{1}{3} + \frac{2}{3} \times 5/11$ or 7/11 without spinning, so that no spinning is superior. At shot two, no spinning gives odds of $1/5 + (4/5) \times (5/11) = 31/55$, making no spinning the better percentage play. It follows that the first player should deny his opponent the opportunity of electing not to spin and should spin prior to his first shot, giving himself maximum odds of 6/11.

Plan Your Move(s), Kid!
Those familiar with Sam Loyd's celebrated Fifteen Puzzle, which appears on page 96 in this book, in which the solver is challenged to manipulate the numbers until they have been placed in proper numerical sequence, may have quickly concluded that the PLAN YOUR MOVE, KID! arrangement is impossible to attain. The Fifteen Puzzle has been proven impossible to solve, based on the fact that regardless of the number of manipulations, the number of 'exchanges' performed is always even. On the other hand, those unfamiliar with the impossibility of the Fifteen Puzzle are likely, after patient manipulation, to have ungarbled the PLA YOUR MOVE, KID! puzzle successfully. How can this be? The puzzles are different! The difference is in the fact that the letter **O** appears twice. Thus an even number of exchanges can be effected by interchanging the two **O**s as well as the **D** and the **I**. If the solver begins by interchanging the **O**s as quickly as possible, he will find that the ungarbled message falls into place.

Seven No Trump
By the rules of the game, a player, according to the diagram, may either move right along a row or up along a column. Thus the five bids indicated by the dots are 'safe' in that:

1 When you make a safe bid, your opponent is always forced to make an unsafe bid.
2 In response to your opponent's unsafe bid, you can always raise the contract to a higher safe bid.
Thus the winning responses to the opening bid are:

opening bid:
1 club
1 diamond
1 heart
1 spade
1 NT

winning response:
3 clubs
4 diamonds
5 hearts
6 spades
7 NT

The solution of a game problem of this type is generally facilitated by working backward from the winning objective.

Trump Management
If the trumps split 3–2, you'll make your contract regardless of how you play them, losing exactly three trump tricks. So you must be prepared for a 4–1 split. In this event, if the 5 of hearts is the singleton, the contract is down, period. If the 8 of hearts is the singleton, a high-trump lead will secure the contract, and if a trump honour is singleton, a low-trump lead will limit you to three trump losers. Since there are three different trump honours, the odds favour a low-trump lead three to one. However, if you led the 2, 3 or 4 of trumps, you deserve no credit. This novice play would cause you to go down *two* tricks in the event of a 5–0 trump split. Leading the 6 or 7 is the correct solution, since such a lead will result in only a one-trick set in the case of the 5–0 trump split.

Most amateurs miss this one, leading out the jack of hearts almost by instinct. The more experienced players see the virtue of the low-trump lead, but very few avoid the pitfall of leading the deuce.

SAM LOYD CLASSICS
page 152
1 The Puzzle of the Red Spade

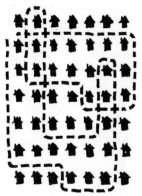

2 The Canals of Mars
The fifty thousand readers who reported 'There is no possible way' had all solved the puzzle, for that is the sentence that makes the round trip tour of the planet.
3 After Dinner Tricks
That odd little sleight-of-hand performance with the four empty and four filled glasses can readily be remembered by the following rule: One long move, two short ones, then one long one. First move **2** and **3** to the extreme end; then fill the gap with **5** and **6**. Fill gap with **8** and **2**; then finish with **1** and **5**.
4 Against the Wind
The popular answer to problems of this kind is to halve the total time to obtain an average speed, assuming that the wind boosts the rider's speed in one direction just as much as it retards it in the other direction. This is incorrect, because the wind has helped the rider for only three minutes, and hindered him for four minutes. If he could ride a mile in three minutes with the wind, he could go 1 and one-third miles in four minutes. He returns against the wind in the same four minutes, so he could go 2 and one-third miles in eight minutes, with the wind helping him half the time and hindering him half the time. The wind can therefore be ignored and we conclude that without the wind he could go 2 and one-third miles in eight minutes, or one mile in 3 and three-sevenths minutes.

5 Diminishing Power
The car travelled $71\frac{3}{8}$ miles for the first hour, $63\frac{5}{8}$ miles the second hour, $55\frac{7}{8}$ miles the third hour, and $48\frac{1}{8}$ the fourth. The difference between each hour is $7\frac{3}{4}$ miles.
The problem can be solved by letting **x** stand for the mileage of the last hour,
x plus y for the third hour,
x plus 2y for the second hour, and **x plus 3y** for the first hour. We now have two linear equations
(1) **2x plus 5y equals 135** and
(2) **2x plus y equals 104**.
6 The Patrolman's Puzzle
The route shown here will take Clancy past all of the houses!

QUESTIONS OF SCIENCE
page 154

1

An Elementary Quiz

Ag silver
Au gold
Cu copper
Fe iron
Hg mercury
K potassium
Mg magnesium
Na sodium
Pb lead
Ra radium
Sn tin
W tungsten

2

ABC

aduncate 10
biramous 16
cassideous 12
dystocia 13
eidograph 17
fluviatile 14
gutnik 2
hickie 19
iridotomy 4
julaceous 18
knaur 3
lentic 15
megaparsec 24
navarho 11
obconic 1
petrail 6
quilo 25
royalette 22
sherardizing 26
tentilla 23
ultor 5
vittate 20
warfarin 7
xiphoid 9
YIG 21
ziram 8

3

Material Anagrams

argon
arsenic *and* cerasin
astatine
erbium
lead
neon
nitrogen
radon
rhenium
terbium
formalin
decalin
ethanol
garnet
ruby
casein

cocaine
antimony
dahline
elastin

4

Ologies

algology *seaweeds*
argyrothecology *moneyboxes*
balneology *medicinal baths*
cartology *maps*
coleopterology *beetles*
desmology *ligaments*
exobiology *life on other planets*
herpetology *reptiles*
ktenology *putting to death*
metrology *weights and measures*
nephology *clouds*
nephrology *kidneys*
oology *birds' eggs*
otology *ears*
pedology *soils*
pomology *fruit*
pteridology *ferns*
spermology *seeds*
tocology *obstetrics*
xylology *structure of wood*

5

Who Invented It?

adding machine *Blaise Pascal*
bakelite *Leo Backeland*
ballpoint pen *John Loud*
barbed wire *Joseph Glidden*
carpet sweeper *Melville Bissell*
diesel engine *Rudolf Diesel*
elevator *Elisha Otis*
fountain pen *Louis Waterman*
gramophone *Thomas Alva Edison*
jet engine *Sir Frank Whittle*
laser *Charles Townes*
lightning conductor *Benjamin Franklin*
machine gun *Richard Gatling*
electric razor *Jacob Schick*
safety razor *King Gillette*
revolver *Samuel Colt*
safety pin *William Hunt*
spinning jenny *James Hargreaves*
tank *Sir Ernest Swinton*
zip *Whitcomb Judson*

ROUND IN CIRCLES
page 156

1

In our diagram the dotted lines represent the circumference of the red circle and an inscribed pentagon. The centre of both is C. Find **D**, point equidistant from **A**, **B**, and **C**, and with radius AD draw the circle **ABC**. Five discs of this size will cover the circle if placed with their centres at **D**, **E**, **F**, **G** and **H**. If the diameter of the large circle is 6 inches, the diameter of the discs is a little less than 4 inches, or 4 inches 'to the nearest half-inch'.
It requires a little care and practice correctly to place the five discs without shifting, unless you make some secret markings that would not be noticed by others.
If readers require a closer approximation or further information as to the way of solving this puzzle, I cannot do better than refer them to a paper, *Solutions of Numerical Functional Equations, illustrated by an account of a Popular Puzzle and its Solution* by Mr Eric H. Neville, in the Proceedings of London Mathematical Society, Series II, Vol. 14, Part 4. I will just add that covering is possible if the ratio of the two diameters exceeds .6094185, and impossible if the ratio is less than .6094180. In my case above, where all five discs touch the centre, the ratio is .6180340.

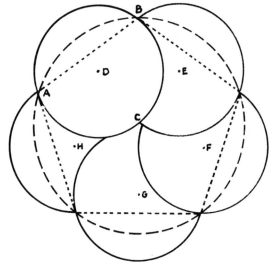

2 The Three Fences
To divide a circular field into four equal parts by three fences of equal length, first divide the diameter of the circle in four parts and then describe semicircles on each side of the line in the manner shown in the diagram. The curved lines will be the required fences.

3 The Circling Car
Since the outside wheels go twice as fast as the inside ones, the circle they describe is twice the length of the inner circle. Therefore, one circle is twice the diameter of the other, and since the wheels are 5 ft apart, the diameter of the larger circle is 20 ft. Multiply 20 ft by 3.1416 (the familiar approximate value of 'pi') to get 62.832 ft as the length of the circumference of the larger circle.

4 Sharing a Grindstone
The first man should use the stone until he has reduced the radius by 1.754 in. The second man will then reduce it by an additional 2.246 in. leaving the last man 4 in. and the aperture. This is a very close approximation.

5 Squaring the Circle
If you make a rectangle with one side equal to the diameter, and the other three times the diameter, then the diagonal will be something near correct. In fact it would be 1 to $1\sqrt{10}$, or 1 to 3.1622+. The method we recommend is the following:

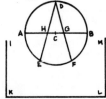

In the diagram, AB is the diameter. Bisect the semicircle in D. Now with the radius AC mark off the points E and F from A and B, and draw the lines DE and DF. The distance DG added to the distance GH gives a quarter of the length of the circumference (IK) correct within a five-thousandth part; IKLM is the length of the complete straight line. There is another way, correct to a seventeen-thousandth part, but it is a little more difficult.

WEIGH OUT
page 158

1
The blonde weighs **7 stone 6 lb**, the brunette **8 stone 8 lb.** Since the dog and the blonde weigh the same as the brunette, you could replace the brunette in the top picture by Fido and an extra blonde. The two blondes would weigh 16 lb (i.e. the dog's weight) less than the man, i.e., 14 stone 12 lb. So one blonde must weigh half of this: viz. 7 stone 6 lb, and the brunette 16 lb more.

2
The weights are 10, 11, 12, 13, and 14 stones.
C is obviously the heaviest at 14 stones, so D must be 13 stones, and E 11. This leaves A at 10 and B at 12. So we have:

A B C D E
10 12 14 13 11 stones

Using algebra, this can be done in one minute.
Say let x = A,
then E = x + 1.
B = x + 2.
C = x + 4.
D = x + 3.

3
a 1.6 kilometers *a mile*
b 28 grams *an ounce*.
  0.45 kilogram *a pound*
c 44.1 kilograms *seven stone*.

4
If a dozen apples weigh 3 kilograms, then each one weighs 250 grams, 7 apples weigh 1750 grams and 3

6 The Wheels of the Car
The circumference of the front wheel and the rear wheel respectively must have been 15 ft and 18 ft. Thus 15 ft goes 24 times in 360 ft and 18 ft 20 times — a difference of four revolutions. But if we reduced the circumference by 3 ft then 12 goes 30 times, and 15 goes 24 times — a difference of 6 revolutions.

apples weigh 750 grams. Thus the weight of the apples in combination with 8 bananas and 3 grapefruits is 1000 grams more than the weight of the apples combined with 6 bananas and 6 grapefruits. The difference between the weights of the bananas and grapefruit in the two groups must be equal to this 1000 grams. The heavier combination has 3 more grapefruit and 2 fewer bananas than the lighter, and we know that the weight of each banana is $\frac{2}{3}$ the weight of the grapefruit. We can say then that the difference between the two groups of fruit, 1000 grams, is equal to the weight of 1 grapefruit (the weight of 3 grapefruit less the weight of 2 bananas).

Therefore each grapefruit must weigh 600 grams, and a banana weighs $\frac{2}{3}$ of that, 400 grams.

5
There is only one possible combination -- **he must add four grapefruit to his order.** The original order adds up to 6300 grams, and the weight of the bananas was 2400 grams. There is no way to exactly replace this 2400 grams with apples which weigh 250 grams each, so there must be at least 1 grapefruit. This leaves 1800 grams still to replace, and since this cannot be made up entirely with 250 gram

apples, there must be at least 2 grapefruit. The remaining 1200 grams also cannot be made up with apples, nor can the 600 grams left after adding 3 grapefruit. The only answer then is to add 4 grapefruit to make up for the lost bananas.

6
With the 5 lb and 9 lb weights in different pans weigh 4 lb.
With that 4 lb weigh a second 4 lb, and then a third 4 lb. Weigh a fourth 4 lb and the remainder will also be 4 lb.
Divide each portion of 4 lb in turn equally on the two sides of the scales.

7
If the scales had been false on account of the pans being unequally weighted, then the true weight of the cake would be 154 oz and it would have weighed 130 oz in one pan and 178 oz in the other. But the pans weighed evenly and the error must be in unequal lengths of the scales' arms. Therefore, the apparent weights were 121 oz and 169 oz, and the real weight 143 oz. Multiply the apparent weights together and we get the square of 143 – the geometric mean. The lengths of the arms were in the ratio 11 to 13.
If we call the true weight x in each case, then we get the equations:

$$(\tfrac{9}{11}x+4)+(\tfrac{9}{11}x+52)=x, \text{ and } x=154$$
$$\overline{2}$$

$$\sqrt{(\tfrac{9}{11}x+4)\times(\tfrac{9}{11}x+52)}=x, \text{ and } x=143$$

8
Timmy found the nuggets weighing 154, 101 and 17 ounces. As for the others, Tom must have found the 46, 22, and 16 ounce nuggets (totalling 84) and Tam the 19, 13 and 10 ounce nuggets (totalling 42).

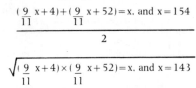

CROSSLAND'S CROSSWORDS
page 160
A Crossland Opener
ACROSS
1 Smuggler
6 Video
10 Put one's foot in it
11 Instigate
12 Issue
13 Hosanna
16 Soldier
17 Horatio
19 Locusta
20 Tramp
21 Electoral
24 Misapprehension
25 Sider
26 Nasality
DOWN
2 Mates
3 Genii
4 La Scala
5 Rioters
6 Vitriolic
7 Dynasties
8 On the bread line
9 Up with the times
14 Surpassed
15 Notepaper
18 Overrun
19 Leeches
22 Tonal
23 Roist

Give and Take
The correct form of definition word is in brackets
ACROSS
1 Check-list (*inventory*)
6 Doric (*style*)
9 Amigo (*Spain*)
10 Gentleman (*noble*)
11 Pectoral (*Breast's*)
12 Stroke (*caress*)
14 Cape (*head*)
15 Filter-tips (*gaspers*)
18 Allocation (*placing*)
19 Stir (*move*)
21 Topers (*revel*)
23 Battered (*fritters*)
26 Spaghetti (*pasta*)
27 Grimm (*tales*)
28 Dated (*old*)
29 Pendragon (*chief*)

A Crossland Standard
ACROSS
1 Valentine
6 Cards
9 Gavin
10 Turntable
11 Bolster
12 Satsuma
13 Nickelodeon
17 Chanticleer
20 Accurse
21 Eye-flap
23 Profiteer
25 Cynic
26 Orson
27 Dismissal
DOWN
1 Vagabond
2 Lovelace
3 Nonet
4 Interpolate
5 Ear
6 Catatonic
7 Rub out
8 Shebat
12 Sweethearts
14 Excursion
15 Ceilings
16 Tropical
18 Sappho
19 Scoops
22 Elchi
24 End

DOWN
1 Clasp (*grip*)
2 Episcopal (*see's*)
3 Kronos (*God*)
4 Ingratiate (*favour*)
5 Tang (*smack*)
6 Dilatory (*slow*)
7 Romeo (*lover*)
8 Confessor (*priest*)
13 Etiolation (*pale*)
14 Chastened (*chiding*)
16 Interning (*locking*)
17 Scorched (*parched*)
20 Stager (*actor*)
22 Plant (*factory*)
24 Demon (*imp*)
25 Stop (*ban*)

Printing Errors
Corrected form of definition word in brackets
ACROSS
1 Bumpkin (*yokel*)
5 Dormant (*sleeping*)
9 Attribute (*property*)
10 Playa (*basin*)
11 Break (*interval*)
12 Suspected (*doubted*)

MENTAL GYMNASTICS
page 164
1
From the clue, if you were told any of the letters in MOD then you would not be able to determine whether the number of vowels in the special word was one or two. So none of the letters in MOD is in the secret word. The word cannot, therefore, be AIM, DUE, MOD, or OAT — so it must be the word TIE.
2

From **d** neither Babe nor Clay occupies dressing room II. From **a** Vera does not occupy dressing room II. So either Adam or Dawn occupies dressing room II. Suppose Adam occupies dressing room II; then, from **c**, one of the following sets of occupation must exist:

13 Experiment (*test*)
16 Fete (*gala*)
18 Song (*aria*)
19 Prospectus (*guide*)
22 Carmelite (*monk*)
24 Utter (*speak*)
26 Irons (*evens*)
27 Entrecote (*steak*)
28 Nascent (*born*)
29 Latency (*hid*)
DOWN
1 Bramble (*bush*)
2 Mitre (*crown*)
3 Knickers (*panties*)
4 Nouns (*names*)
5 Dressings (*plasters*)
6 Ripper (*Jack*)
7 Apartment (*flat*)
8 Twaddle (*rot*)
14 Penurious (*wanting*)
15 Merriment (*joy*)
17 Tegument (*covering*)
18 Section (*part*)
20 Sorcery (*spells*)
21 Nessie (*monster*)
23 Extol (*lift*)
25 Thorn (*thistle*)

A – Adam
C – Clay
D – Dawn

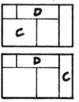

But, from **b** each of these sets of occupation is impossible. So Dawn occupies dressing room II. From **c** one of the following sets of occupation must exist:

But from **b** the first of these sets is impossible. So the second set is the correct one and from **c** Vera occupies dressing room IV. From **d** Babe occupies dressing room I. So Adam occupies dressing room V. From **a**, **Adam killed Vera.**

3
$140 \div 3 = 46\frac{2}{3}$ **days.** Because in one day the wife drinks
$$\frac{1}{14} - \frac{1}{20} = \frac{3}{140}$$
Therefore it takes her $\frac{140}{3}$

days to finish the barrel.

4
Four years ago.
Let **x** represent the unknown
number of years.
$40 - x = 4(13 - x) = 52 - 4x$
$\therefore \ 3x = 12$
$\therefore \ \ x = 4$

5

6
4 lines as follows:

7

```
    1   1   7
    3   0   7
    8   1   9
3   5   1
3   5   9   1   9
```

8
B must be equal to 1 and I is
therefore 0. We then have:

```
9   –   –   –
1   –   –   1

1   0   –   5   –
```

From this it follows that
M=2 and O=3.
We then have:

```
9   4   3   2
1   3   2   1

1   0   7   5   3
```

9 The year is **1992**.
10
The clerk gave back $5 and
kept $25. The boy gave each
man $1 and kept $2. Each
man paid $9 less the $2 to
the boy which makes the
$25 given to the clerk.
11 108 trees.

AN OLIO OF ORTHO-GRAPHICAL ODDITIES
page 166
1 Geographical Anagrams
Maine, Yemen, Crete, Italy,
Seoul, Spain, Paris, Nepal,
Niger, Burma, Essex, Texas,
Sudan, Angola, Denver,
Naples, Israel, Dorset,
Cyprus, Detroit, Athlone,
Tangier, Tijuana, Arundel,
Chelsea, Romania, Ontario,
Dresden, Chester, Cremona,
Bermuda, Trieste, Surinam,
New York, Tangiers, San
Diego, Savannah, Illinois,
Las Vegas, Hastings,
Lancaster, Maidstone,
Greenland, Minnesota,
Greenwich, Leningrad,
Singapore, San Marino,
Argentine, Washington.
2 Word Squares

```
S  Q  U  A  B
O  U  N  C  E
N  I  T  R  E
G  R  I  E  F
S  E  E  D  Y

M  A  R  S  H
I  R  A  T  E
L  E  V  E  R
K  N  E  A  D
Y  A  N  K  S

C  R  I  M  E
H  A  R  E  M
A  D  O  R  E
R  A  N  G  E
D  R  Y  E  R
```

3 What's Special?
The ten-letter words are all
composed of five pairs of
different letters; the twelve-
letter words are all composed
of six pairs of different letters;
and the fourteen-letter words
are all composed of seven
pairs of different letters. List 2
is extra special because the
first half of each of the words
contains all the different
letters in the word. No
examples longer than fourteen
letters are known.
4 Words Within Words
Tomb, car or cart, cocoa,
debate, ruin, urge, vacate,
elation, fun, fag, hies, lit,
tutor, last, male, pure,
ramble, rain, rule, sated.

CEREBRAL SEREBRIAKOFF
page 168
1 Unorthodox Neighbours
Shapes **24** and **25**.
Some of the patterns are
undercut; if you cut them out
you would have to *lift* them
out, you could not *slide* them
our. The pattern is 'two
undercut, one not'; 24 and
25 are the only two not
under-cut which are together.
2 Cube of Cubes
Mark B.
The three dimensions are size
shape and colour, and the
large black circle logically
goes in the hidden far corner
cube.
3 Missing Pattern
Pattern C.
Squares shrink downwards
and rotate quarter right-
wards. Ellipses grow downwards and rotate eighth
rightwards.
4 All Bounce
180 mph.
The iron plate on the train
and the ball collide at a
speed of 120 mph and the
elastic deformation which
occurs absorbs the energy of
this collision. The energy
imparted therefore forces the
ball to bounce back at this
speed from the surface of the
plate on the train. But the
plate is itself moving at 60
mph so the total speed
relative to the ground *or the
boy* will be three times the
initial speed or 180 mph.
5 Irresistible, Immovable
My friend Isaac Asimov says
that any universe which
contains an immovable
object cannot also contain
an irresistible force and
vice versa. But as Isaac
has not examined this
universe in real detail, yet
alone all possible universes,
we could put this another
way and say that he cannot
conceive of a universe which
contains both. So, in the
same kind of terms as the
question is posed, we can
answer the question very
simply. What happens when
an irresistible force meets an

immovable object is an
inconceivable event.
6 As Easy as Pie
The most obvious answer is
to fit a 1 at either end but I
think the second most
obvious answer, especially in
view of the heading. 'Easy as
Pie' is 0 at the beginning and
9 at the end which then
gives the answer
π (pi) i.e. $= 3.14159 = \pi$
**7 Egging Them On by
Calling Them 'Chicken'**
The answer, about which
there is absolutely no doubt,
is that **the egg came first**. To
illustrate this, let us go back
through time, passing a
succession of eggs and
chickens on our way. Unless
we reject the theory of
evolution, we shall be looking
at birds which differ more
and more from that class of
birds which we call 'chickens'.
Eventually we shall find some
early ancestor of the chicken
which is so dissimilar that we
must reject it as a member of
the class 'chicken'. We shall
have to go back a very great
deal further before the objects
lain by these pre-chickens
cease to be classified as 'eggs'.

COUNTDOWN/COUNTUP

page 170

If you remove one counter, leaving twelve, you can ensure a win by responding to your opponent's moves as follows: If he takes one counter, you take three; if he takes two, you take two; if he takes three, you take one. Thus the next three exchanges of moves will each reduce the pile by four counters, and yours will be the last move.

Generalising, let N be the limiting number of counters removable on a single play. If N+1 is not a factor of the original number of counters, then the first player should remove exactly the number required to make the remainder a multiple of N+1. This is the only 'safe leave'. The winning strategy now is to parry the removal by your opponent of K counters by removing N+1−K counters. Thus each exchange results in the removal of N+1 counters, guaranteeing you the win.

What are the winning first moves, starting with a pile of thirteen, if the option on each turn is to remove one or two counters? One, two, three, or four counters? Any number of counters from one to five? In the first case N=2, making N+1 a factor of 12. Remove one counter; then parry each of your opponent's moves by removing 3 minus the number removed by him. In the second case (N=4), N+1 is a factor of 10. Start by removing three counters, and when opponent removes K, remove 5−K. In the third case N+1=6, a factor of 12. Remove one counter and parry K with 6−K.

Now that you have the idea, you should be able to win the Second Player Option game.

Second Player Option

The solution to Triskidekaphilia provides the clue. Since a winning leave occurs when the number of counters left is a multiple of N+1, you will, by declaring an N of 12, be effectively creating a winning leave. Whatever number of counters your opponent removes, you remove thirteen minus that number − that is, the remainder of the counters. Twelve is the only value of N which gives you an advantage. The table below provides the winning first moves for your opponent for all other values of N, starting with a pile of thirteen counters.

Limiting Number N	Winning First Move
1	1
2	1
3	1
4	3
5	1
6	6
7	5
8	4
9	3
10	2
11	1
13 or more	13

Triskidekaphilia Misere

Forcing your opponent to take the last counter is equivalent to securing the next-to-last counter for yourself. So Misere with thirteen counter is played like regular Triskidekaphilia with twelve counters. Since N+1=5, you play to leave a multiple of 5 (plus one additional counter). Your winning play, therefore, is to remove two counters, leaving eleven. You parry your opponent's removal of K by removing 5−K. Following your third move, he will be left with the losing counter.

Nim

Nim has been well analyzed and generalised to any number of piles and any number of counters in each pile. The key is to partition each pile into distinct powers of two. Thus, there is 1 triangular counter, 1+4 circular counters, and 2+8 square counters. A winning leave is created by leaving your opponent a partitioning in which no power of two appears an odd number of times. When forced to play on a winning leave, a player will always present his opponent with a losing leave, and the latter can always be converted to another winning leave.

The 8 must be eliminated, so your first play must be on the square counters. The only winning leave is created by removing 6 square counters, leaving the partitions 1, 1+4, and 4.

Tsyanshidzi

Working backward, one can generate a table of winning leaves:

(1,2)
(3,5)
(4,7)
(6, 10)
(8,13)
(9,15)
(11,18)
(12,20)
(14,23)
(16,26) etc.

The first member of each pair is the smallest positive integer that does not appear in a previous winning leave. To obtain the second member, follow the rule that the difference between the two members is always one more than that for the previous winning leave. So the game is actually rather simple to analyze. There is even a formula for the *n*th winning leave, which is based on the well-known Fibonacci ratio. In the game under consideration, the correct play is to subtract five chips from each pile, leaving the winning pair (4,7). Just for diversion, see how quickly you can determine the three alternative winning plays when confronted with piles of fifteen and twenty chips.

The Last Prime

A Five-Finger Exercise

The objective is to be the player who first reaches a total that is a prime at least 6 less than the next highest prime. Then the opponent will be stymied. The first such prime is 23. Since you wish to arrive at this total, you want your opponent to arrive at a total of 19. Reasoning backward, the desired sequence is **23**, 19, **17**, 13, **11**, 7 and **5**, with your totals in bold type. Thus your first play should be five fingers.

CRISS CROSS
page 172
Four-letter Words

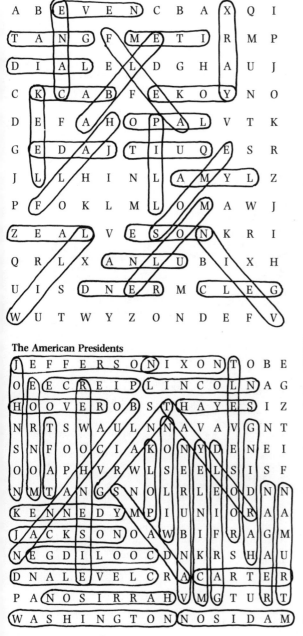

```
A B E V E N C B A X Q I
T A N G F M E T I R M P
D I A L E L D G H A U J
C K C A B F E K O Y N O
D E F A H O P A L V T K
G E D A J T I U Q E S R
J L L H I N L A M Y L Z
P F O K L M L O M A W J
Z E A L V E S O N K R I
Q R L X A N L U B I X H
U I S D N E R M C L E G
W U T W Y Z O N D E F V
```

The American Presidents

```
J E F F E R S O N I X O N T O B E
O E E C R E I P L I N C O L N A G
H O O V E R O B S T H A Y E S I Z
N R T S W A U L N N A V A V G N T
S N F O O C I A K O N Y D E N E I
O O A P H V R W L S E E L S I S F
N M T A N G S N O L R L E O D N N
K E N N E D Y M P I U N I O R A A
J A C K S O N O A W B I F R A G M
N E G D I L O O C D N K R S H A U
D N A L E V E L C R A C A R T E R
P A N O S I R R A H V M G T U R T
W A S H I N G T O N N O S I D A M
```

Drinks

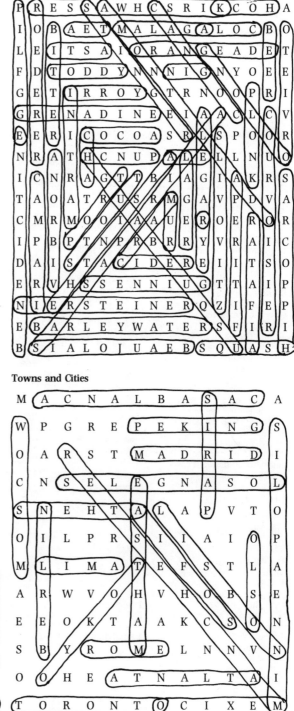

```
P R E S S A W H C S R I K C O H A
I O B A E T M A L A G A L O C B O
L E I T S A I O R A N G E A D E T
F D T O D D Y N N N I G N Y O E E
G E T I R R O Y G T R N O O P R I
G R E N A D I N E E I A A C L C V
E E R I C O C O A S R I S P O O R
N R A T H C N U P A L E L L N U O
I C N R A G T T B I A G I A K R S
T A O A T R U S R M G A V P D V A
C M R M O O I A A U E R O E R O R
I P B P T N P R B R R Y V R A I C
D A I S T A C I D E R E I I T S O
E R V H S S E N N I U G T T A I P
N I E R S T E I N E R Q Z I F E P
E B A R L E Y W A T E R S F I R I
B S I A L O J U A E B S Q U A S H
```

Towns and Cities

```
M A C N A L B A S A C A
W P G R E P E K I N G S
O A R S T M A D R I D I
C N S E L E G N A S O L
S N E H T A L A P V T O
O I L P R S I I A I O P
M L I M A T E F S T L A
A R W V O H V H O B S E
E O K T A A K C S O N N
S B Y R O M E L N N V N
O O H E A T N A L T A I
T O R O N T O C I X E M
```

FOR THE NUMERATE
page 174
Digital Delights

1 $50\frac{1}{2} + 49\frac{38}{76}$

2 4368

3 Arrange the figures in the following way:

173 85
4 92
——— ———
177 177

4 All you need do is proceed as follows:

$7 - 7101449275362318840579$

$\overline{1014492753623188405797}$

Divide 7 by 7, carry the 1 to the top line, divide again by 7 and carry the 0 to the top line, and so on until you come to a 7 in the bottom line without any remainder. Then stop, for the correct number is found.

5 Taking the six numbers in order, the sums of their digits are:

46 31 42 34 25 34
1   4   6   7   7   7

Adding, where necessary, the digits until we reach a single figure, we get the second row of numbers, which we call the digital routes. These may be combined in different triplets in eight different ways.

146 147 167 177
2   3   5   6

467 477 677 777
8   9   2   3

The digital route of every square must be either 1, 4, 7, or 9 so that the required numbers must have the roots 4, 7, 7, to be a square. The two 7's may be selected in three different ways. But if the fifth number is included, the total of the three will end in 189 or 389, which is impossible for a square, as the 89 must be preceded by an even figure or 0.

Therefore the required numbers must be:
$2,494,651 + 1,385,287 + 9,406,087 = 13,286,025$
which is the square of 3,645.

6 $7 + 1 = 8$
$9 - 6 = 3$
$5 \times 4 = 20$

7 989,010,989 multiplied by 123,456,789 produces 122,100,120,987,654,321, where the last nine digits are in the reverse order.

8 The smallest number that fulfills these conditions is 35,641,667,749. Other numbers that will serve may be obtained by adding 46,895,573,610, or any multiple of it.

9 In four exchanges: 7 with 3, 3 with 4, 4 with 8, and 2 with 5, we can get 157,326,849 which is the square of 12,543. But the correct solution is 1 with 5, 8 with 4, and 4 with 6, which gives us the number 523,814,769, the square of 22,887 which uses only three moves.

10 In every one of the following eight sums all the nine digits are used once, and the difference between the successive totals is, throughout, 9:

243 341 154 317
675 586 782 628
——— ——— ——— ———
918 927 936 945

216 215 318 235
738 748 654 746
——— ——— ——— ———
954 963 972 981

11

1 hectoliters
2 °F
3 inches
4 cm.dynes
5 ft.
6 radian
7 cu. ins.
8 cu. ins.
9 lbs. water/min.
10 gals/min.
11 cu. cm.
12 gals (liq)
13 cu. ft.
14 seconds
15 revs/min.
16 °C
17 amperes
18 cm.
19 lbs/sq. ft.
20 cm/sec.
21 m.p.h.
22 milliliters
23 feet
24 cu. ins.
25 cu. ft/hr.
26 grams
27 dynes
28 sq. ft.
29 bushels
30 ft. lbs/min.
31 mm.
32 lbs/sq. in.
33 dynes
34 ft. lbs.
35 ft. lbs/sec.
36 ft.
37 m.p.h.
38 ft. lbs/sec.
39 ft. lbs.
40 ft/hr.
41 cu. ins.
42 inches
43 ft.
44 ft/sec.
45 parts/million
46 fluid oz.
47 inches
48 grams
49 litres
50 cu. cm.
51 dynes
52 g/sq. cm.
53 cu. ins.
54 sheets
55 minutes
56 sheets
57 degrees/sec.
58 ft.
59 lbs. (mass)
60 sq. ins.
61 sq. m.
62 sq. cm.
63 acres
64 sq. ft.

ALPHAMETICS AND CRYPTARITHMS
page 176
An Introduction to Cryptarithmetic

a In the second partial product, we see D×A=D, hence A=1

b D × C and E × C both end in C, hence C = 5.

c D and E must be odd. Since both partial products have only three digits, neither can be 9. This leaves only 3 and 7. In the first partial product, E×C is a number of two digits, while in the second partial product, D×B is a number of only one digit. Thus, E is larger than D, so E=7 and D=3.

d Since D×B has only one digit, B must be 3 or less. The only two possibilities are 0 and 2. B cannot be 0 because 7B is a two-digit number. Thus B=2

e By completing the multiplication, F=8, E=7 G=6

f The answer is $125 \times 37 = 4625$

Other Problems 1

a T must equal 1 and W less than or equal to 4, since THREE contains five digits

b E=4 because 44 is the only combination of two equal digits that terminate in a square. Hence, O=2 or 8

c The answer is TWO=138, THREE=19,044

Other Problems 2

a None of the digits is zero because each gives a product

b Since A×C ends in A and B×C ends in B, C must be either 1 or 6. But since the first product contains four digits, C is greater than 1, so must be 6

c A and B are even (but not 6), hence A and B are 2, 4, or 8. Now, A cannot be 4 or 8 since the second product contains three digits, hence A is 2

d B must be 4 or 8. B cannot be 4 because the last product contains four digits. Hence B is 8

e The multiplication is 286×826

Other Problems 3

R must equal zero. 2U+F is less than or equal to 9, hence U=1, 2, 3 or 4. And USA= 178, FDR=230, NRA=408, and TAX=586

Prime Problems 1

a The first equation indicates that R^2 has two digits. Since R is prime, it must be 5 or 7. If R=5, the second equation indicates A=zero (which is impossible) or A=5=R (which is impossible). Hence, R=7

b 49×NIG terminates in 7, so G=3

c The other numbers are A=1, N=2, L=4, E=5, D=6, O=8, I=9, and T=zero

Prime Problems 2

Since each letter is a final digit, they must all be odd: 1, 3, 7 or 9. A and C must be 1 or 7, otherwise the numbers ADDD and AACA would be divisible by 3. Thus B and D must be 3 or 9. Under these conditions, BCDB can be written in four ways:

B=3 D=9 A=7 C=1
3193, divisible by 31

B=3 D=9 A=1 C=7
3793, prime

B=9 D=3 A=7 C=1
9139, divisible by 13

B=9 D=3 A=1 C=7
9739, prime

In both cases where a prime results, C=7 and A=1. BDAC must be either 9317 or 3917 as B and D equal 9 and 3. But 9317 is divisible by 7 whereas 3917 is prime. Thus A=1, B=3, C=7, and D=9.

Prime Problems 3
The four primes are **1483, 4813, 4831** and **8431**

Prime Problems 4
The square of C ends in C, thus C must be 0, 1, 5 or 6. Since ABC is prime, C=1. For the square BC to end in BC, B must equal 0. ABC can be 101, 401, 601 or 701. And only **601** is prime

Printer's Devilry
a=1 can be rejected
a=2 gives:
$2^b \times c^2 = 2bc2$
Set up the first nine powers of 2 **(I)** and the squares of the first nine numbers **(II)**. The product of a number from **(I)** and a number from **(II)** must end in 2 and have four digits

$2^5 \times 9^2 = 2592$
For a=3, the first eight powers of 3 (four digits maximum) and the cubes of the first nine numbers must give **3bc3**. There is no such solution

inx Problem
S=1, P=4, H=2, I=8, N=5 and X=7. Thus, SPHINX represents the recurring period of the fraction one seventh

Two More Problems 1
Since **REDACTIONS** contains all ten digits, it is divisible by 9. Also, the sum of the digits of the product, 9T+2S, is divisible by 9 or zero. Only the value S=zero will give the solution:
8641975230×9=777777777070

Two More Problems 2
If the numbers are written in the decimal (base-10) system:
$$(E+8N+64N+512A)-$$
$$(E+5N+25N+125A)=$$
$$E+7N+49N+343A$$
Or: 44A−14N=E
A, N and E are less than 5 and E is even. The only solution is ANNE=1332

POETS CORNER
page 178
1 a Sir Walter Raleigh
  b Edmund Spenser
  c William Shakespeare
  d Francis Beaumont
  e John Milton
  f William Blake
  g Robert Burns
  h Lord Byron
  i John Keats
  j Lord Tennyson

2 All the names are those of poets born in the twentieth century, except for T. S. Eliot, who was born in 1888, and Bernie Schwarz who is a dentist living in Oswego, New York.

3 Chaucer, Frost, Auden, Dickinson, Keats, Greville, De La Mare, Chesterton, Poe, Yeats.

4	1 Young	15 Milton
	2 Dr. Johnson	16 Bailey
	3 Pope	17 Trench
	4 Prior	18 Somerville
	5 Sewell	19 Thompson
	6 Spenser	20 Byron
	7 Daniel	21 Smollett
	8 Raleigh	22 Crabbe
	9 Longfellow	23 Massinger
	10 Southwell	24 Crowley
	11 Congreve	25 Beattie
	12 Churchill	26 Cowper
	13 Rochester	27 Davenant
	14 Armstrong	28 Grey

5 a *Wandering*   *Worshipper*
    O'er   *Of*
    Rich   *Reflection*
    Day-dreams   *Thus*
    Such   *High*
  b *Wondrous*   *Such*

Armed   *Character*
Like   *Of*
The   *The*
E'en   *Thy*
Resemblance
d *Lays*   *Excelsior*
  Oft   *Life's*
  Now   *Longings*
  Grief   *O'er*
  Far   *While*

NEVER SAY DIE
page 180
Guessing the Sum of Spots on Hidden Faces
The top and bottom of the middle die add up to 7; the top and bottom of the bottom die add up to 7 more. The bottom of the top die is 3 (7 minus the top of the top die). There are two ways of numbering the faces of a die so that opposite sides add up to 7. Each is a mirror image of the other (*see figure*). Modern dice are numbered as shown on the right, with 1, 2 and 3 reading counter-clockwise around their common corner. Thus you need only see two adjacent faces of a die to know what the other four faces are.

The Three Dice
Mason's chance of winning was one in six. If Jackson had selected the numbers 8 and 14, his chances would have been exactly the same

A Trick with Three Dice
The sum to be guessed is the number of points on the upper faces of the three dice in their final position plus the sum on two opposite faces of a die. The latter is 7

Turning the Die
The best call for the first player is either '2' or '3', as in either case only one particular throw should defeat him. If he called '1', the throw of either 3 or 6 should defeat him. If he called '2', the throw of 5 only should defeat him. If he called '3', the throw of 4 only should defeat him. If he called '4', the throw of either 3 or 4 should defeat him. If he called '5', a throw of either 2 or 3 should defeat him. And if he called '6', the throw of either 1 or 5 should defeat him. It is impossible to give here a complete analysis of the play, but I will state that if at any time you score either 5, 6, 9, 10, 14, 15, 18, 19 or 23, with the die any side up, you ought to lose. If you score 7 or 16 with any side up, you should win. The chance of winning with the other scores depends on the lie of the dice.

In What Order are the Dice Arranged?
Let A be the original three-digit number. The second number is 777−A, and the six-digit number is 1,000A+ 777−A=111 (9A+7). Divide by 111, subtract 7, and divide by 9, and you get A again

POLYOMINOES
page 182

1 A Domino Problem

The answer is **no**.
The standard chess-board contains 64 squares of alternating black and white colours. On this board, each domino will cover one black square and one white square. Thus, **n** dominoes (any specific number of dominoes) will cover **n** black squares and **n** white squares; that is, a number of each equal to the total number of dominoes. However, the defective chess-board has more black squares than white squares, so it cannot be covered.

2 A Tetromino Problem

The diagram shows how the four allowed tetrominoes can be used to cover quarters of the chess-board. Any one quarter can be repeated to

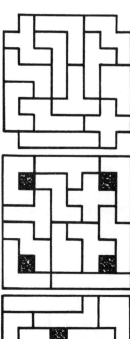

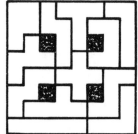

cover an entire eight-by-eight chess-board.

3 Pentomino Problems

Sample solutions are shown in the illustrations. There are alternatives to all of these, however.

4 Bigger Polyominoes

There are
35 different hexominoes
108 different heptominoes
369 different octominoes
1285 different nonominoes
and 4466 different dekominoes.

5 Polyominoes with Holes

The six 'hole-y' octominoes are shown in the illustration. They are quite simply derived by just adding an extra square to the single 'hole-y' heptomino in various positions.

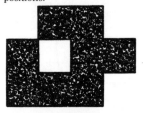

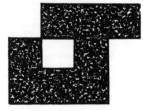

A ROSS ECKLER'S CRYPTOLOGY
page 186

Puzzle Number One

If we number the letters of
G O L D E N B I N A R Y
from 1 through 12, we see that the final arrangement is either
10 6 8 9 2 12 1 11 5 4 7 3
or
10 9 8 6 2 12 1 11 5 4 7 3
depending upon the positions of the two Ns. The intermediate arrangement can be easily deduced with a little trial and error. For example, assume that the first number is 2; then the second number must be 10 in order to ensure that two successive operations convert 1 into 10. Eventually one discovers that the second permutation given above is the result of two applications of the permutation
3 5 10 11 9 7 12 4 2 8 6 1
which yields the message
L E A R N   B Y   D O I N G.

Puzzle Number Two

If we make all possible assumptions for 2 and 8 and form the fragment 2 2 8 2, eliminating all assumptions leading to three spaces in a row, five or more dots and dashes in a row with no space, or an impossible combination (dot dot dash, dash, dot dash dot dash,

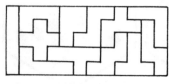

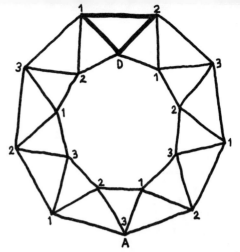

dash, dash dash dot, dash dash dash dash), we are left with a small number of possibilities. Extending these to the fragments 3 2 2 8 2 3 by making all admissible assumptions for 3, again eliminating the impossible sequences, and continuing with 9 and 1, we are soon able to eliminate everything except WELL BEGUN IS HALF DONE.

Puzzle Number Three
From the data, we see that B, K and U are in the first row of the square, and A, E and O in the first column. Likewise, T is in the fourth row, and I in the fourth column. Also, C and S are in the same row as the column containing J and U. Proceeding in this way and using all the information about the rows and columns containing the other letters, we are able to construct a number of squares containing 15 letters which satisfy all the conditions. The sixteenth letter must be the missing W. However, only these two squares permit a word to be constructed from TMUCHRBNSSE, namely, JOURNALIST.

E	L	N	J		A	R	H	I
E	L	N	J		A	R	H	I
A	H	R	I		E	N	L	J
M	T	C	S		M	C	T	S

Puzzle Number Four
The initial T is most likely to be followed by H. If we line up the H in position 13, we get good letter pairs until the end when we come across WW. Although there are words with two consecutive Ws (GLOWWORM, for example), this combination seems unlikely. It is more probable that we have passed a one-letter word which would throw off the spacing. Skipping a space for A (the only candidate) and continuing with the third column, we get, with a little juggling, because of short words,

THERE IS NO FRIGATE LIKE A BOOK TO BEAR US WORLDS AWAY.

Puzzle Number Five
Note that B in the original alphabet translates to I in in the message, I in the original alphabet translates to L in the message, and so on, forming a chain. The longest such chain is J R I L E N. Let us assume in turn J = A, B, …… Z and trace through the letters so determined, until an inconsistency develops. We find that the only consistent sequences are E..RY…UD.A.A…V..LI..N. and E…Y…UT.A.A…V.RLI..N. Continuing in this way, we find the second letter is P, V or X, the third letter is E, etc. We soon learn that EVERY CLOUD HAS A SILVER LINING.

Puzzle Number Six
The original prices were $36.75, $49.50 and $81.25, representing a mark-up of 8 per cent. The system of letter equivalents is seen to be based on the words PENCIL MARK.

Puzzle Number Seven
1 arrested offender
2 truthful aviatrix
3 sinister werewolf
4 civilian monopoly
5 colorful visitors
6 gullible warriors
7 surprise clemency
8 restored clavicle
9 seacoast skirmish
10 artistic painting

NOUGHTS AND CROSSES ?
page 188

Crosses and Noughts
The key is symmetry. Your first move should be to take the centre square and to counter each of your opponent's moves by 'reflecting' them through the centre. The outcome is inevitable. Either your opponent will lose (though he will have to play suicidally to do so), or the game will end in a tie. It has been said that the initial play of the centre square is the only one that will guarantee a tie against best play, but there doesn't seem to be a proof of it. The game tree is sufficiently profuse to make complete analysis difficult. But a determined and diligent reader might enjoy settling the question. (Against a corner opening, it seems that the second player can ensure a win by taking a square a 'knight's move' away. *What about a side opening?*)

Quick-Tac-Toe
Mark all three squares in the second column and the game is yours. Playing second is not a dubious advantage at all. The second player will always win if he follows this strategy: if the first player starts by marking one square, the second marks two to form a connected right angle. If, instead, the first player starts by marking two or three squares, the second player counters by marking as many squares as are necessary to complete either a T, an L, or a cross containing five squares.

The reader should verify that this strategy insures a quick victory for the second player.

3 × 3 × 3 Noughts and Crosses
This restricted version enables the second player to win easily against any opening. Whether the first player starts out aggressively or defensively, and regardless of his initial choice of squares, the second player should move into B5. He will then easily counter any threat by the first player, and in so doing will invariably produce a double threat when the first player's attack peters out.

In a more restricted version in which B5 is permanently prohibited to both players, the first player has an easy win. Among other winning openings, he may take A1, creating a starting position in three different planes. If now the second player blocks him in the plane of tier A by taking A5, the first player can take C1, forcing the response B1 and winning with the double threat generated by A7.

All this suggests the real question: *can you devise a set of restrictions that will make an interesting game out of 3 × 3 × 3 Noughts and Crosses?*

Connecto
It is not difficult to see that every closed boundary must contain at least one pair of perpendicular segments forming an L. Consequently, you can avoid defeat by completing each of your opponent's potential L's, drawing the foot whenever your opponent makes a vertical connection and the upright one whenever your opponent makes a horizontal one.

However, the triviality of the game disappears if Connecto is generalised to a three-dimensional lattice. Here one is tempted to believe that first play confers a winning advantage.

Fortress diagram above Number the vertices as shown. Working backward from the fortress, it can be seen that a winning strategy for either player is to move always to a vertex labelled with the same number as that which his opponent presently occupies.

Since the initial positions are both labelled 3 and the attacker moves first, the defender has the winning advantage. Therefore take the defender's role, adopt the equalising strategy, and you will inevitably capture the attacker, if he doesn't force himself into a cul-de-sac.

97

CLASSIC CROSSWORDS
page 190
Elizabeth Kingsley's Double-Crostic
'Ulysses'   Alfred Lord Tennyson
And tho'
We are not now that strength which in old days
Moved earth and heaven; that which we are, we are;
One equal temper of heroic hearts,
Made weak by time and fate, but strong in will
To strive, to seek, to find, and not to yield.

Torquemada's Torture

Definitions concealed in the verse were as follows:

ACROSS
 1 warning
10 praise
13 lair
14 newly wed
16 notches
18 befall
19 disinherit
21 and 24 tree
22 glean
23 weird
26 Michaelmas daisy
28 pot-stick
32 custom
33 bird
34 rev. deadly disease
35 little Edward
36 glacial snow

DOWN
 1 swing
 2 regret
 3 extends
 4 move away
 5 swift
 6 coin
 8 tear
 9 rev. coin
11 and 7 a snail is
12 seat
15 little
17 rev. slip
20 soft
24 beer
25 and 30 crustacean's thorax
27 may (maid) sheep
28 and 31 threefold
29 concealed.

Afrit's Afright

ACROSS
 1 nomad *no, Scots for not*
 4 parker *Nosey P*
 8 malodour *anag*
 9 oiled *Oi, Irish for I*
11 sodium *anag*
12 calends *contains ends*
13 abstract *anag*
14 tarry *two meanings*
15 cheroots *ends with roots*
19 renegade *anag*
22 gnome *anag*
24 villager *contains lager*
27 embrace *em-brace*
28 unfelt *anag*
29 dixie *'dear old Dixie'* and *camper's can*
30 secretes *SE-Crete-S*
31 dandle *anag*
32 herds *anag*

DOWN
 1 nabob *n, name – a bob, shilling*
 2 monitor *mo-ni-tor*
 3 dogma *dog, follow – ma, mother*
 4 practise *pra-ct-ise*
 5 roulette *let, hindrance, in route*
 6 kinema *ma after kine, cows*
 7 rendered *rend, tear asunder plus anag. of reed*
 8 mosaic *two meanings*
10 dusty *anag.*
16 handmaid *sounds like hand-made*
17 overawed *O Vera, wed!*
18 traverse *rev. of art plus verse*
20 grafter *g-rafter*
21 earths *foxes' lairs*
22 greed *anag. of degre(e)*
23 margin *mar-gin*
25 lurch *'left in the lurch'*
26 elves *end of themselves*

Ximenes

Definitions misprinted in the clues are given in *italics*.

ACROSS
 1 Perse. per-se
 5 vanes-s.a.
10 anag: *rump*
11 anag: *warmer*
12 ups-tart
13 cannon: three meanings
15 =shirker: *dies*
17 rev. of reel: *look*
18 soap-test: so-aptest
21 stra-teg-y
22 bone: three meanings
24 three meanings: *pucker*
26 MO-hair: *cloth*
28 t-ide-rip
29 O-lid: *niffy*
30 che-mother-apy: cheapy=not deary!
31 i.e. more Helly: *slater*
32 anag: *carriage.*

DOWN
 1 pet-as-us
 2 ethe plus anag of emotions: *fish*
 3 real-gar: *red*
 4 anag: *Porch*
 5 vous-soir
 6 sound of high plus son: *tea*
 7 smut
 8 surge-on-ships
 9 a-stir: *moving*
13 men-age
14 no-tour
16 hag-taper
19 anag: *rhyme*
20 tweed-le
22 *dog*
23 moron: sounds opposite of less on
25 *boat*
27 idea(l).

Shuckburgh Reynolds Ltd acknowledge the assistance of the following in the design and production of this book:
Maxwell Boam, Franco Chen, Rene Eyre, Naomi Games, Lucina dellaRocca Hay, Bridget Heal, Susan Hitches, Mike Jarvis of SX Composing Ltd, Dinah Lone, Elizabeth Pring, Carol Suffling, Jeremy Watkiss, Janet Watson and John Woodcock.

256